Emmanuel Joseph Sieyès

Studies in the History of Political Thought

VOLUME 9

The titles published in this series are listed at *brill.com/ship*

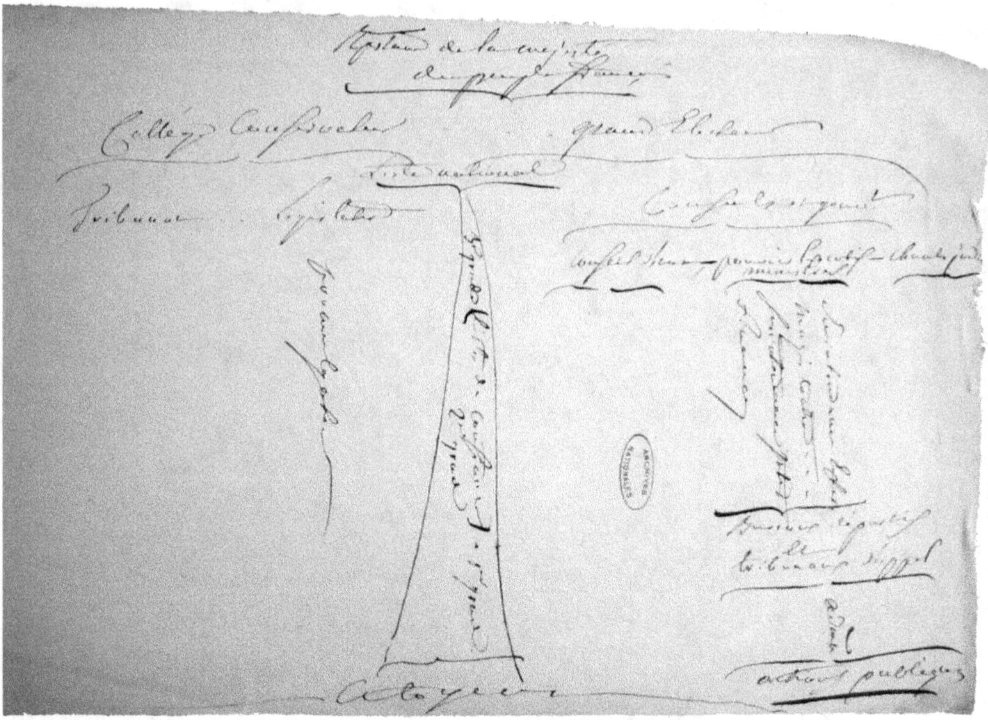

Sieyès's illustration of his constitutional draft in 1799, reproduced from the Archives Nationales (Paris): folder Sieyes (= 284 AP), box 5, dossier 2, sheet 6

Emmanuel Joseph Sieyès

The Essential Political Writings

Edited, with an introduction and historical annotations by

Oliver W. Lembcke
Florian Weber

BRILL

LEIDEN | BOSTON

Cover illustration: Portrait of Emmanuel Joseph Sieyès (ca. 1780); ©istockphoto.com, Hulton Archive.

Library of Congress Cataloging-in-Publication Data

Sieyès, Emmanuel Joseph, comte, 1748-1836.
[Works. Selections. English]
Emmanuel Joseph Sieyès : the essential political writings / edited, with an introduction and historical annotations by Oliver W. Lembcke, Florian Weber.
pages cm. – (Studies in the history of political thought, ISSN 1873–6548 ; volume 9)
Includes bibliographical references and index.
ISBN 978-90-04-22571-8 (hardback : alk. paper) – ISBN 978-90-04-27399-3 (e-book) 1. Sieyès, Emmanuel Joseph, comte, 1748-1836. 2. Political science–Philosophy. 3. State, The. 4. Constitutional law–France. 5. Constitutional history–France. 6. France–Politics and government–1789-1815. I. Lembcke, Oliver, editor. II. Weber, Florian, 1978- , editor. III. Title.

JC179.S5313 2014
320.1–dc23

2014009254

This publication has been typeset in the multilingual "Brill" typeface. With over 5,100 characters covering Latin, IPA, Greek, and Cyrillic, this typeface is especially suitable for use in the humanities. For more information, please see www.brill.com/brill-typeface.

ISSN 1873-6548
ISBN 978-90-04-22571-8 (hardback)
ISBN 978-90-04-27399-3 (e-book)

This book is printed on acid-free paper.

Contents

Foreword IX
Note to the Reader XI
Acknowledgements XII

Introduction to Sieyès's Political Theory 1
Oliver W. Lembcke and Florian Weber

1 What Is the Third Estate? 43

2 Reasoned Exposition of the Rights of Man and Citizen 118

3 Controversy between Mr. Paine and M. Emmanuel Sieyès 135

4 Of the Gains of Liberty in Society and in the Representative System 144

5 Sieyès's Views Concerning Several Articles of Sections IV and V of the Draft Constitution [First Thermidorian Intervention] 152

6 The Opinion of Sieyès Concerning the Tasks and Organization of the Constitutional Jury, Submitted on the Second Thermidor [Second Thermidorian Intervention] 170

7 Constitutional Observations 186

Bibliography 195
Index 202

Foreword

Emmanuel Joseph Sieyès was much more than a political pamphleteer. No other intellectual exerted such an influence over the different phases of the French Revolution, and left his mark on so many areas of policy-making—from constitutional design and administrative organization, to educational theory, military strategy and diplomacy. The beginning and the end of the Revolution not only frame the rise and fall of Sieyès's political career. Rather, instigating *and* terminating the Revolution were the major goals of his political life. Accordingly, his corpus entails theories of constitutional rupture *and* constitutional formation. For Sieyès, the legitimacy of the Revolution—as a political act that furthers human rights—was always predicated on the ultimate establishment of a stable, liberal political order.

Today, Sieyès is remembered primarily as a revolutionary agitator, especially through his concept of a forceful *pouvoir constituant*. But this narrow reading has produced a one-sided focus on Sieyès's early writings. His comments on the *Third Estate*, his *Essay on Privilege*, and his *Reasoned Exposition of the Rights of Man and Citizen* have been reprinted, and circulated in many languages, since their first publication in 1788 and 1789, yet his later writings have remained almost completely unstudied. This volume, by contrast, presents a representative sample of his political writings from across the revolutionary decade. Aside from his reflections on the *Third Estate* and his *Reasoned Exposition of the Rights of Man and Citizen*—both of which appeared in 1789—it features the *Controversy between Thomas Paine and Emmanuel Joseph Sieyès* (1791), his essay *Of the Gains of Liberty in Society and in the Representative System* (1793), both of his *Thermidorian Interventions* (1795), and his *Constitutional Observations of the Year VIII* (1799).

This book arose in the course of the editors' research into Sieyès's political thought, and was inspired by the meticulously researched edition of the *Groupe d'Études Sieyèsienne*, especially Christine Fauré, Jacques Guilhaumou and Jaques Valier. For their financial support, we would like to thank the Ernst Abbe foundation and the Friedrich Schiller University, Jena. The hospitality of the German Historical Institute in Paris (GHIP)—and their support in the form of a generous research grant—allowed us to study Sieyès's manuscripts in the *archives nationales*. It was also incredibly helpful to be able to assemble our findings and our initial thoughts in the *Forum du mardi: recherches en cours* of the GHIP. Moreover, we are grateful to Michael Sonenscher for insightful comments on the relationship between Rousseau and Sieyès. For fruitful discussions of our topic we are thankful to Harald Bluhm, Roland Lhotta, Ulrich

Thiele, Daniel Schulz, Werner Greiling, Hans-Werner Hahn, Bernd Klesmann, and Marcus Llanque. Our thanks also to Jörn Leonhard for including our project in the "Studies in the History of Political Thought," and for advising us with generosity from the outset. Finally, we would like to thank Felix Koch, who translated the texts of the later Sieyès from French into English, and James Wagner, Jonathan Green and Karen Hug, who lent us their advice on the nuances of English expression.

Oliver W. Lembcke and Florian Weber
Hamburg and Berlin, March 2014

Note to the Reader

This book contains two sets of footnotes, one indicated numerically and the other alphabetically. The numeric footnotes are part of Emmanuel Joseph Sieyès's original text whilst the alphabetic footnotes indicate the editors' notes, with one exception: the alphabetic footnotes of the first chapter entitled 'What is the Third Estate?' are the original annotations by S.E. Finer.

Acknowledgements

'What is the Third Estate?' is translated from the original French version ('Qu' est-ce que le Tiers État?') by Mrs. M. Blondel. This text was first published in Emmanuel Joseph Sieyès, *What is the Third Estate?* Edited, with historical notes by Samuel E. Finer, with an introduction by Peter Campbell (London and Dunnow, 1963). The editors of this volume have made all reasonable efforts to trace the copyrights holder of the Pall Mall Press '63 translation used for this chapter. Communications from copyright holders are welcome, so that the appropriate acknowledgements can be made in future editions, and to settle other permission matters.

'Reasoned Exposition of the Rights of Man and Citizen' is translated from the original French version ('Reconnaissance et exposition raisonnée des Droits de l' Homme et du Citoyen') by Marc Allan Goldstein. It was first published in *Social and Political Thought of the French Revolution. 1788–1797. An Anthology of Texts*, ed. Marc Allan Goldstein (New York et al., 1997), pp. 134–150.

'Controversy between Mr. Paine and M. Emmanuel Sieyès' is reprinted from *The European Magazine and London Review*, vol. 20 (1791), pp. 129–133. A French edition of this controversy (with a translation of Paine's letter by his French companion Condorcet) can be found in *Œuvres de Sieyes*, ed. Marcel Dorigny (Paris, 1989), vol. 2, no. 29 and 30.

'Of the Gains of Liberty in Society and in the Representative System' is translated from the original French version ('Des intérêts de la Liberté dans l'état social et dans le système représentatif') by Felix Koch. The essay was originally published on 8 July in the *Journal de l'instruction social*, vol. 2 (1793), pp. 33–48. It is reprinted in *Œuvres de Sieyes*, ed. Marcel Dorigny (Paris, 1989), vol. 3, no. 32.

'Sieyès's Views concerning several Articles of Sections IV and V of the Draft Constitution' is translated from the original French version ('Opinion de Sieyès, sur plusieurs articles de titres IV et V du projet de constitution') by Felix Koch. This text is reprinted in *Œuvres de Sieyes*, ed. Marcel Dorigny (Paris, 1989), vol. 3, no. 40. A critical edition can be found in Paul Bastid, *Les Discours des Sieyès dans les débats constitutionnels de l'an III* (*2 et 18 thermidor*) (Paris, 1939).

'The Opinion of Sieyès Concerning the Tasks and Organization of the Constitutional Jury, Submitted on the Second Thermidor' is translated from the original

French version ('Opinion de Sieyès, sur les attributions et l'organisation du Jury Constitutionnaire, proposé le 2 thermidor') by Felix Koch. It is reprinted in *Œuvres de Sieyes*, ed. Marcel Dorigny (Paris, 1989), vol. 3, no. 41. A critical edition can be found in Paul Bastid, *Les Discours des Sieyès dans les débats constitutionnels de l'an III (2 et 18 thermidor)* (Paris, 1939).

'Constitutional Observations' is translated from the original French version ('Observations constitutionnelles') by Felix Koch. Sieyès never published this manuscript. It is available in *Des manuscrits de Sieyès 1773–1799*, vol. I, ed. Christine Fauré, Jacques Guilhaumou and Jacques Valier (Paris, 1999), pp. 519–526.

Introduction to Sieyès's Political Theory

Oliver W. Lembcke and Florian Weber

Throughout his lifetime, Emmanuel Joseph Sieyès[1] never had the leisure to systematize a coherent political theory. Working in the medium of pamphlets and speeches, he learned how to harmonize dispassionate analysis with fervent polemics. Sieyès's body of work consists of a bundle of such papers, the results of a long education in political thought and philosophy. The most important of these papers are presented in this volume, along with a preface introducing the reader to Sieyès's life, political theory, and the context of his writings.

Some Notes on Sieyès's Political Biography

Both the beginning and the end of the French Revolution are linked to Sieyès. His passionate rallying of the Third Estate and his calculated appeal for the Estates-General to transform itself into a National Assembly are as well known as his conspiracy with Napoleon, whom he saw as the guardian of the Revolution, yet whose 'will to power' he underestimated. His political fate was interwoven with that of the Revolution. Before 1789, and after 1799, he was a political nobody, leading the life of a reclusive hermit, absorbed in philosophical studies that were not meant for the outside world; his was a contemplative rather than political existence. Unlike other prominent revolutionary campaigners who promoted the Enlightenment prior to the Revolution (such as the Marquis de Condorcet, who belonged to the circle of encyclopædists and held leading positions at the *Académie des sciences* and the *Académie française*) or who guarded the legacy of the Revolution during the Restoration (such as Benjamin Constant, one of the leading liberals of the French *Vormärz*), Sieyès's political influence was singularly limited to the decade of the Revolution.

His life prior to the Revolution was marked by resignation in the face of social immobility in a corporatist, estate-based society. His youthful hopes for

1 Sieyès's works are cited as follows: *Écrits* = *Écrits politiques*, ed. Roberto Zapperi (Paris et al., 1985); *Œuvres* = *Œuvres de Sieyès*, ed. Marcel Dorigny, 3 vols (Paris, 1989); *Manuscrits I* = *Des manuscrits de Sieyès 1773–1799*, vol. I, ed. Christine Fauré, Jacques Guilhaumou and Jacques Valier (Paris, 1999); *Manuscrits II* = *Des manuscrits de Sieyès 1770–1815*, vol. II, ed. Christine Fauré, Jacques Guilhaumou and Jacques Valier (Paris, 2007).

 | DOI: 10.1163/9789004273993_002

an ascent in the church hierarchy, which had moved his father to allow the talented pupil to pursue a religious career, proved to be illusory. In a letter to his father dated June 1773, Sieyès openly expressed his disgust at the spoils system: "I give as little credence to the promises of all those people as to the prophecies of the almanac. But because I cannot do otherwise, I act as though I believe them."[2] He offered a retrospective on the social confinement of his youth in an autobiography that he wrote in the third person and published anonymously in 1795:

> It is not surprising that in this situation, which disagreed with his temperament, he was stricken with a deep melancholy, accompanied by a great, almost stoic indifference with respect to his own person and future.[3]

For Sieyès, the Revolution promised personal liberation from a life determined by outside forces. His deep hatred for the aristocracy, which can be seen in his polemical *Essay on Privileges*[4] and *What Is the Third Estate?* (see text 1 of this compilation), compelled him to advocate for the disenfranchised. When a newly revised version of the *Third Estate* was published under his name for the first time in May 1789—the text had been distributed as early as January, and had been reprinted multiple times—, the bourgeois Estate in Paris selected Sieyès as a representative to the Estates-General, an office that the clergy of the commune Montfort-l'Amaury had denied him the previous March. The sweeping success of Sieyès's polemics, which stood out in a torrential flood of late-1780s political pamphlets, stemmed from his unique zeal: the churchman became an undisputed spokesman for the bourgeoisie even before the session began. Like no other writer of his day, Sieyès united the visionary force of a philosopher-legislator with the practical expertise of an administrative specialist. At once *législateur* and *administrateur*, Sieyès articulated a widespread anger against the old elites that, like a magnifying glass, focused inchoate popular *ressentiment* into a conflagration that consumed the *ancien régime* in the summer of 1789.

2 Octave Teissier (ed.), *La jeunesse de l'abbé Sieyès. Documents inédits* (Marseille, 1897), p. 8.—Unless otherwise indicated, all French and German citations have been translated by the editors.

3 Sieyès, *Œuvres III*, no. 36, p. 7 ('Notice sur la vie de Sieyès, membre de la première Assemblée nationale et de la Convention').

4 Sieyès, *Œuvres I*, no. 1 ('Essai sur les privilèges').

In its initial phase, the Revolution of 1789 followed the logic of the *Third Estate* as if taking stage directions from a "script."[5] Sieyès won over the revolutionary camp with his radical proposal to blow up the corporatist system of representation[6] and to entrust the drafting of a new constitution to the Third Estate. The success of his proposal can perhaps be seen most clearly in the convention's adoption of a title he had demanded as early as 1788: *Assemblée nationale*.[7]

This phase, in which Sieyès possessed the popular authority of a revolutionary prophet—Mirabeau[8] called him a new "Mohammed"[9]—, did not last long. The revolutionary script written by Sieyès, that fierce critic of privilege, did not foresee the National Assembly's total abolition of the feudal system, at least not in the rash way that the deputies caused the foundations of traditional social order to collapse on the night of 4 August 1789. In his speech of 10 August regarding the status of church lands, Sieyès criticized the elimination of the benefice system and the ecclesiastical tithe.[10]

He claimed that the National Assembly had deprived the First Estate of its material foundation, even though the clergy had a public educational mission and, unlike the aristocracy, did not lead a 'parasitic' existence. Like a didactic teacher reading renegade pupils the riot act, he reproached the Assembly: "You want to be free and do not understand how to be just!" In so doing, he exhausted his moral credibility among many of his supporters: "The Assembly didn't know what had happened to it. The oracle of the Revolution had treated it as no deputy had ever before dared."[11]

---

5 William H. Sewell, *A Rhetoric of Bourgeois Revolution. The Abbé Sieyès and What is the Third Estate?* (Durham et al., 1994), p. 53.

6 Keith M. Baker, *Inventing the French Revolution. Essays on French Political Culture in the Eighteenth Century* (Cambridge, 1990), pp. 224–251.

7 Sieyès, *Œuvres I*, no. 2, p. 7 ('Vues sur les moyens d'exécution dont les Représentants de la France pourront disposer en 1789').

8 Mirabeau and Sieyès entertained a close relationship at the beginning of the Revolution. Mirabeau was a prominent figure among the supporters of Sieyès's constitutional ideas and his concept of national representation via a process of elections at different levels. On this see Michael Sonenscher, *Sans-Culottes. An Eighteenth-Century Emblem in the French Revolution* (Princeton and Oxford, 2008), pp. 47, 304.

9 Étienne Dumont, *Souvenirs sur Mirabeau et sur les deux premières assemblées législatives* (Paris, 1832), p. 295 and *passim*.

10 Sieyès, *Œuvres II*, no. 11 ('Observations sommaires sur les biens Ecclésiastiques').

11 Jean-Denis Bredin, *Sieyès. La clé de la Révolution française* (Paris, 1988), p. 197.

The public rebuke that greeted 'Padre' Sieyès, who seemed to have placed personal interests before his principles,[12] did not lead to his departure from politics. Instead, he simply withdrew from public life—a life to which he did not feel called anyway, if his *Biographical Notes* are to be believed.[13]

For Sieyès, public acclaim was merely a road to political relevance; most fundamentally, he saw himself as a framer of commissions and committees. Rarely, and only when the gravity of the situation demanded it, did he stand at the lectern of the National Assembly—as, for instance, in the debate of September 1789 on the royal veto, which, according to Sieyès, put the legitimacy of the new political order to the test.[14] Thus despite the resistance that met his proposals (which, because of popular antipathy toward him, he occasionally allowed his allies to propose), he succeeded in putting his mark on the Revolution in three different respects. The *Declaration of the Rights of Man and Citizen* (text 2) as a founding document of bourgeois society; the dissolution of the old administrative system and the organization of the nation into territorial departments;[15] the establishment of a post-corporatist system of representation based on elections[16]—these are the three load-bearing columns of Sieyès's new political architecture.

For this reason, Sieyès has rightly been called the father of the first Revolutionary Constitution of 1791. He was unable, however, to convince his compatriots on one crucial point: the role of the monarch. For Sieyès, the king symbolized the unity of the state and occupied the role of head of government, but held no further power to shape politics. In contrast to other variants of constitutional monarchy, Sieyès's blueprint placed legislative power firmly in the hand of a democratically legitimated parliament. Sieyès advocated this position consistently, both in the fall of 1789, in opposition to demands for a royal veto, and in the summer of 1791, in opposition to Condorcet's and Paine's demands for a French republic in the wake of Louis XVI's attempted flight (text 3). He proffered his vision of constitutional monarchy one last time—once again unsuccessfully—during the debate on constitutional revisions[17] prior to

12 Sieyès, *Œuvres II*, no. 11, p. 1 and *passim* ('Observations sommaires sur les biens Ecclésiastiques').

13 Sieyès, *Œuvres III*, no. 36, p. 43 ('Notice sur la vie de Sieyès, membre de la première Assemblée nationale et de la Convention').

14 Sieyès, *Œuvres II*, no. 12 ('Dire de l'abbé Sieyès sur la question du veto royal').

15 Sieyès, *Œuvres II*, no. 8 ('Quelques idées de constitution applicables à la ville de Paris').

16 Sieyès, *Œuvres II*, no. 12 ('Dire de l'abbé Sieyès sur la question du veto royal').

17 Cf. Pierre Brunet, *Vouloir pour la nation. Le concept de représentation dans la théorie de l'État* (Paris, 2004), pp. 221ff.

the dissolution of the National Constituent Assembly.[18] For his part, although he supported the new constitution, he saw it as precarious: destabilized by the compromise that resulted from the veto dispute. When the Revolution became more radical, his skepticism proved prescient. The outraged populace deposed the king on 10 August 1792, robbing the new constitutional order of its validity de facto. Sieyès accepted this overthrow with great sobriety. Claiming that the monarchy had been irreparably discredited in the public mind by Louis XVI's abuses, he declared himself a "republican by reason" and, in January 1793, voted for the death of the monarch. Subsequently, Sieyès did not play a major role in the National Convention's drafting of a new constitution.[19] At the behest of his allies, who deemed his criticism of Condorcet too vehement, his counterproposal to the Convention's adopted constitution remained unpublished. Sieyès disliked the directly democratic elements of Condorcet's proposal, which were irreconcilable with the fundamental principle of his constitutional theory—i.e. representation.[20] When his plans for educational policy and a military constitution[21] also failed, he declared himself weary of the enduring public hostility directed towards him, and draped himself in a "philosophical silence."[22]

During the Reign of Terror, Sieyès disappeared from the political stage, although he continued to take part—silently—in the meetings of the Convention "in order to show that he had not emigrated," as he later explained to Wilhelm von Humboldt.[23]

---

18 'Représentation et élections' (1791), published in Pasquale Pasquino, *Sieyès et l'invention de la constitution en France* (Paris, 1998), pp. 171–173.

19 Sieyès was an opponent not only of the Robespierrists but also of the Feuillant wing of the Jacobin club. For his hostile relations with Duport and Barnave see Sonenscher, *Sans-Culottes*, pp. 304, 327.

20 On Sieyès's distinctly modern theory of representation see Colette Clavreul, 'Sieyès et la génèse de la représentation moderne', in *Droits. Revue française de théorie juridique* 6 (1986), pp. 45–56.

21 Sieyès, *Œuvres II*, no. 33 ('Du nouvel établissement de l'Instruction en France'); Sieyès, *Œuvres II*, no. 35 ('Rapport du Comité de Défense générale pour organiser le Ministère de la Guerre').

22 Sieyès, *Œuvres III*, no. 36, p. 39 ('Notice sur la vie de Sieyès, membre de la première Assemblée nationale et de la Convention').

23 Wilhelm von Humboldt, *Tagebücher 1788–1798*, vol. I, in *Gesammelte Schriften*, vol. XIV, ed. Albert Leitzmann (Berlin, 1968), p. 472.—As for how he escaped the furious guillotine despite being the target of Jacobin hostilities, he explained to Humboldt that a "revolutionary superstition" had prevented the Robespierrists from killing him. Had they executed the murderer of the king, it would have given the hated aristocrats "too much pleasure" (ibid.).

Sieyès's experience of the Terror marked him deeply. His opponents' machinations, which portrayed him as an enemy of the Revolution and damaged his reputation well beyond the French political elite, stoked up Sieyès's contempt for the Jacobin leadership. Four years after Robespierre's death, Sieyès still could not utter his name without adding "five or six epithets one after the other: *the hideous, the ignorant, the childish, the ridiculous, the smug Robespierre*."[24] As late as 1832, while suffering from a fever, he instructed his attendants to tell Robespierre he was not at home.[25]

As his confidant Constant later noted in his ruminations on the Revolutionary decade, the Abbé's ire toward his opponents and his fear of their attacks were his dominant traits: "After hate, fear was his greatest passion. Always and everywhere he believed himself threatened."[26]

Sieyès survived the Terror, but the rumors spread by the Jacobins to impugn his character—that he was an agent of the church and an enemy of the people, that he had colluded with the aristocracy, that he favored a British form of constitutional monarchy—made any resumption of his political career highly tenuous. For this reason, his return to the political stage was choreographed to coincide with the release of an autobiography intended to rehabilitate him as a public figure. He became a member of the Committee of Public Safety, which took charge of state business after Robespierre's fall. Although he was not part of the new constitutional commission appointed in the spring of 1795, he supported it in an advisory capacity.[27] Since reservations on both sides (Jacobins, Royalists) made cooperation difficult, it is not surprising that Sieyès was unsuccessful in winning majority support for his constitutional plans, despite two speeches before the Convention in which he criticized the commission for its anglophilic preference for a balance of powers (text 5), advocated the fusion of the legislative and executive branches, and proposed to install a "guardian of the constitution" (see text 6). Nevertheless, the parliament was as hostile to his proposals as the commission had been, and his bill was unanimously rejected. Beaten and humiliated, Sieyès saw his defeat as a personal disgrace. He interpreted his rejection by the Thermidorians, with whom he shared fundamental liberal convictions, as a flat insult. As a result, he refused to accept his election

---

24 Ibid.

25 Bredin, *Sieyès*, p. 737.

26 Benjamin Constant, 'Fragments des mémoires de Madame Récamier', in *Œuvre*, ed. Alfred Roulin (Paris, 1957), pp. 931 ff.

27 Cf. Sieyès, *Manuscrits I*, pp. 478–480 ('Préface des 4 à 5 conférences que j'ai eues avec le Comité des 11 dans les 1er jours de messidor, l'an 3, au sujet de la Constitution').

to the Directory, the new executive branch of the Republic. Aside from his deputation to the parliament, he never held another political office.

This abstinence from politics in the early stages of the Thermidorian Republic turned out to be fortuitous. As an advocate of strong executive authority, Sieyès was not tainted by the stigma that soon befell the powerless new government, pulverized by hostilities from left and right.[28] Ironically, it was a near-fatal misfortune that returned Sieyès to the political stage. On 11 April 1797, he was the victim of an assassination attempt. But, providentially, he only got slightly injured. In the context of the ongoing political crisis fomented by the Royalists, republicans saw the attempt on Sieyès's life as symbolic of the reactionaries' attack of the Revolution. Emboldened by public sympathy and encouraged by a flood of condolences,[29] Sieyès once again grasped at power. After the showdown between the republican majority of the Directory (supported by the army) and the royalist majority of the parliament was decided in favor of the former, Sieyès leapt to the Directory's defense, and proposed the deportation of enemies of the state. His fight against the royalists became a personal vendetta, one that allowed him to turn his back on his political principles in case of emergency. At that moment, he was constrained by neither the constitutional prohibition against the deployment of the army in the interior nor his egalitarian convictions about civil rights. The bourgeois class thanked him for it: in November 1797, Sieyès was elected president of the lower house of parliament, which had been "purified" of royalist opposition.

It was in this parliamentary role that he met Napoleon for the first time in December 1797, at a banquet honoring the general in the wake of the Treaty of Campo Formio. The two had much to discuss. As a public servant in the diplomatic corps of the Committee of Public Safety after Robespierre's fall, Sieyès had developed an interest in European diplomacy. Moreover, he admired Bonaparte's expansionary and hegemonic ambitions. The diplomatic expertise that Sieyès demonstrated in crafting peace with Holland led him to the office of French Ambassador to Prussia, which he assumed in June 1798.[30] Specifically,

28 Bronsilaw Baczko, 'L'expérience thermidorienne', in *The Political Culture of the French Revolution*, vol. II of *The French Revolution and the Creation of Modern Political Culture*, ed. Colin Lucas (Oxford et al., 1987), pp. 339–370.

29 These letters can be found in the folder Sieyès (= 284 AP) of the Archives Nationales, Paris, box 11, Dossier 2, sheet 3; henceforth cited as A.N. 284 AP 11, 2(3).

30 For Sieyès's time in Berlin see Marcelle Adler-Bresse, *Sieyès et le monde allemand* (Paris, 1977). For his influence on the contemporary German political debate, which is mirrored in Kant's *Perpetual Peace* as well as Fichte's *The Closed Commericla State*, see Isaac Nakhimovsky, *The Closed Commercial State. Perpetual Peace and Commercial Society From*

the foreign minister Talleyrand instructed him to obtain Prussian neutrality in France's conflict with Austria. Ultimately, Sieyès was unsuccessful: he was unable to negotiate an agreement of reassurance in Berlin. But as France's relations with European powers were generally deteriorating at this time, Sieyes's failure did not damage his reputation in Paris. When he was summoned back to Paris in the summer of 1799, his reception did not lack pomp. He was considered a father of the Revolution and guarantor of its success. As the tensions with other European powers escalated into crisis, the people placed their last hopes for the Revolution in him; as Constant told Sieyès, "I believe in the Revolution, because I believe in you."[31] Sieyès was elected to the Directory, where, alongside Barras, he became a strong leader. As a result of his successful suppression of the royalist opposition, he controlled majorities in both chambers of parliament, and skillfully pitted his enemies in the Directory against one another. It was not long, however, before Sieyès fell out of favor with the left-wing majority that had brought him to power. Driven by a paranoia spawned by the neo-Jacobins' campaign of personal defamation against him, weary of the perpetual infighting among the various political factions, sobered by the incompetence of the government, which frequently resorted to illegal measures in order to maintain power, and further motivated to make amends for his failure in the Thermidorian constitutional debate, Sieyès arranged a *coup d'état* in order to put an end to the prevailing anarchy and to establish a new constitution. By 1799, he had learned his lesson: one cannot attain a stable majority with arguments alone. Hence, Sieyès forged coalitions in advance of his *coup*, filling key positions with confidants, and allied himself with Napoleon, putatively the most civilian of the military officers. The connection between the two amounted to an alliance of convenience. Sieyès possessed the trust of the political elite, and Bonaparte that of the army, on whose support—and here Sieyès held no illusions—the leadership of the government had long been dependent. In late 1799, each man needed the other. The task of steering the ship of state into calmer waters Bonaparte reserved for himself. Sieyès's new constitution,

---

Rousseau to Fichte (Princeton and Oxford, 2011), ch. 1, pp. 15–62; see Jean Delinière, Karl Friedrich Reinhard, introducteur de Kant auprès de Sieyès, in *Revue d'Allemagne* 12 (1980), pp. 481–496 and also Michael Sonenscher, *Before the Deluge. Public Debt, Inequality, and the Intellectual Origins of the French Revolution* (Princeton and Oxford, 2007), p. 70, n. 139. Fichte even "served as an intermediary to help find a publisher for the German edition of Sieyes's works" (ibid., p. 38), which were translated by Johann Gottfried Ebel and prefaced with an introduction by Konrad Engelbert Oelsner.

31 Letter of 9th July, published in Norman King and Etienne Hofmann (eds.), 'Les lettres de Benjamin Constant à Sieyès', *Annales Benjamin Constant* 3 (1983), pp. 89–110.

which was drafted overnight after the successful coup d'état, had support in both chambers of parliament, but was remodeled by Napoleon to serve his own ambitions. He hollowed out its liberal substance.

Sieyès had failed for the last time, and withdrew from politics. Bonaparte, who feared Sieyès's influence and did not want to anger him, gilded his path of retreat. Sieyès received considerable properties from the state, was made an officer of the Legion of Honor in 1804, and in 1813 became a Grand Cross of the Imperial Order of Reunion. His overt penchant for honors and distinctions even led him to accept the title of *comte* in 1808.

Yet Sieyès was not granted the leisure to enjoy his wealth and fame without disturbance. After the return of the Bourbons, the murderer of the king had to flee into exile to Brussels. Only after the July Revolution did he return to Paris, frail and wearied. When he died in 1836 at the age of 88, he was nearly forgotten. Whereas the funeral for Constant in 1830 resembled a state ceremony, Sieyès's burial rite involved only his closest family. He departed life in silence, a private man. His star had faded long ago, in the early days of the Napoleonic era.

Main Elements of Sieyès's Political Theory

Evaluated solely in light of the principles of his constitutional theory and of his intentions to stabilize Revolutionary France, Sieyès failed as a politician. And yet, this curt assessment does not adequately represent his talent for reconciling political thought with practical action. No other practitioner so influenced the various phases of the Revolution as did Sieyès. Like Machiavelli, he aspired to enlist theory in the service of praxis. But whereas, in his retirement, Machiavelli reached for his pen, Sieyès wrote his major works as a politician in waiting. For him, writing was not a substitute for but a precondition of his political work. Although he read, studied, quoted and debated his entire life, his published writings all originated during the Revolutionary period: they represent his intellectual preparation for oncoming political engagements. "That he should have written merely theoretically about politics was out of the question for him in France," as Wilhelm von Humboldt noted in his diary after a conversation with Sieyès.[32] Yet, nevertheless, a theory of politics may be reconstructed from Sieyès's writings. The main elements of his political thought may be sketched out in the following five categories: freedom and society, legal community, democratic sovereignty, political authority, and mixed government.

---

32 Humboldt, *Tagebücher*, p. 470.

Freedom and Society

In Sieyès's view, society rests on the division of labor.[33] Riches do not emerge solely from the soil, as the physiocrats claimed; rather, it is "labor that creates wealth."[34] The natural principle of efficiency achieves maximal utility not by privileging agriculture, but by organizing labor across the entire society. For Sieyès, as for Adam Smith, this is accomplished by the division of labor, "which follows the law: increase production, reduce costs."[35] Unlike Smith, however, Sieyès concerns himself with the sociological repercussions of organized labor, rather than its economic consequences.[36] He is interested in what constitutes a society, understood as a continuation and consummation of the *ordre naturel*: what binds it together. He searches for the principle or "force" of social integration, and finds it in general labor: "General labor is thus the foundation of society, and social order is nothing other than the best possible ordering of labor."[37] Sieyès describes labor as the "nimble force" (*force vive*) of prosperity, the production of which is unleashed through its division and organization.

Sieyes's general labor (*travail général*) serves an analogous function to Rousseau's general will (*volonté générale*). In Sieyes's social theory, representatively organized labor guarantees socialization; in Rousseau's theory, the moral integration of the community via a general will that cannot be represented performs this function.[38] The differences between Sieyès and Rousseau become most clear in their opposing accounts of the connection between socialization and freedom. Whereas for Rousseau the formation of society leads to the gradual erosion of freedom, according to Sieyès, freedom attains its fullest development in society. As Larrère aptly notes, "Contrary to Rousseau, Sieyès reverses the balance of freedom's profits and losses in the transition from the state of nature to that of society."[39] This relationship—the subject of Sieyès's

---

33 "[Sieyès's] starting point was a radical reformulation of the idea of representation so that it referred, initially, to something more basic than was usually implied by established legal or political usage. In Sieyès's usage, anyone acting on someone else's behalf was acting as that person's representative." Sonenscher, *Deluge*, p. 12.

34 Sieyès, *Manuscrits I*, pp. 171–184; p. 175 ('Lettres aux Économistes sur leur système de politique et de morale').

35 Ibid., p. 176.

36 Cf. Sieyès, *Manuscrits II*, pp. 305–361 ('Cahiers Smith').

37 Sieyès, *Manuscrits I*, p. 176 ('Lettres aux Économistes').

38 Sieyès, *Écrits*, p. 62 ('Travail ne favorise la liberté qu' en devenant représentatif'); cf. Sewell, *Rhetoric*, p. 95.

39 Catherine Larrère, *L'invention de l'économie au XVIIIe siècle. Du droit naturel à la physiocratie* (Paris, 1992), p. 311.

essay *Of the Gains of Liberty* (text 4)—is twofold. On the one hand, the representative organization of labor increases "negative freedom" by relieving the individual's obligation to perform a variety of necessary occupations via specialization. Therefore, though it perpetuates the social interdependence that results from economic differentiation, specialization does not lead to a freedom-endangering form of dependence. On the other hand, the division of labor also allows for the emergence of a positive "freedom of assets"—i.e. the means to satisfy our needs.

Against Rousseau's qualitatively positive concept of freedom as autonomy, Sieyès posits a quantitative definition of positive freedom—namely, the expansion of the realm of individual action, i.e. as an enlarged social space for ordered activity, based on the principle of representation. For his own part, Rousseau does not deny that society makes an increase in the means of satisfying individual needs possible. But this admission misses the point of his critique of modernity. Due to the "differential" structure of desire that arises during socialization, Rousseau claims that human needs inevitably increase faster than the means by which they can be satisfied. Sieyès does not deny this danger; to guard against it, he supplements his belief in progress with a neo-Stoic ethic of modesty.[40]

His concept of freedom—i.e., the right to satisfy one's needs—is qualified in two ways. Firstly, every individual is free to define for himself the ends of his freedom. As a result, Sieyès's concept of needs is free of any teleological paternalism:

> Yet his obligation to unite with his peers in no case gives him [sc. man] the right to impose his own views upon others. As much as their own interest drives and binds them to community [association], and especially to a form of community that best corresponds to their common interest, yet they never lose the freedom not to pursue their own happiness, whether out of ignorance or by their refusal to do so.[41]

Secondly, freedom is subject to the condition of reciprocity, which Sieyès, invoking the commandment *neminem laede*, counts among the principles of natural law. As opposed to the physiocratic understanding of natural law, however, Sieyès insisted that equality must be put into effect by a legislator in order to guarantee the legitimate exercise of freedom: "[D]o no injustice to

40 See his 'Of the Gains of Liberty' (text 4).

41 'Études sur Helvétius', A.N. 284 AP 2, 3(3).

others […] is the greatest natural law, which the legislator dispenses in a piecemeal fashion, as it were, by applying it in its particulars to the proper order of society; all positive laws emerge in this way."[42] For the state of nature is ruled by de facto inequality, which must be overcome through the establishment of a community under law. Sieyès's concept of law is not informed by the natural law tradition, which treats law as an expression of a pre-existing normative order. Rather, he spells out a distinctly modern perspective of normativity, according to which law is the instrument of a legal order that must be recreated, in which the circumstances of life, insofar as they concern freedom and property, are regulated according to the principle of juridical equality.

For Sieyès there exists no physiocratic *ordre naturel* that must be simply reproduced by the lawyer. Indeed, Sieyès inverts the physiocratic distinction between legitimate *législation* (which reproduces natural law: *loi-rapport*), and politically dysfunctional *légisfaction* (which institutes compulsory positive law: *loi-commandant*).[43] His notion of civil equality seeks not to effect a positive good embodied in a system of order, but to prevent the evils invariably attendant on the abuse of freedom.

Legal Community

In Sieyès's social theory, society does not exist to pursue specific, collective ends, but is rather an end in itself. It allows its members to pursue their own particular interests. Yet the individual gains that stem from the division of labor (which, recall, frees him from the mundane and variegated concerns of everyday life) can only be reached via voluntary and mutual agreements, i.e. through contracts. For Sieyès, human rights existentially precede their codification as classical (i.e. legal positive) personal liberties by a political constitution in which they are sanctioned by the state in order to serve as safeguards against government action. It is clear from the introduction to his draft of the *Declaration of the Rights of Man and Citizen* (text 2) that Sieyès conceives of human rights as the structural principle of human sociality, which the philosopher extrapolates "in an analytic way"[44] from the fundamental datum of human socialization. All human rights can be traced to the basic, natural, legal principle that others may not be coerced, but may be bound only by free and

---

42 Sieyès, *Œuvres I*, no. 1, p. 3 ('Essai sur les privilèges').

43 Larrère, *L'invention*, p. 202.

44 'Manuscrit inédit de Sieyès sur les déclarations des droits de l'homme', in *Les déclarations des droits de l'homme de 1789*, ed. Christine Fauré (Paris, 1988), pp. 403–408, p. 406.

willing agreement: they articulate the essential "equality that brings together two people in free accord."[45] Rights establish a framework for the successful coexistence of many individuals, a framework that nevertheless conduces to the needs of each particular individual. Vis-à-vis their content, however, any specific account of human rights is dependent upon a given society's stage of development and its cultural peculiarities. Inherent to the differentiation of human rights is their irreducible historicity: the exact content of human needs, and thus rights, cannot fully be derived from the nature of man, whose character is anterior to the formation of the state. Nor, however, do individuated human rights have their source in laws. Their formalization adds nothing to the principle of equal freedom; as Sieyès writes, "the consequences which follow from them [the principles of natural law—OWL/FW] are merely explicated within the framework of the new relations in which socialized man once again is found."[46] What is at issue here is not only—indeed, not even primarily—the definition of human needs in terms, but rather the construction of a mode of legal coexistence in which a modern society recognizes an equality of rights among the citizenry. Life within this social mode is predicated on civility, the ability to recognize right for its own sake. Such social intercourse engenders a value-neutral public space in which different individuals can pursue their desires and fulfill their needs as they see fit; it does not compel citizens towards a particular conception of flourishing or happiness. According to Sieyès, political constitutions are just the instruments by which such a mode of social existence can be effected and maintained. This does not preclude government action in the social sphere; rather, it demands such intervention—not, however, from government's absolute authority, but through its credible representation of the communal interests that give form to the *volonté générale*. For Sieyès, this means enfranchising all citizens, not only those who can afford it. Obviously, the society which Sieyès rejects here is oligarchy, in either its aristocratic (i.e. privilege of birth) or plutocratic (i.e. privilege of wealth) form. The return to a society of privilege would be a horror; Sieyès's aim is equal rights for all citizens. Whichever citizen distinguishes himself by his achievements has a claim to social distinction, and whichever poor citizen cannot take advantage of his rights deserves the solidarity of society, which otherwise could not claim to recognize all citizens as equals.[47] In this way, the *Declaration of the Rights of Man and Citizen* gives form to the social contract; it establishes human rights

45 Ibid. p. 404.

46 Ibid., p. 404.

47 A.N. 284 AP 5, 4(2); cf. Pasquino 1998, pp. 122 f.

as both the "foundation" and "end"[48] of society. The location and function of human rights in Sieyès's political theory are described this way as well. As the *foundation* of society, rights belong to the civil sphere and concern first and foremost the relationships of individuals to each other. Only secondarily are they to be applied, vis-à-vis protective, negative personal liberties, to the relationship between the individual and the state. That Sieyès at the same time speaks of human rights as an *end* signifies that their normative content is not exhausted in their delineation and protection of spheres of negative freedom. Rather, bound up in the idea of human rights is a teleological drive towards liberal optimization: rightful governments must not only ensure but expand the domain of freedom for their citizens.

Sieyès derives the rights of man from the natural legal axiom of equal freedom (see text 1). Freedom, in his view, is the right to satisfy one's needs; need-satisfaction, in turn, enables the pursuit of well-being and happiness. In continuity with Locke,[49] Sieyès believed that every human being is "proprietor of his person" (art. III). The concept of property once again makes clear that freedom for Sieyès is not first created or realized within the political community but already exists in the civil sphere. Civil freedom has two dimensions which can be differentiated analytically. *Negative* freedom refers to the individual's right against the arbitrary exercise of power. It is expressed in defining one's needs and choosing their means of satisfaction. *Positive* freedom, on the other hand, involves the social organization and allocation of resources. This right, too, primarily concerns the civil realm, which is anterior to the state, and therefore pertains to political organization only secondarily. In contrast to republican tradition, positive freedom for Sieyès is not identical with political participation.

The limits of freedom are circumscribed by the freedom of others. Consequently, the obligation to respect the rights of others arises only as a result of legal relationships. Indeed, legal equality—a conceptual component of freedom rightly understood—is first realized in society. Accordingly, there exists a pre-legal obligation correspondent to this precept—namely, to leave the state of nature, where might makes right. Human rights mark the first step towards the formalization of natural law. As fundamental norms, they precede constitutions. They obligate the state in three ways:

48 Sieyès, *Manuscrits I* ('Base et fin de la société = respect de la liberté individuelle').

49 On Sieyès's relation to Locke, see Pierre-Yves Quiviger, 'Sieyès as a Reader of John Locke: Metaphysics, Politics and Law', in *Locke's Political Liberty: Readings and Misreadings*, ed. Christophe Miqueu and Mason Chamie, (Oxford, 2009), pp. 127–142.

(1) *Limitative function*: Human rights are the foundation of society. As such, the state's first task is to protect its citizens' freedom. Human rights thus serve to limit government power. In the draft of his *Declaration of the Rights of Man and Citizen*, Sieyès enumerates the classical, state-based personal rights (with the notable exception of religious freedom): a government that acts in accordance with the rule of law, freedom of occupation and of trade, freedom of movement, protection of private property, and freedom of expression and of the press. In addition, he champions a right to challenge despotic rule (i.e. a right to resistance) and a right to (periodically) revise the constitution (which prevents constitutional authority from being absorbed by the *pouvoirs constitués* without an express mandate).

(2) *Compensatory function*: For Sieyès, human rights do not only guarantee personal liberties, they furthermore ensure that individuals in need are entitled to help. Fundamental social rights are not established indirectly in order to provide positive freedom vis-à-vis material aid, but rather arise directly as a result of the social contract, which aims for "the greatest good for everyone" (art. II). According to Sieyès, social welfare administered by the state ensures equality of positive right, and also promotes equality among the citizenry—for Sieyès, a legal end in itself. He is nevertheless aware that an entitlement society may hypertrophy into a social welfare state. Thus he notes in Article XXXV:

> As for public charity, it is clear that it must only be distributed to those persons who are truly unable to provide for their needs; and this word is to be understood as referring to real needs, not the needs of vanity, for tax payers never intended to deprive themselves—sometimes of a part of what they truly require—so that a pensioner of the state live in luxury. Moreover, it is necessary that charitable assistance cease as soon as the disabilities that justified it come to an end.

(3) *Constitutive function*: In addition to their limitative and compensatory functions, human rights for Sieyès also serve a third, constitutive function: they compel political officeholders to enact policies which conceive of human rights as the *purpose* of society. In effect, it is the task of politics not only to "guarantee" rights and "serve" them, but also to "realize" them. This demand was ultimately included in the French Declaration of the Rights of Man and Citizen that was adopted on 26 August 1789. This declaration not only limited—like its American equivalents (e.g. the Virginia Bill of Rights)—but also legitimized the political order. This function is, among others, expressed in the centrality of the concept of laws as concrete interpretations of the principles of human

rights, which are supposed to optimize human rights as ends in themselves.[50] In contrast to the current material interpretation of fundamental rights by constitutional courts, Sieyès has in view not concrete sociopolitical decisions, but rather the parameters of such decisions. The Declaration of the Rights of Man thus provides legislators with a normative guide for organizing political power, defending a separation of powers that accounts for the division of labor as a criterion of political organization. A human-rights-oriented constitution must ensure that political decisions are made rationally and can be implemented efficiently.

Democratic Sovereignty

According to contractualist logic, nothing except voluntary consent has the force of obligation. Perhaps no other social contract theorist submitted voluntarism to such a systematic scrutiny as Jean-Jacques Rousseau. Only the consent of individual citizens can validate the social contract through which these citizens assume the dual role of *citoyen* (self-legislator) and *sujet* (who must recognize the binding force of external law). The legislative *volonté générale*, which is born as a collective agent through the original contract, is sovereign. Even still, "there is in the state no fundamental law [...] which cannot be repealed, not even the social pact."[51]

This construction inevitably raises the question of the aim of socialization. Rousseau placed this question at the center of his political philosophy, with a critical eye toward Hobbes's (and Locke's) theory of the social contract, which in his view was nothing more than a theory of obligation.[52] If political community is founded on the particular will of an individual, the origin of all laws—including that of the social contract—necessarily remains extrinsic to the citizen. For this reason, state decisions are tantamount to compulsory norms, from which self-determined citizenship cannot emerge. Rousseau believed to have solved this fundamental problem of social contract theory through the concept of the *volonté générale*. Willed consent, through which a civil society becomes a community of free citizens, finds its orientation vis-à-vis the common good, which, strictly speaking, can be recognized as such.[53] The problem of communal obligation disappears once the individual understands the

50 For a critique of the sovereignty-based understanding of rights see Marcel Gauchet, *La Révolution des droits de l'homme* (Paris, 1989).

51 Jean-Jacques Rousseau, *Du Contrat Social*, ed. Pierre Burgelin (Paris, 1992), III/18, p. 129.

52 Ibid., I/2–4, pp. 29–37.

53 Ibid., IV/1, pp. 133–135.

community as the foundation of his existence and brings his particular will in line with the *volonté générale*.

Sieyès vaguely echoes Rousseau in his pamphlet on the *Third Estate*, wherein he emphasizes the unbounded freedom of nations. A thorough reading of the text, however, shows that Sieyès does not adopt Rousseau's *volonté générale* wholesale. Rousseau's construction attempts to reconcile the modern phenomenon of subjectivity with the conception of corporate agency at the heart of ancient political systems. Sieyès points to this effort as a *ré-totale*, a conflation of the state and society that demands too much of the moral capacities of the citizen. The Rousseauian paradox that "men, before laws existed, would have to be what the laws themselves should make them"[54] exposes the root of this problem: his *original* contract demands a moral maturity that rightfully *follows* from successful socialization. Spinoza denounced such views as philosophical naïveté: a practical political theory must begin with "human nature as it actually is,"[55] not with man as he ought to be. Sieyès's program of *l'art social*,[56] which distinguishes between natural/organic and artificial/mechanical principles in society, assesses social developments similarly. Ultimately for Sieyès, in contrast to a naturalistic "logic of socialization," it is primarily positive law that is adaptive. With this instrument, incentives may be instituted to influence individual needs and interests.

The distinctions between a political system founded on morality and one founded on law are manifest in the very order of the commonwealth. When Rousseau speaks of legislation as the basis of order, he means the adoption of a constitution—an act so broad as to require a God-like *législateur*, who knows all human passions and is subject to none. Rousseau's constitution, in modern political theoretical rhetoric, is a fundamental order: a rational expression of the citizens' identity, a font of meaning and the existential root of their community. For Sieyès, on the other hand, constitutions create parameters: they establish the rules that organize the state and, to a lesser extent, the civic community. Nonetheless, Sieyès does not ignore Rousseau's insights about the moral foundations of the social contract. Rousseau calls on legislators to give the commonwealth the "best possible form."[57] And his drafts of constitutions for Corsica and Poland argue for the significance of political culture; the

54 Ibid., II/7, pp. 64 ff.

55 Baruch de Spinoza, *Tractatus politicus*, ed. Wolfgang Bartuschat, Latin-German, 2nd ed. (Hamburg, 2010), I/4.

56 Cf. Sonenscher, *Deluge*, pp. 259 f.

57 Rousseau, *Contrat Social*, II/12, pp. 78 ff.

législateur must take into account a nation's character and habits in order to create institutions that reflect its true *Geist*.

Both aspects, albeit in modified form, found their way into Sieyès's theoretical approach as matters of institutional organization. The personality of Rousseau's *législateur* finds its counterpart in Sieyès's constituting power (*pouvoir constituant*)—not to be confused with the general constituted powers (*pouvoirs constitués*) of Sieyès's legislature.[58] Similarly, Sieyès appropriates Rousseau's (and Montesquieu's) insight that constitutions must be adapted to the nation's stage of historical development. In this sense, Sieyès differentiates between the processes of *adunation* and *assimilation*.[59] Whereas assimilation denotes the general unification of the customs, values and views of a given society, adunation instead refers to the articulation and aggregation of diverse individual and collective interests within a society. The common social denominator, for Sieyès, is sifted out through the adunative and assimilative process of the formation of political will. Both processes are interrelated but do not permit simple correlation (i.e. inferring similar interests from common values). In Sieyès's view, rather, institutional mediation is required.[60] Moreover, the moral foundations of society can be strengthened (to a limited extent) through enlightenment, education and culture. If mediation of the two processes of assimilation and adunation is successful, the result is a tight bond between ethics and politics—ultimately even the domination of virtue in politics, which Sieyès terms *éthocratie* (following the Baron d'Holbach).[61] Under no circumstance, however, can the political realm be collapsed into the moral, or vice versa. Political activity remains dependent on moral attitudes—a

58 See Sonenscher, *Deluge*, p. 234.

59 Cf. Pierre-Yves Quiviger, *Le principe d'immanence. Métaphysique et droit administratif chez Sieyès. Avec des textes inédits de Sieyès* (Paris, 2008), pp. 301 ff., pp. 366 ff.

60 In his approach, Sieyès anticipates Hegel's distinction between the civil society (based on *Moralität*) and the political state (based on *Sittlichkeit*). Both spheres are different, though mediated—and it belongs to the fundamental insights of Hegel's political philosophy that they are treated that way, so that a societal plurality of interests can be maintained without endangering necessary political unity. Viewed against this backdrop, Sieyès's work can be seen as a sort of (Hegelian) 'Aufhebung' of Rousseau's *contrat social*, which not only allows for, but rather demands, two complementary perspectives: one that stresses continuity between Rousseau and Sieyès (see Sonenscher, *Deluge*, 234–237), the other that highlights Sieyès's focus on institutional arrangements (with recourse to Hobbes) and their impact on the political decision-making process.

61 Sieyès, *Manuscrits II*, pp. 544f. ('Ethocratie'). Sieyès refers to Paul Henri Dietrich d'Holbach, *Ethocratie, ou le gouvernement fondé sur la morale* (Amsterdam, 1776).

thoroughly corrupt civil service, for instance, presents a substantial burden for the state—, yet the viability of the state must be proven precisely when the ethical consensus which undergirds it grows tenuous.

Rousseau would have criticized such an institutionally-mediated coupling of morality and politics; it presupposes an internal division between citizens' moral and political identities that he finds subversive to community. The general will, an actual relationship between governing and governed, is in his view the only true form of democratic sovereignty. As a result, however, he is unwilling to debate the general will: it is primary. For Sieyès, such a conception of community is as wrongheaded as it is dangerous, as it assumes that the people exist as a collective subject and are capable of acting as such when necessary. Yet will is necessarily individual, oriented toward the particular. Rousseau therefore commits a category error: his general will wrongfully imparts general agency to a necessarily particular phenomenon.[62] For this reason, Sieyès sees political consensus as nothing more than the effective unanimous aggregate of individual wills (Rousseauian *volonté de tous*). No separate collective will can exist over and above the will of the individual citizens. Accordingly, Sieyès's understanding of democratic sovereignty does not entail the immediate unity of all citizens in the one, indivisible, indestructible, inalienable general will. Instead, democratic sovereignty lies in the representation of civic multiplicity—i.e. the expression of the divergent individual wills of each citizen, which only become a unified entity via their aggregation. The nation is, for Sieyès, a political unit whose commonalities must be articulated discursively (not, as for Rousseau, a metaphysical unity). Sonenscher emphasizes that, "as Sieyès understood it, a nation was not a body, but an abstraction represented by a body."[63] Were representation understood as merely symbolic rather than the actual expression of individual political wills, the democratic foundation[64] of the nation would be chimerical. Of course order and unity are secondarily necessary in Sieyès's theory, since an organized state and well-constituted political institutions are required in order to articulate agreement.

Sieyès's appreciation of voluntary sovereignty arises from a different understanding of democracy than Rousseau's. It is not the general will, shorn of the particular, that is exalted, but rather the nation *qua* legal entity, grounded

62 Patrick Riley, 'A Possible Explanation of Rousseau's General Will', *American Political Science Review* 64 (1970), pp. 86–97.

63 Michael Sonenscher, 'The Nation's Debt and the Birth of the Modern Republic: The French Fiscal Deficit and the Politics of the Revolution of 1789. Part II', in *History of Political Thought* 18 (1997), pp. 267–325, p. 314.

64 'Démocratie', A.N. 284 AP 5, 2(3).

equally in social pluralism and state unity. Despite this, Carl Schmitt, in his reading of Sieyès's theory of the *pouvoir constituant*,[65] focuses on the "formlessness" of the sovereign decision the nation makes about its own political form. Yet this reading completely misses the actual point of Sieyès, who understood politics first and foremost as creating order by giving form. Schmitt, on the other hand, hears only the decisionist tone of Sieyès's remarks on the nation. The following passage, in which Schmitt cites the Abbé's statement that "[i]t suffices that the nation wants,"[66] is characteristic of this. To continue from the same point:

> This statement from Sieyès most clearly gets at the essence of this process [of the nation's decision about its political form]. The constitution-making authority is not bound to legal structures and procedures; it is always 'in the state of nature' when it emerges in this inalienable quality.

According to Sieyès, however, the nation—not the authority to craft a constitution—exists in the state of nature. This is an important distinction, as the *pouvoir constituant* is a sophisticated entity, predicated on the division of labor and charged to create a new political form. Later, Sieyès gave the will to authorize the *pouvoir constituant* its own institutionalized form, which he termed the *pouvoir commettant*. Nevertheless, no substantial feature of his theory changed between the *Third Estate* and the draft of the *Declaration of the Rights of Man and Citizen*. As before, the nation endows a representative assembly with many powers, but not omnipotence. There is no mention of a sovereign *pouvoir constituant*, even in the state of nature. Rather, sovereignty is circumscribed by juridical boundaries and is organized according to the division of labor. Sovereignty is not characterized by "formlessness," but by a freedom of form.[67] Certainly, that the nation is free to decide if it wants to remain a nation, and if it wants a constitution (and if so, what kind). Yet does this freedom of form recognize normative restrictions through, say, natural law? Sieyès ultimately prized natural law over the nation in his pamphlet on the *Third Estate*. A blind faith in natural law is irrelevant, however, if it lacks sufficient individuated definition to compel particular behaviors in accordance with natural norms. Fundamental human rights are more promising, given Sieyès's dependence on the *jury*

---

65 Carl Schmitt, *Verfassungslehre*, 8th ed. (Berlin, 1993), pp. 77–80.

66 Ibid., p. 79.

67 Udo Steiner, *Verfassunggebung und verfassunggebende Gewalt des Volkes* (Berlin, 1966), pp. 216 f.

constitutionnaire, which includes jurisdiction over constitutional matters as well as human rights (see text 6). Sieyès's constitutional thought is predicated on an extensive arsenal of legal instruments that limit state action: a distinction between constitutional and sub-constitutional law, various methods of inter- and intra-supervision of government bodies, and so on.[68] For Sieyès, however, these efforts do not guarantee that the nation will never will itself a different political form—as the French Revolution emphatically demonstrated, not only in 1789 but through the constitutional experiments of the following years (1791, 1793, 1795 and 1799). As a constitutionalist, Sieyès consistently believed that the legal limitation of state power contributes significantly to the legitimacy of state action. As a contractualist, he championed the Rousseauian insight that the social contract must be democratic in nature.

Sieyès departed from democratic constitutionalism only at the end of the Revolution, when, after the Brumaire coup, his constitutional framework replaced indirect democratic elections with a co-optative selection process. Up to this point, he considered democratic sovereignty to be the sole legitimizing foundation of political order. Democracy creates an "unbroken chain of legitimacy"[69] that pervades the structures of a polity. According to Sieyès, this construction rests on three pillars:

(1) *Authorized power instead of absolute power*: Sieyès championed the idea—essential to the idea of a chain of legitimacy—that every public office requires authorization, that every public authority expresses the will of the nation that adopted the constitution. In connecting the principle of public office[70] to popular sovereignty, he turned Rousseau's *volonté générale* on its head. If republican principles are made to serve democratic self-determination, the nation's sovereignty attains a constitutional form that it cannot abandon without falling into a performative self-contradiction. This is a central feature of Sieyès's political theory—essentially, that sovereignty obtains legitimacy via representation. From this basic principle emerges a sovereignty whose internal logic is not absolute power but authorized power. Restrictions to democratic sovereignty thus do not follow from the yoke of natural law. Nor do they require a fictive juridical imputation that admits popular sovereignty only as a regulative ideal—for it is empirical individual wills that come to bear on the frame-

68 Karl Loewenstein, *Political Power and the Governmental Process* (Chicago et al., 1965), chaps. 6–9.

69 Ernst-Wolfgang Böckenförde, *Staat, Verfassung, Demokratie. Studien zur Verfassungstheorie und zum Verfassungsrecht*, 2nd ed. (Frankfurt a. M., 1992), p. 302.

70 On the concept of authorized power in office cf. Pasquino, *Sieyès*, pp. 52, 67.

work of the adoption of a constitution. It is the empirical will of the majority that appoints representatives via elections, and expresses trust or distrust in them based on their actions. The fiction of imputation only applies to elected officials and officeholders themselves, and to their self-understanding as representatives of the nation—i.e., insofar as this fiction ought to be made reality. Therefore, the modern effort to demarcate an 'empty space' for sovereignty is unnecessary: for Sieyès (anticipating Hegel),[71] sovereignty 'resides' in the nation.

(2) *Ré-publique*: The legitimacy of democratic sovereignty is only relevant with regard to political order. In other words, for Sieyès, democracy is not a normative *social* principle. How else could he justify the distinction in his pamphlet on the *Third Estate* between active and passive citizenship, except via a definition of nationhood as an economic association of shareholders who establish the necessary preconditions for political determination? This idea is further elaborated in *Of the Gains of Liberty* (text 4), where these shareholders are called 'entrepreneurs'—i.e., men who facilitate a sociopolitical state in order to profit from the gains of freedom. According to Sieyès, if they had devoted this profit to the service of the state, they would have entered into a misguided, totalizing political relationship between governing and governed. Such a *ré-totale* would unravel the normative constellation of public office, duty and authorization. Sieyès's republican concept of authorized power also holds true for potential political crises in which the nation again faces a breakdown of the political order. It would find itself in a state-of-nature-like situation and the circumstances of the *pouvoir constituant* would be literally extraordinary. Examples are situations in which, firstly, consensus on the old order has evaporated, or, secondly, the constitution is incomplete and must be augmented, or, thirdly, the consitution must be amended to match empirical realities. Sieyès's solutions for the two latter situations show his inclination for the concept of authorized power: they can be negotiated on the basis of the existing constitution through the establishment of a *jury constitutionnaire*,[72] which is, according to Oelsner, one of the "finest discoveries"[73] of the *art social* à la Sieyès.

71 See Sonenscher, *Deluge*, p. 89.

72 On Sieyès's jury see Marco Goldoni, 'At the Origins of Constitutional Review: Sieyès' Constitutional Jury and the Taming of Constituent Power', *Oxford Journal of Legal Studies*, 32 (2012), pp. 211–234.

73 Konrad-Engelbert Oelsner, *Des opinions politiques du citoyen Sieyès, et sa vie comme homme public* (Paris, 1799/1800), p. 255.

(3) *Circularity of democratic politics*: Functional requirements that provide lasting incentives to observe the constitutional rules offer a more effective protection against totalizing sovereignty than normative guidelines. Recall that Sieyès understands differentiation as a sort of social and political lifeblood. Society attains through political order qua representation a unity that it could not bring about on its own. The state, on the other hand, obtains via adunation the rich social matrix from which common interests and concerns emerge, the implementation of which is the task of politics. According to Sieyès, the social and political dynamics of distinction and interconnectedness find particular expression through organicist rhetoric, which supplements ideas of adunation and representation with the language of "regeneration."[74] The interplay of multiplicity and unity, which takes the human body as its model, finds a secondary expression in the personhood of the sovereign: in the people themselves, and in their representatives. Yet only the lasting regeneration of this representative relationship allows the political organism to remain viable. It is circulation itself, not the head or heart, which defines the life of a state. Sovereignty is not a matter of hierarchy, but collaboration. Whoever excludes himself forfeits his place in the new body of the nation.

Political Authority

For Sieyès, the division of labor demands positive law, so that social coherence can permeate and infuse the state. The legally-defined arena of state action serves as a foil to the contractually-defined social sphere. While in society everyone has a right to satisfy his needs, state actors require legal authorization. This explains why Sieyès wants human rights placed *before* the constitution (see the preface to text 2). A constitution is the means by which a state is established. Human rights, on the other hand, link the individual's needs to natural rights. State and society are linked above and beyond laws, which make a just life in society possible. Such is the lesson of the Declaration of the Rights of Man.[75] In the state, contrariwise, laws are the end of political action. The character of divided labor is thereby fundamentally changed. If division gives a natural structure to the multiplicity of interactions in society, it is palpably artificial in the realm of state. Absolutist rule creates "a political monster," as

74 Antoine de Baecque, *Le corps de l'histoire. Métaphores et politique* (1770–1800) (Paris, 1993), p. 118, pp. 123 ff.

75 See Jean-Denis Bredin, 'L'influence de Sieyès sur la Déclaration des droits de l'homme de 1789', in *Revue des Sciences morales et politiques* 144 (1989), pp. 253–264.

Sieyès puts it in his *First Thermidorian Intervention* (text 5). Yet the nation is also ill-advised when—out of fear of such a monster, as it were—it burdens itself with the exercise of government, thereby losing the original liberating benefits of political life. That is to say, as indeed Sieyès did in his *Of the Gains of Liberty* (text 4), freedom is attained not through independence, but through representation. Hedging against the dangers of such representative freedom—namely, defective and tyrannical political systems—is the paramount task of the constitutionalist. The *art social* protects the state from two evils, "excessive unity" and "excessive division"—the former would mean "despotism," the latter "anarchy." A proper constitution combines these two principles in an appropriate admixture.

For Sieyès, the right of the *pouvoir constituant* to implement a new constitution is granted solely by national mandate. His distinction between task and mandate is based on the amalgamation of two normative principles—namely democratic legitimacy, which originates in politically active citizenry, and republicanism, in which officeholders act within their authorized legal powers. Sieyès saw these two elements as the foundation of a representative order, which he explicitly set in opposition to the concept of a "democratic" constitution:

> In a democracy, the citizens themselves make the laws and appoint their public officials directly. In our conception, citizens elect—more or less directly—their delegates to the constitutional convention. The legislature is thus no longer democratic, but rather *representative*. The people exert a lasting influence on the [selection of their] representatives—no one can become a representative of the people who does not have the trust of his constituents—, yet the people themselves can in no case pass laws, let alone take the implementation of those laws into their own hands.[76]

In Sieyès's political thought, a democratic mandate refers to the political endorsement of active citizenry. Together with passive citizenry, the citizens form the national community in the state of society. National unity, however, is only a framework of the political process and for political action. The decision-making process must not assume a self-evident uniformity among the citizenry: it must take individual wills into account. For this reason, Sieyès is hostile to democracy because it sees the formation of national will and political

76 Sieyès, *Œuvres II*, no. 8, p. 3 ('Quelques idées de Constitution applicables à la ville de Paris').

decision-making as matters for citizenship.[77] Instead, these processes must be kept separate. Common interests must be generated *within* political discourse (and prove themselves to be of general interest) before they can be legitimately imbued with the binding force of law. A state is well-constituted, according to Sieyès's *First Thermidorian Intervention*, if its politics are characterized by the dual dynamics of "ascension" and "descension." Ascending movement requires a politically active citizenry, which authorizes its representatives to act on its behalf. To order this ascension, Sieyès advocated elections first and foremost. Commensurate with his distinction between civil and political rights, he always advocated restrictions to universal suffrage.[78] His restricting criteria, however, were not rooted in property but in the citizens' willingness to engage politically. The citizens' voluntary contribution to the public serves for Sieyès as evidence of a robust republican community spirit, which undergirds a politically active citizenry.[79] Property-restricted suffrage rights would be at odds with such a goal. Instead, Sieyès favored a number of sliding-scale electoral procedures to reduce democratic influence on the political process. Most importantly, he proposed a selection mechanism whereby citizens determine their choice of representative indirectly, via an electoral body that picks from a prescreened list of suitable candidates.[80] Sieyès held onto this electoral instrument his entire life: it appeared in his drafts of the constitution for the French consulate, which are marked by a profound skepticism toward the electorate.[81] In 1799 he went further, preventing this ascending movement from appointing representatives at the national level at all. Instead of direct election of electors, Sieyès favored indirect elections of lists of candidates, from which the *collège des conservateurs* could select members of parliament (text 7).

In this later model, it is fruitless to talk of democratic *processes*. In contrast to Sieyès's previous writings, however, one can detect the adunation behind indirect elections: they are an attempt to link an aggregation of individual interests with the appointment of political representatives. To this end, the process of building a political will is internally organized by election bodies that bind together three distinct elements—firstly, the community of politically

77 See the fragment 'Observations constitutionnelles', in *Manuscrits I*, pp. 19, 23, 116.

78 Sieyès, *Œuvres II*, no. 13, pp. 19 f. ('Observations sur le rapport du comité de Constitution, concernant la nouvelle organisation de la France').

79 Ibid., pp. 20–22.

80 This idea is not exclusively Sieyèsian. It can be traced back to Rousseau. It was then taken up by Mirabeau and advocated by Sieyès's companion Roederer. Cf. Sonenscher, *Deluge*, pp. 15, 69, 77 f., 80–90.

81 Cf. 'Démocratie', A.N. 284 AP 5, 2(5).

active citizens; secondly, the bond between factions of active citizens and their preferred candidates; and thirdly, the leveling of fringe interests via the narrowing of the electoral process itself, which produces something very like a meritocratic elite.[82]

The centrality of the democratic *principles*, however, is reflected—despite the centralizing tendencies in Sieyès's thought throughout the Revolution—in Sieyès's hierarchization of state powers. Like the relationship between the voter and his representative, the democratic laws of the national assembly function as a mandate for administrators. Sieyès grants normative priority to laws over the decisions of other state actors, tacitly assuming that laws represent the popular will of the active citizenry. This priority arises not from any particular obligation that the assembly holds to its constituents, but solely from its role as the existential representative of the community of politically active citizens. The purpose of Sieyès's multistage electoral process is precisely to ground a common national perspective on pertinent questions of state. Ideally, what ought to emerge from this process is a substantial agreement about answers to such questions (the 'what'), if not a consensus on the means of their resolution (the 'how'). This view is expressed above all in his apology for an independent mandate. Without an independent mandate, he claimed, the representatives of the national assembly would be unable to do their work properly.[83]

Other state organs are bound not by the mandate of voters, but by laws. Following Sieyès's hierarchization of norms,[84] legislative acts carry less weight than the constitution, but more weight than the individual acts of law-enforcing institutions (i.e. government, administrators, and courts). This does

82 Sonenscher highlights its artificial character: "[T]he meritocratic hierarchy [...] would be compatible both with those human qualities associated with admiration or respect and with all the ordinary economic and social arrangements likely to arise in a state of natural liberty. It would leave every kind of quasi-natural [i.e. property-based; OWL/FW] social hierarchy intact and form another, largely artificial hierarchy alongside of them, keeping a door permanently open for entry from the former to the latter [...]." (*Deluge*, p. 79).

83 Sieyès, *Œuvres I*, no. 7 ('Intervention de Sieyès dans le débat sur les mandats impératifs confiés aux Représentants par leurs électeurs').

84 Pasquino, *Sieyès*, pp. 75ff. compares Sieyès's approach to that of Hans Kelsen. See also Quiviger, *Principe*, p. 362.—A critical perspective which denies similarities between Sieyès and Kelsen can be found in Michel Troper, 'Sieyès et le jury constitutionnaire', in *Mélanges et l'Honneur de Pierre Avril. La République*, ed. Michel Ameller (Paris, 2001), pp. 265–282 and Troper, 'Sieyès et la hiérarchie des normes', in *Figures de Sieyès*, ed. Pierre-Yves Quiviger, Vincent Denis and Jean Salem (Paris, 2008), pp. 25–42.

not imply a deductive relationship between these norms, however: constitutional law and statutory legislation are too concrete to be explained in terms of one another (unlike natural law, which is indeterminate). Indeed, constitutional and statutory law are concrete enough to be regularly cited in legal disputes. Nevertheless, Sieyès believed that judicial power is necessary to adjudicate cases of ambiguity. From this insight—significant for the development of the modern constitutional state—he draws a distinction between government (*gouvernement*), which debates and plans, and administration (*pouvoir exécutif*), which executes and implements.[85] The government is legislator (*législature d'exécution*), grappling with state decisions and making decisions that can be standardized. Likewise, Sieyès distinguishes between offices that are bound by directives, and those that are independent of them. The discretionary powers of directive-independent government offices do not represent a necessary evil, but are in fact intended; yet, at the same time, they raise difficult questions of responsibility and accountability. Which instruments are at the disposal of the *pouvoir exécutif* to carry out the function of the office and to exert its appropriate influence, while still maintaining responsibility for this influence?[86]

Sieyès relies on positive law to validate the normative principles upon which political order is based. Positive law supports the decision-making process via the individualization of laws from the top down, and the process of forming political will via the selection of representatives from the bottom up. Accordingly, Sieyès sees in the legal containment of political power an essential feature of his representative constitutionalism. In his numerous drafts of constitutions, he spells out a system of government in which officeholders are representative, but nevertheless restrained while in power. Moreover, the independence of representatives is circumscribed to ensure that they remain sensitive to the needs of the citizenry. In the relationship between representative and represented, grounded in the self-determination of the nation, the representative form becomes a legal reality.

For Sieyès, both (complementary) "movements" of the political process, which stand above positive law in a "circular mechanism," are necessary if the division of labor is to avoid despotism and anarchy. The full meaning of ascending and descending movement is revealed through political processes that encompass the local and the regional levels. Sieyès conceives of adunation

85 Cf. Sieyès, *Manuscrits I*, pp. 399f. ('Notion du gouvernement').

86 The best analysis of the role that the executive plays in Sieyès's thought is presented by Quiviger, *Principe*.

as a form of political decentralization.[87] His three-step model of representation, which divides the French nation into eighty provinces (or departments) and 720 municipalities (or districts), each with nine cantons (or city districts), seeks to accomplish ascension and descension on multiple discursive planes. With his rigorous (and rather disconcerting) geometric structure, Sieyès pursues two goals. Firstly, his mathematically exact division of the nation stems from his belief in legal equality, which applies not only to citizens but to the nation's administrative entities as well. These entities undergird political representation and must thus be subject to strict apportionment. This includes fixed representation according to region, since a standard size demands consistent representation. Yet, as Sieyès notes, the size of a region must be considered alongside its number of active citizens, their ability to pay taxes, and the level of their republican fervor—all relevant variables for the purpose of proportional balance.

Secondly, Sieyès means to annihilate the traditional administrative structures of the *ancien régime* without jeopardizing its efficiency. The process of democratic will-building must, according to Sieyès, be augmented by forms of communal self-administration. Citizen assemblies therefore assume an important function extrinsic to their formal *raison d'être*: they are sites of political integration. Here issues are debated, various citizens' interests and needs are discussed, and representatives are assessed. Moreover, assemblies compile the candidate registers that are essential for indirect elections. Representative assemblies are a precondition for politically active citizens to select representatives of their trust. Sieyès labels these political referees "the essential driving force of society."[88] Thanks to the small scale of citizen assemblies, citizens are not only able to possess the knowledge necessary to debate politically, but are able to bring their personal abilities to bear on public questions. Accordingly, their registries ideally spring from complementary interests and virtues. At this personal level, citizens can authentically place their trust in the person standing for election, and in his ability to represent their interests. The candidate is able to demonstrate his moral fiber to his constituents. The interplay of moral trust and political power is critically important for Sieyès.[89]

87 Sieyès, *Manuscrits I*, pp. 485f. ('Arrêter l'influence de Paris dans l'ordre politique').
88 Sieyès, *Œuvres II*, no. 8, p. 22 ('Quelques idées de Constitution applicables à la ville de Paris').
89 Consider the beginning of his draft for a 'Constitution of Paris': "For the governed must be able to have respect for and trust in the governing. This attitude arises from the people voluntarily; at the same time, it is indispensable to maintaining good order." Ibid., p. 4.

Sieyès's conceptual link between trust and power strengthens for him the bond between democratic mandate and a republican notion of political representation. They build on his principle of divided labor in the political realm, and give form to the idea that the basis for trust is not weakened, but confirmed, by divided labor. According to the principles of the division of labor, a hired man must possess the requisite expertise for his task. Because Sieyès sees the distinction between state and society as a self-conscious decision among the members of society to divide their labor, it is unsurprising that, for Sieyès, the validity of the political process is predicated on expert knowledge as well. Indeed, he scorned the nobility precisely because of their baseless claims for themselves of exalted positions that rightly belonged to experts. Sieyès contrasts an aristocracy of birth with an intellectual aristocracy of talent, which he deemed the "true nobles."[90] Among these elites are specialists who possess political expertise, and are capable of using their talents for the common good. Whoever can justify himself as a true meritocrat has earned his place on the electoral register: he can court the public trust with good conscience. The final decision over whether a candidate indeed possesses intelligence and conscience must be decided in the assemblies. The people themselves must recruit the elites; that is to say, they are responsible for the quality of their government. In this way, Sieyès's constitutionalism promoted theoretical debate about political questions and practical discussion about representative personnel at all levels of government, even as it vested active citizens with a modicum of real power.

Mixed Government Revisited

Whereas Sieyès's normative principles aimed to simultaneously legitimate and delimit political order, his functional principles optimized interaction between political institutions. In his *First Thermidorian Intervention* he distinguished between two functional models: an ineffectual "system of equilibrium" and a fluid "system of cooperation" (also called a model for "organized unity"), which he favored.[91] In his view, the equilibrium model was profoundly misguided, since it erroneously assumed that two distinct governmental bodies can exercise the same political function. Yet, Sieyès writes polemically, nobody would have the walls of his house erected twice, by two different masons. Such

90 Cf. Sieyès, *Manuscrits I*, p. 449 ('Nobles'). See also his 'Essai sur le meilleur moyen de détruire la noblesse féodale, gentilhommière et royale' (1789), cf. A.N. 284 AP 4, 8(3).

91 See Sieyès, *Manuscrits I*, pp. 489 ff. ('Fragments politiques').

redundancy would not only be wasteful: in the realm of state, divergent actions by government officials can damage consensus about the common good. At the very least, if two government bodies are charged with the same function, a higher arbitrator capable of resolving the deadlock must be appointed. Otherwise the political order undermines its own stability: the structural possibility of obstructionism will inevitably provoke constitutional crises. To spell out this danger, Sieyès describes the systemic flaws of three common constitutional models.

(1) *Bicameralism*: Sieyès takes neither the American constitution—though it proceeded from a liberal revolution—nor the English system—highly praised by Montesquieu—as his model. The House of Lords, a second chamber alongside the Commons, is anathema to him, since it presupposes an estate-based segmentation of society. Yet he likewise rejects what he calls the 'bourgeois' variant to the Lords—namely, the Senate of the United States. Since the American House of Representatives and Senate each possess distinct legislative rights, decision-making must be arduously synchronized, or else remain fruitless. That this institutional division attempted a representative compromise regarding the competing claims of population and statehood discredits this arrangement for Sieyès. Unlike the American states, France is not a federation but an indivisible nation,[92] the unity of which must be expressed by its political order.

(2) *Veto power*: For Sieyès, the bitter fight over the royal veto in September 1789 is most fundamentally about how to represent national unity in a constitution—a function that, in his view, lies within the purview of the monarch. Sieyès opposes any monarchial veto over parliament, thereby rebutting not only the anglophiles' demand for an absolute veto but also the majority's preferred suspensive veto. Such arrangements are incompatible with free and equal representation, he claimed; the royal will cannot rightfully counteract the will of the nation. "[T]hen the law would be the expression of a single will; then the king would be able to declare himself the *single* representative of the nation."[93] This privilege does not belong to him: he is the embodiment, not the creator, of the will of the nation. It is precisely this representative function that precludes the monarch's separation from the general community. As a citizen, he can express his will. As the representative of the nation, however, he may not legislate unilaterally on behalf of the nation, for law is

92 Sieyès, *Œuvres II*, no. 12, p. 10 ('Dire de l'abbé Sieyès, sur la question du veto royal').

93 Ibid., p. 6.

the amalgam of the individual wills of the governed. The monarch may certainly advise legislators, but if he conspires to legislate himself, he oversteps his bounds. From this sinister mixing of functions, despotism arises all too easily. One should not surrender to the illusion, Sieyès argues, that there is a categorical difference between 'making' and 'obstructing' laws: the veto allows the government to override the will of the majority so that laws must conform to *its* will.[94]

(3) *Collective executive body*: Sieyès's rejection of the veto in no way sought to delegitimize the monarchy. Rather, he repeatedly defended the existence of the monarchy against no less a critic than Thomas Paine, the celebrated radical publicist of the two revolutions.[95] Sieyès's monarchism was rooted in his understanding of republicanism. Paine understands a republic as a system of representative democratic rule.[96] Sieyès is concerned that political power and legal responsibility be harmonized such that the basis for state action is solely the will of the people. His essential dilemma lies in the proper organization of the exercise of state power. The government must be able to take up and represent a multiplicity of interests. Yet it must also embody the unity of the nation. Republics are unbalanced toward multiplicity, monarchies toward unity. Therefore, the solution to their excesses is a government that mediates multiplicity and unity. Here begins Sieyès's critique of Paine's republicanism. A government must choose between monarchical leadership (hereditary or elective) or a republican governing body. If there is no central head of government, the political decision-making process will be unable to smooth a plurality of interests into a unified will. Sieyès calls this state of affairs "polyarchy"; he sees in its division and incompetence essential structural problems of republican government.

---

94 In this light, Sieyès's later attempts to reconcile the constitutional practice of 1791 with his theoretical groundwork seem unpersuasive. Cf. Sieyès, *Manuscrits I*, pp. 413 ff. (Idée exacte et précise des pouvoirs publics dont l'ensemble forme la Royauté en France, suivie d'un nouveau plan de constitution ministérielle, etc.).

95 Oliver W. Lembcke and Florian Weber, 'Sieyès' Konzept der Staats- und Regierungsform', in *Volkssouveränität und Freiheitsrechte. Emmanuel Joseph Sieyès' Staatsverständnis*, ed. Ulrich Thiele (Baden-Baden, 2009), pp. 139–165.

96 For a detailed analysis of Paine's republicanism, see Richard Whatmore, '"A Gigantic Manliness": Paine's Republicanism in the 1790s' in *Economy, Polity, and Society. British Intellectual History 1750–1950*, ed. Stefan Collini, Richard Whatmore and Brian Young (Cambridge, 2000), pp. 135–157.

In his form of divided government, Sieyès fused the advantages of monarchy with those of a republican ministerial cohort. As Michael Sonenscher states: "The outcome would be a system of government that would join the unity of monarchy to the pluralism of a republic and, by doing so, would bypass the need to have to make a choice between the two."[97] At the apex of his government stands a monarch who merely appoints and removes ministers subordinate to him—much like the monarch in Hegel's philosophy of right.[98] The monarch's scope of duties is limited, and his political power is minimal. Nevertheless, insofar as Sieyès and Hegel see the monarch as an expression of *auctoritas* rather than *potestas*, they anticipate the role of the head of state in modern constitutional democracies. The actual significance of the monarch is hidden. He is bound to no party, and monitors decision-making within his ministries as the trustee of the nation.[99] His presence symbolizes that the government does in fact make decisions in the name of, and for the good of, the people. Whereas ministers concern themselves with technical matters, the monarch embodies the whole government.[100]

In his *First Thermidorian Intervention*, Sieyès claims that state decisions should lead to an *unité d'action*, but not an *action unique*. The end of the political process should be a unified decision to which various actors have contributed. Such unity cannot precede institutional interactions—not even in a substantial commonality (*ré-totale*)—and therefore no single actor can claim that the government's actions are his alone (*action unique*). Rather, effective state action involves parallel processes of cooperation. Firstly, the politically active citizenry engages in a hierarchical process of democratically appointing legal officeholders. Secondly, heterarchical ministerial bodies make, implement, and apply the law. The separation of these processes is an expression of the *ré-publique*, i.e. self-limiting power. Accordingly, the principle of suspension of incompatibility common to parliamentary governments finds no support from Sieyès. In his view, governments tend toward despotism, and to create a "temporary parliamentary dictatorship" in this way would be foolhardy and illiberal. The functions of government may not be mixed, not even indirectly via the accumulation of offices.

97 Sonenscher, *Deluge*, p. 13.

98 Oliver W. Lembcke, 'Institutionalisierung eines pouvoir neutre? Oder: Wie Hegel aus dem Klumpen einen Knoten machte', in *Staat, Politik und Recht beim frühen Hegel*, ed. Michael Henkel (Berlin, 2002), pp. 85–123.

99 Sieyès, *Œuvres II*, no. 12, p. 7 ('Dire de l'abbé Sieyès, sur la question du veto royal').

100 On the role of the monarch see Sieyès, *Manuscrits I*, pp. 428 ff. ('Qu'est-ce que le roi?').

Nevertheless, efficiency remains an essential challenge. Here especially, Sieyès claimed, mixed-constitutional models predicated on "equilibrium" struggle. For this reason, though he believed in a strict separation of powers, including an incompatibility of appointive and elective offices, he guards against the ill-effects of divided government. Sieyès prizes a constitutional model equidistant from both the efficient yet potentially despotic systems of "unity" and the representative but inefficient systems of "division"—to wit, a mixed-constitutional model of "organized unity," for only "[d]ivision and unity combined can serve to provide the sort of political guarantee without which freedom is in constant danger." He thereby established what Richard Whatmore aptly calls "a French 'third way', entailing neither mixed government nor forms of economic or political despotism."[101]

The Context of His Political Writings

With his polemical *What Is the Third Estate?* (text 1), Sieyès executed a rare feat for public intellectuals: he composed a substantive text that resonated in the political arena. This pamphlet, the most extensive he ever published, can well be compared to the *Federalist Papers* or the *Communist Manifesto* and their respective significance in American constitutionalism and socialist thought. The *Third Estate* belongs to a flood of pamphlets that appeared in 1788 and 1789, the crisis years of the *ancien régime*. The volume of French political pamphlets had increased steadily since the 1770s as a result of the liberalization of the press under the late-monarchical period. Pamphlet dissemination increased particularly dramatically when Louis XVI summoned the Estates-General to address a growing French financial crisis. Sieyès's tremendous productivity helped him to stand out among the crowd of pamphleteers: on the eve of the Estates-General he published three tracts, each of them written within a couple weeks.[102] His work ethic and encyclopaedic knowledge of politics, philosophy, and economics stemmed from his many years of study in seminary during the mid-1770s. Sieyès drew from this breadth of knowledge his entire life. At the end of 1788, he published his *Views of the Executive Means Available to*

---

101 Richard Whatmore, 'Enlightenment Political Philosophy', in *The Oxford Handbook of the History of Political Philosophy*, ed. George Klosko (Oxford/New York, 2011), pp. 296–319, p. 314.

102 For a reconstruction of the concrete political background, see Sonenscher, *Deluge*, pp. 283ff.

the Representatives of France in 1789[103] and his *Essay on Privileges*,[104] both of which paved the way for the brilliant success of his *Third Estate*. More than thirty thousand copies of the pamphlet were sold in the weeks following its publication in January 1789; within six months, four editions had appeared in France. Only on the printing of the extensively revised and supplemented third edition in May 1789 did Sieyès reveal himself as the author. All told, perhaps as many as 300,000 copies of the essay were printed, reaching upwards of one million readers. Overnight, the publication turned the Abbé into a celebrity: at the opening of the Estates-General, he was an indisputable star among his fellow revolutionaries.

Sieyès's political successes followed fast on the heels of his success in the realm of letters. Indeed, the initial steps of the constitutional revolution seemed a vindication of his *Third Estate*. On 10 and 11 June 1789, Sieyès challenged the clergy and aristocracy of the First and Second Estates to join the Third Estate, which alone represented "the entire nation." Two weeks later, at the prodding of a capitulating Louis XVI, a majority of the first two Estates' representatives complied with Sieyès's demands. By this time, the logic of representation had irrevocably destroyed the logic of aristocratic privilege. On 17 June, the newly amalgamated Third Estate declared themselves a National Assembly and swore on the royal tennis court not to disband until they had established a written constitution for France—just as Sieyès had urged.

The political potency of Sieyès's pamphlet lay in its mixture of polemic and policy prescriptions. Alongside his biting critique of estates-based society, which he further developed in his *Essay*, Sieyès explicated the practical features of a political order based on the sovereignty of the nation. Simultaneously, he outlined a scheme for the transfer of powers to the people and the rearrangement of aristocratic institutions. This combination of principle and practice makes the *Third Estate* a handbook for the revolutionary foundation of a new political order—equal in this respect to the *Federalist Papers*.

The comparison between Sieyès and the American Founders may perhaps seem odd: Sieyès has a reputation for concerning himself only with theoretical questions of legitimacy, whereas the pragmatic American Founders are often seen as prizing political stability. These popular perceptions are misguided: With his doctrine of constituent power, Sieyès created a sword of Damocles that could vanquish vested powers at the will and pleasure of the

---

103 Sieyès, *Œuvres I*, no. 2 ('Vues sur les moyens d'exécution dont les Représentants de la France pourront disposer en 1789').

104 Sieyès, *Œuvres I*, no. 1 ('Essai sur les privilèges').

people. The doctrine of *pouvoir constituant* was radical insofar as it was oriented against the old regime, yet its true accent for Sieyès lay not in its revolutionary implications, but in its potential for constituting political community.

The work of constitution-making, to which the Third Estate bound itself with its Tennis Court Oath, began with a debate on human rights. Sieyès offered to this conversation his *Reasoned Exposition of the Rights of Man and Citizen* (text 2). On 9 July 1789, General Lafayette—the hero of the American War of Independence—introduced a draft of a French declaration of human rights, and thereby inaugurated a debate that raged for over six weeks and concluded with the *Declaration of the Rights of Man and Citizen* on 26 August. Lafayette's draft drew heavily on the bills of rights of the New England colonies; it was short and prosaic, written in a juridical style, and divided into articles. He was unable to bring the National Assembly behind his proposal, however. Although the American example shone bright in the minds of the deputies, they were also aware of the circumstantial differences between America and France. American constitutional debates codified existing civil rights and liberties in a new and largely undiscovered country; in France, legislators sought to construct a free and equal political order on the ashes of centuries of privilege and class distinction. Therefore a French declaration of rights had to accomplish more than the American bills of rights: it had to establish foundations for a new political order. The rights of man were to be the origin and aim of all political action.

This right-based political agenda was the subject of fierce debate. The French debate on human rights in the summer of 1789 was an early battle in the struggle to politically define the Revolution. Even before the National Assembly began debating individual rights, deputies wondered if the Declaration of the Rights of Man should be promulgated before the constitution, or be included as the constitution's first section. Should the Declaration take the form of a philosophical treatise, or a collection of juridical articles? Could the Declaration stand on its own legitimacy, or did it require a corresponding Declaration of Obligations?

Sieyès's counterproposal to Lafayette of 21 July claimed that the Declaration should be independent of the constitution, so as to serve as a foundation and benchmark for constitutionalist (self-) understanding. Most fundamentally, he hoped that the Declaration would establish a political foundation that sprang from the needs inherent in human nature. Sieyès thus reluctantly included in his remarks a short outline of needs-oriented rights, in order to satisfy the majority. He mentioned nothing about obligations, however; he believed that legal obligations would emerge naturally from the symmetrical structure of rights.

The National Assembly ultimately decided on a Declaration in the form of articles, promulgated independently of the constitution and without a complementary declaration of obligations. In this early debate, Sieyès won out against conservatives who demanded a list of obligations to parallel any declaration of rights. Sieyès's influence on the Declaration's character and form was likewise profound, even if his handwriting is not immediately recognizable in the document's rhetoric.[105]

Yet with regard to contemporary discussions of human rights, which often invoked the French Declaration of the Rights of Man as a seminal discursive moment, Sieyès seems obsolete. His anthropological explanation of human rights, which bears both naturalistic and utilitarian characteristics, has been eclipsed by discursive and deontological neo-Kantian models. Likewise, the tension between sovereignty and the authority of laws remains unsettled in his writings. However, Sieyès's theory of rights merits study in two particular respects. Firstly, Sieyès sees in human rights a social dimension; in contrast to a (mere) liberal conception of rights, he talks explicitly of a right to social welfare. Secondly, he demands that the state fulfill its obligation to realize rights. His remarks on the complementarity of rights and needs anticipate a Rawlsian liberalism that encourages legislators to account for the conditions necessary for the optimization and flourishing of rights.

After adopting the Declaration of the Rights of Man and Citizen on 26 August 1789, the National Assembly dedicated itself to basic questions of state organization. In the summer of 1789, none of the revolutionaries questioned the monarchy. Only after Louis XVI's failed escape attempt, which ended with his arrest in Varennes on the night of 21 June 1791, did the radicals begin calling the office into question. At this point, the constitutional monarchy was in crisis at any rate: Louis had never accepted his new constitutional role and had entertained thoughts of fleeing since October 1790. In the wake of his treason, what arguments existed in favor of the monarchy? This question was the subject of a *Controversy between Thomas Paine and Sieyès* (text 3). In mid-July 1791, a portion of the populace demanded the deposition of the king at demonstrations in Paris. Radical republicanism began to seep into the discussions of the political elite, as the establishment of the *Société républicaine* attests. The Marquis de Condorcet, philosopher and confidant of Sieyès, was among its founding members, as was Thomas Paine, whose pamphlet *Common Sense* sparked revolution in America, much like Sieyès's *Third Estate* did in France. Persecuted after his return to England in 1786, Paine fled into exile to France. He received French

105 On this question see Bredin, *L'influence*.

citizenship on 26 August 1792 (as did George Washington and Friedrich Schiller, incidentally) and was later elected to the National Convention. Alongside Condorcet, Paine had called for the foundation of a French Republic as early as the summer of 1791.

Despite the king's perceived perfidy, a large majority of the deputies stood by Louis XVI early in the Revolution, including Robespierre himself. The Jacobins' accusation that Sieyès was antimonarchical and partial to the republicans was calculated to paint him as a fickle vacillator, and to undermine his political authority. Sieyès confronted their slander directly with a challenge in the *Moniteur* on 6 July, in which he called for a debate. He proved his Jacobin bona fides by claiming that citizens are freer in a monarchy than in a republic, a provocation that Paine readily contested. On 8 July, he released a merciless assault on monarchical governments, a work translated into French by Condorcet and published in the first issue of the Republican Society's journal, *Le Républicain*. Poised for a vigorous counterattack, Sieyès vindicated the "hell of monarchy" from Paine with a long response in the *Moniteur* on 16 July. He meticulously disarmed Paine, arguing instead that monarchy is most truly republican, i.e. the freest form of government.

Sieyès argued that a unitarian state could be held together only by a presidential or monarchical system of government. The efficiency of state action made possible by a unitary executive would disburden the citizens and thereby increase their freedom. His case for monarchy stemmed from his belief in the functional, rather than institutional separation of powers—an idea that he would define more precisely in his *First Thermidorian Intervention*.

In the summer of 1791, the republicans were too few to topple the monarchy. Instead, a committee was appointed to revise the constitution. This committee, to which Sieyès also belonged, left the monarchy unmolested; instead, it raised the financial preconditions for suffrage in reaction to the popular unrest and intermittent martial law of the previous summer. The National Assembly finished its work in peace and presented it to the king, who swore an oath to the constitution on 14 September.

The triumph of the monarchy would prove Pyrrhic. Less than one year later, the storming of the Tuileries on 10 August heralded the demise of Louis XVI, whose fate was sealed on 21 September with the proclamation of the Republic. A new constitutional convention was assembled—but, in this assembly, Sieyès did not play a decisive role. He participated in these debates only as a *homme public*, via his article *Of the Gains of Liberty in Society and in the Representative System* (text 4). This piece first appeared in the second issue of the *Journal de l'instruction sociale* on 8 June 1793, a journal published by Sieyès with Marie Jean Antoine Nicolas de Caritat Condorcet and Jules-Michel Duhamel.

The journal sought to fill the lacuna created when the *Journal de la Société de 1789* was discontinued in September 1790 due to lack of funds. The new journal hoped to introduce *art social* to a broad public, thereby contributing to enlightenment and civic education.[106] In his essay, Sieyès proposed to interrogate the idea of freedom. With eerie prescience he asked how self-evidently oppressive political measures could be promulgated in the name of liberty. In opposition to the collectivist Rousseauian understanding of freedom as an expression of the general will, he distinguished between negative and positive freedom. Unlike Isaiah Berlin—who often takes credit for this distinction—Sieyès granted positive freedom an irreducible place within his liberal theory.

With his *Thermidorian Interventions* on 2 and 18 Thermidor in the third year of the Republic (20 July and 5 August 1795), Sieyès joined parliamentary debates on the third Revolutionary constitution, again unsuccessfully. The convention adopted the constitution on 22 August without Sieyès's proposals, and the people ratified it in primary assemblies on 6 September.

After the fall of Robespierre on 9 Thermidor II (27 July 1794) the Jacobin constitution of 1793 was widely viewed as illegitimate. Leading politicians called for a new political order. The Jacobins' opponents saw the previous constitution as too democratic, an ineffective system that paved the way for a new dictatorship. On 3 April 1795 Sieyès was appointed to a committee charged to determine whether the constitution should be reformed or rewritten. As a member of the Committee of Public Safety—the de facto executive branch of the Republic in the wake of Robespierre's dictatorship—he felt ill-suited to answer this question. Accordingly, he relinquished his seat on the constitutional committee. Eventually known as the Commission of Eleven, this group began working toward a new constitution on 20 and 21 May.

On 23 June, the commission presented a constitution designed to prevent a new Terror: firstly, by introducing property-based suffrage, which excluded the poor from politics; secondly, by creating a second chamber of parliament to check parliamentary majorities; and thirdly, by instituting an independent executive power.

In his *First Thermidorian Intervention* (text 5) of 20 July 1795, Sieyès criticized the committee's anglophilic balance of powers via bicameralism. Against this *equilibrium model*, Sieyès suggested a *model of cooperation* that internally differentiated the various departments of government but nevertheless connected

106 For a reconstruction of the "art social" project and the innovative role political language plays therein, see Jacques Guilhaumou, *Sieyès et l'ordre de la langue. L'invention de la politique moderne* (Paris, 2002).

them functionally.[107] Thus he segmented the legislative process into discrete stages—proposal, deliberation, adoption, promulgation—but still preserved a unicameral legislature that could not be counteracted by a veto. In the sphere of executive action he distinguished between a government that legislates and an executive administration—a division now a central feature of modern parliamentary systems.

Yet Sieyès's proposals fell on deaf ears; indeed, only his plan for a constitutional jury was considered. In the enthusiasm for moderated bicameralism, his critique found few sympathetic readers. His complex institutional design was intellectually impenetrable for many members of parliament. Having kept a low profile during the assembly of the constitutional commission only to emerge as a critic afterwards, Sieyès seemed arrogant to the Commission of Eleven, many of whom had actively sought his advice during their work. As his political brother-in-arms Benjamin Constant later wrote of Sieyès, "He lectures, but he does not discuss."[108] Indeed, his rhetorical style allowed his enemies to marginalize him politically. His cavalier attitude suggested neither a calculating political mind, nor the steadfastness necessary to forge coalitions to implement his agenda. Sieyès's biographer Jean-Denis Bredin has gone so far as to claim that the Abbé had no practical intentions whatsoever; rather, his writings were composed for the enlightened intelligentsia of Paris, and for posterity. In this light, Paul Bastid considered the *First Thermidorian Intervention* the most important speech of Sieyès's career.[109] It enumerates a plan for stable constitutional order in the wake of the Terror, even as it demonstrates a fluid continuity with his earlier political writings: in particular, his critique of totalistic theories of sovereignty found expression in his juxtaposition of *ré-publique* and *ré-totale*.

When Sieyès delivered his *Second Thermidorian Intervention* (text 6) on 18 Thermidor III (5 August 1795), he knew he was fighting a losing battle. The Commission of Eleven had rejected his earlier reformist proposals, claiming that his concerns had already been addressed by their constitutional draft. This claim must have seemed absurd to Sieyès: large swaths of his *First Thermidorian*

---

107 Cf. Lucien Jaume, 'Sieyès et le sens du jury constitutionnaire: une réinterprétation', in *Droits. Revue française de théorie juridique* 36 (2002), pp. 115–134.

108 See Marc Lahmer, 'Sieyès lors des débats constituants en l'an III. Autopsie d'un échec', in *Figures de Sieyès*, ed. Pierre-Yves Quiviger, Vincent Denis and Jean Salem (Paris, 2008), pp. 43–82, p. 82.

109 Bredin, *Sieyès*, p. 517; Paul Bastid (ed.), *Les discours de Sieyès dans les débats constitutionnels de l'an III* (2 et 18 thermidor) (Paris, 1939).

Intervention criticized the Commission's bicameralist parliamentary model in favor of his preferred unicameralism. As Sieyès's authority within political circles was clearly fading, he also entertained little hope for his constitutional juridical scheme.

Nevertheless, in his *Second Thermidorian Intervention* he argued that an institutional "guardian"—his constitutional jury—must protect the foundations of any constitutional order. He tasked his jury with three responsibilities: firstly, as a *court of cassation*, the jury was to interpret the constitution, and to judge whether particular legislation was constitutional; secondly, as a *committee for reform*, the jury was to collect proposals for constitutional reforms every ten years, and to submit these reforms to the primary assemblies; and thirdly, as a *human rights court*, the jury was to ensure that complete equity pervaded French jurisprudence.

The Commission initially favored a constitutional jury for reviewing the constitutionality of laws (an idea, incidentally, that anticipated modern constitutionalism). But the Commission also believed that charging this institution with reforming the constitution and ensuring the equity of jurisprudence would make its powers too great.

The idea of an institution dedicated to monitoring the constitutionality of legislative, executive, and judicial action did not originate with Sieyès but with the journalist Roch-Henri Prévost de Saint-Lucien, under his proposal for a *jury constitutionnel*.[110] The Abbé picked up on this idea, which had been debated since early 1795, in his second Thermidor speech. He watered down the potency of Saint-Lucien's proposal, however, to accommodate critics who saw in the jury an inordinate restriction of popular sovereignty.

Whereas his *First Thermidorian Intervention* granted the constitutional jury a material right to preemptively examine resolutions of the legislative assembly (i.e. laws that had been passed but not yet promulgated), in his *Second Thermidorian Intervention* the constitutional jury was restricted to merely monitoring the legislature's compliance with the constitution. Whether such a constitutional formalization of democracy is desirable remains a fundamental question of political theory to this day, typically debated as the 'counter-majoritarian difficulty.'

Sieyès's constitutional jury became a reality several years later—not in France, but in the United States—when the American Supreme Court recognized the Constitution as the supreme law of the land, and declared itself the arbiter of constitutional disputes. In France, on the other hand, popular

110 See Lahmer, *Sieyès*.

sovereignty remained unrestrained by restrictions, despite Sieyès's frequent concessions in his model for a constitutional jury. Even later iterations of the institution were unanimously rejected by the convention.

Disappointed, Sieyès turned his back on politics. When he was elected to the five-member Directory after the constitution had been adopted, he refused to serve. He disappeared from politics, only to reemerge four years later to join constitutional debates one last time. He aligned himself with Napoleon, whose rise he aided yet whose power he hoped to check with an effective constitution. The greatest innovation of his *Constitutional Observations* (1799) (text 7) was his new *Grand Electeur*, a republican "king" who represented the unity of the nation. The *Grand Electeur* would function as head of government and appoint consuls, but would not directly govern. A consul for foreign affairs and a consul for domestic affairs, each at the head of a state council (*Conseil d'État*), would handle practical political matters, with the *Grand Electeur* as the arbiter of jurisdictional disputes between the consuls. His power of appointment would be limited too: if an officeholder vacates his position, his successor is chosen via lottery from a predetermined group of candidates. This method of appointment stands in opposition to direct-democratic or parliamentary-democratic processes, insofar as only the highest governmental bodies would participate in the selection of the head of state.

Sieyès transferred the leadership role of the executive to a "state council"[111] that would take on the work of government. In addition to introducing legislation as a *conseil de proposition* and regulating administration as a *jury d'exécution*, the state council would also, as a *législateur réglementaire*, have authority over administrative offices not under the control of the ministers. Moreover, the state council would possess an administrative jurisdiction befitting a committee well-versed in questions of administration. The establishment of a state council represents a remarkable progression in Sieyès's constitutional thought. Although he considered parliamentary impeachment a sufficient check on ministers at the beginning of the Revolution, by the turn of the century he had expanded checks and balances to the civil service and integrated oversight measures into the executive branch. With these intra-institutional supervisory measures Sieyès was able to account for fundamental differences between government and administration while remaining faithful to his original theory of a functional separation of powers. The state council would reign in the excesses of the civil service from within the machinery of the political system.

111 On this institution, see Quiviger, *Principe*, pp. 214 ff. and pp. 329 ff.

The task of defending the constitution, which Sieyès had entrusted to the *jury constitutionnaire* in 1795, would be given to a *collège des conservateurs*. In contrast to the jury, the *collège* had no democratic pretenses: members of the college would be determined by co-optation and would be appointed for life. Further undermining the democratic structure of his original constitutional theory, Sieyès supplemented the democratic electoral process with co-optative modes of election, and proposed general changes to suffrage. He suggested that members of parliament be recruited from an electoral register—but rather than being selected by the people (from "below"), they would now be picked by the *collège des conservateurs* (from "above").

Despite its weakening of the democratic principle of popular sovereignty, Sieyès's constitutional draft may still be placed within the tradition of liberal constitutionalism. Of course Napoleon was unwilling to bind himself to the document. The constitution that eventually passed muster excised nearly all the liberal elements of Sieyès's earlier draft. It weakened the guardian of the constitution, strengthened the executive, who held a monopoly on legislation, and replaced the *Grand Electeur* with a dictatorial First Consul who could appoint and depose administrators and judges at his pleasure, and who could declare war and peace equally at will. Thus, under the rule of Napoleon, Sieyès's political thought became largely irrelevant, consigned to academic debates among *philosophes* and aged radicals—and historians of political theory.

CHAPTER 1

What Is the Third Estate?[1]

> As long as the Philosopher does not go beyond the boundary of truth, do not accuse him of going too far. His function is to show us the goal and first, therefore, he must get there. If he stopped and dared to put up his signpost midway, it might misdirect us. The duty of the Administrator is the reverse. He has to set his pace according to the nature of the difficulties ... If the Philosopher has not reached the goal, he does not know where he stands. If the Administrator does not see the goal, he does not know where he goes.

∴

The plan of this book is fairly simple. We must ask ourselves three questions.

1) What is the Third Estate? *Everything.*
2) What has it been until now in the political order? *Nothing.*
3) What does it want to be? *Something.*

We are going to see whether the answers are correct. Meanwhile, it would be improper to say these statements are exaggerated until the supporting evidence has been examined.[a] We shall next examine the measures that have been tried and those that must still be taken for the Third Estate really to become something. Thus, we shall state:

1 This book, composed during the *Notables* of 1788, was published in the first days of January 1789. It can be used as a continuation of the *Essai sur les Privilèges*. [Note by S.E. Finer: This fixes the date of the writing of the pamphlet between November 6 and December 12, 1788. The latest incident referred to in the work is the *Résultat du Conseil* of December 27, 1788. The fact that this reference—despite its importance to Sieyès's general argument—occurs only in a footnote, suggests that by that date the manuscript was already in the hands of the printer.]

a This sentence did not appear in the First Edition.

 | DOI: 10.1163/9789004273993_003

4) What the Ministers have attempted and what even the privileged orders propose to do for it.
5) What ought to have been done.
6) Finally, what remains to be done in order that the Third Estate should take its rightful place.

Chapter 1

The Third Estate Is a Complete Nation

What does a nation require to survive and prosper? It needs *private* activities and *public* services. These private activities can all be comprised within four classes of persons:

1) Since land and water provide the basic materials for human needs, the first class, in logical order, includes all the families connected with work on the land.
2) Between the initial sale of goods and the moment when they reach the consumer or user, goods acquire an increased value of a more or less compound nature through the incorporation of varying amounts of labor. In this way human industry manages to improve the gifts of nature and the value of the raw material may be multiplied twice, or ten-fold, or a hundred-fold. Such are the activities of the second class of persons.
3) Between production and consumption, as also between the various stages of production, a variety of intermediary agents intervene, to help producers as well as consumers; these are the dealers and the merchants. Merchants continually compare needs according to place and time and estimate the profits to be obtained from warehousing and transportation; dealers undertake, in the final stage, to deliver the goods on the wholesale and retail markets. Such is the function of the third class of persons.
4) Besides these three classes of useful and industrious citizens who deal with *things* fit to be consumed or used, society also requires a vast number of special activities and of services *directly* useful or pleasant to the *person*. This fourth class embraces all sorts of occupations, from the most distinguished liberal and scientific professions to the lowest of menial tasks.

Such are the activities which support society. But who performs them? The Third Estate.

Public services can also, at present, be divided into four known categories, the army, the law, the Church and the bureaucracy. It needs no detailed analysis to show that the Third Estate everywhere constitutes nineteen-twentieths of them, except that it is loaded with all the really arduous work, all the tasks which the privileged order refuses to perform. Only the well-paid and honorific posts are filled by members of the privileged order. Are we to give them credit for this? We could do so only if the Third Estate was unable or unwilling to fill these posts. We know the answer. Nevertheless, the privileged have dared to preclude the Third Estate. "No matter how useful you are," they said, "no matter how able you are, you can go so far and no further. Honors are not for the like of you." The rare exceptions, noticeable as they are bound to be, are mere mockery, and the sort of language allowed on such occasions is an additional insult.

If this exclusion is a social crime, a veritable act of war against the Third Estate, can it be said at least to be useful to the commonwealth? Ah! Do we not understand the consequences of monopoly? While discouraging those it excludes, does it not destroy the skill of those it favors? Are we unaware that any work from which free competition is excluded will be performed less well and more expensively?

When any function is made the prerogative of a separate order among the citizens, has nobody remarked how a salary has to be paid not only to the man who actually does the work, but to all those of the same caste who do not, and also to the entire families of both the workers and the nonworkers? Has nobody observed that as soon as the government becomes the property of a separate class, it starts to grow out of all proportion and that posts are created not to meet the needs of the governed but of those who govern them? Has nobody noticed that while on the one hand, we basely and I dare say *stupidly* accept this situation of ours, on the other hand, when we read the history of Egypt or stories of travels in India, we describe the same kind of conditions as despicable, monstrous, destructive of all industry, as inimical to social progress, and above all as debasing to the human race in general and intolerable to Europeans in particular ...?[2] But here we must leave considerations which, however much they might broaden and clarify the problem, would nevertheless slow our pace.[3]

It suffices to have made the point that the so-called usefulness of a privileged order to the public service is a fallacy; that, without help from this order, all the arduous tasks in the service are performed by the Third Estate; that without

2 About Indian castes, see Histoire Philosophique et Politique des deux Indes, Liv I.I.

3 Allow us merely to point out how utterly absurd it is to argue on the one hand that the nation is not made for the head of state and to contend on the other hand that it is made for the aristocrats.

this order the higher posts could be infinitely better filled; that they ought to be the natural prize and reward of recognized ability and service; and that if the privileged have succeeded in usurping all well-paid and honorific posts, this is both a hateful iniquity towards the generality of citizens and an act of treason to the commonwealth.

Who is bold enough to maintain that the Third Estate does not contain within itself everything needful to constitute a complete nation? It is like a strong and robust man with one arm still in chains. If the privileged order were removed, the nation would not be something less but something more. What then is the Third Estate? All; but an 'all' that is fettered and oppressed. What would it be without the privileged order? It would be all; but free and flourishing. Nothing will go well without the Third Estate; everything would go considerably better without the two others.

It is not enough to have shown that the privileged, far from being useful to the nation, can only weaken and injure it; we must prove further that the nobility[4] is not part of our society at all: it may be a *burden* for the nation, but it cannot be part of it.

First, it is impossible to find what place to assign to the caste of nobles among all the elements of a nation.[5] I know that there are many people, all

4 I do not mention the clergy here. If you regard it as a corps charged with a public duty, it belongs to society, since any public service is part of the government. When one says that the clergy is a *profession* rather than an *order*, those ecclesiastics who are still living in the eleventh century, or who affect to think so because it suits their plans, complain that they are belittled. They are wrong. It is precisely because the clergy is a profession that it amounts to something among us. If it were merely an *order*, it would have no substance. As the political and moral sciences advance, the more convincing becomes the proposition that, whatever the society, there exist only private and public activities. Nothing else exists except non-sensicalities, dangerous fancies or pernicious institutions. Thus, when I maintain that the clergy cannot be considered an order, it is not to rank it lower than the nobility. The clergy must not be regarded as an order because there must be no distinction between *orders* within the nation. If, however, such distinctions could be admitted, it would probably be better to grant such a privilege to men who can show proof of a sacerdotal election, rather than grant it to men whose pretensions have no other foundation than a certificate of baptism. For, after all, one can prevent an unintelligent or dishonest man from entering the Church, but how can one prevent him from being born?

5 Caste is the right word. It describes a class of men who although they lack functions and usefulness enjoy privileges attaching to their person by the mere fact of birth. From this, which is the correct point of view, there is only one privileged caste, viz. the nobility. It is truly a nation apart, but a bogus one which, lacking organs to keep it alive, clings to a real nation like those vegetable parasites which can live only on the sap of the plants that they impoverish

too many, who, from infirmity, incapacity, incurable idleness or a collapse of morality, perform no functions at all in society. Exceptions and abuses always exist alongside the rule, and particularly in a large commonwealth. But all will agree that the fewer these abuses, the better organized a state is supposed to be. The most ill-organized state of all would be the one where not just isolated individuals but a complete class of citizens would glory in inactivity amidst the general movement and contrive to consume the best part of the product without having in any way helped to produce it. Such a class, surely, is foreign to the nation because of its *idleness*.

The nobility, however, is also a foreigner in our midst because of its *civil and political* prerogatives. What is a nation? A body of associates living under *common* laws and represented by the same *legislative assembly*, etc.

Is it not obvious that the nobility possesses privileges and exemptions which it brazenly calls its rights and which stand distinct from the rights of the great body of citizens? Because of these special rights, the nobility does not belong to the common order, nor is it subjected to the common laws. Thus its private rights make it a people apart in the great nation. It is truly *imperium in imperio*.

As for its political rights, it also exercises these separately from the nation. It has its own representatives who are charged with no mandate from the People. Its deputies sit separately, and even if they sat in the same chamber as the deputies of ordinary citizens they would still constitute a different and separate representation. They are foreign to the nation first because of their origin, since they do not owe their powers to the People; and secondly because of their aim, since this consists in defending, not the general interest, but the private one.

The Third Estate then contains everything that pertains to the nation while nobody outside the Third Estate can be considered as part of the nation. What is the Third Estate? *Everything*.[6]

---

and blight. The Church, the law, the army and the bureaucracy are four classes of public agents necessary everywhere. Why are they accused of *aristocratism* in France? Because the caste of the nobles has usurped all the best posts, and taken them as its hereditary property. Thus it exploits them, not in the spirit of the laws of society, but to its own profit.

6 An honorable author has tried to be more precise. He stated that: "The Third Estate is the nation *less* the clergy and the nobility." I must confess that I could never have mustered the strength to announce this great truth. Anybody else can come along and say: "The nobility is the nation *less* the clergy and the Third Estate," or "The clergy is the nation *less* the Third Estate and the nobility." These surely are geometrically demonstrated propositions. I am sorry to have to say so; but if you intended to do more than express a rather naive truth; if you have already grasped what a nation is, what its components are, how there are only public

Chapter 2

What Has the Third Estate Been until Now? Nothing

We shall examine neither the condition of servitude in which the People have suffered for so long, nor that of constraint and humiliation in which it is still confined. Its status has changed in private law. It must change still further: the nation as a whole cannot be free, nor can any of its separate orders, unless the Third Estate is free. Freedom does not derive from privileges. It derives from the rights of citizens—and these rights belong to all.

If the aristocrats try to repress the People at the expense of that very freedom of which they prove themselves unworthy, the Third Estate will dare challenge their right. If they reply, "by the right of conquest," one must concede that this is to go back rather far. Yet the Third Estate need not fear examining the past. It will betake itself to the year preceding the "conquest"; and as it is nowadays too strong to be conquered it will certainly resist effectively. Why should it not repatriate to the Franconian forests all the families who wildly claim to descend from the race of the conquerors and to inherit their *rights of conquest*?

If it were purged in this way, I think the nation might well recover from the thought that thenceforward it would be reduced to the descendants of mere Gauls and Romans. When our poor fellow-citizens insist on distinguishing between one lineage and another, could nobody reveal to them that it is at least as good to be descended from the Gauls and the Romans as from the Sicambrians, Welches and other savages from the woods and swamps of ancient Germany? "True enough," some will say; "but conquest has upset all relationships and hereditary nobility now descends through the line of the

---

functions and private activities, and how the Third Estate can carry out all of these without help; if you have observed that the help which the state does receive from the privileged caste to carry them out is exceedingly ruinous; if you have realized that these wretched privileges produce all the errors and evils which distress and will long distress the French nation; if you know that a monarchy, like any other political system, requires only rulers and subjects, and that a caste, which the most stupid prejudice allows to usurp every office and to live off its privileges, will shortly afford nothing but despots and rebels, that it will be the worst burden that Heaven in its wrath could ever impose on a people, and that it will become an almost indestructible obstacle to any plan of return to justice or progress towards social order; if your mind has promptly seized upon all these truths and scores of others which also relate to our theme: why not avow frankly that the Third Estate is everything? How could you conclude such a train of considerations by the cold corollary: "the Third Estate is the nation *less* the clergy and the nobility"?

conquerors." Well, then; we shall have to arrange for it to descend through the other line! The Third Estate will become noble again by becoming a conqueror in its own turn.[b]

But, if we accept that all races are mixed; if the blood of the Franks (none the better for being pure) now mingles with the blood of the Gauls; if the fathers of the Third Estate are the fathers of the whole nation; can we not hope that one day will see the end of this long parricide which one class is proud to commit day after day against all the others? Why should not reason and justice, eventually grown as powerful as vanity, press so hard upon the privileged order that, moved by a new, truer and more social interest, it requests its own *regeneration* within the order of the Third Estate?[c]

Let us pursue our theme. By Third Estate is meant all the citizens who belong to the common order. Anybody who holds a legal privilege of any kind deserts the common order, stands as an exception to the common laws and, consequently, does not belong to the Third Estate. As we have already said, a nation is made one by virtue of common laws and common representation. It is indisputably only too true that in France a man who is protected only by the common laws is a nobody; whoever is totally unprivileged must submit to every form of contempt, insult and humiliation. To avoid being completely crushed, what must the unlucky non-privileged person do? He has to attach himself by all kinds of contemptible actions to some magnate; he prostitutes his principles and human dignity for the possibility of claiming, in his need, the protection of a *somebody*.

---

b Cf. G. Lefebvre, *The Coming of the French Revolution* (New York, 1961), p. 10f.: "What really characterized the nobility was birth; it was impossible to become a noble, but in the eyes of everyone the true nobleman was born. It was from blood that the noble derived his superiority over the 'ignoble' commoners, and hence it followed that noble status was inalienable and that an unsuitable marriage was an ineffaceable blot. The aristocratic literature that flourished in the eighteenth century, more than is generally realised, side by side with the bourgeois philosophy, set itself to fortify this racial phantasmagoria by imaginary portrayals of French social history. To the Comte de Boulainvilliers, the nobles were descendants of the early Germans who had established themselves by conquest as lords over the persons and lands of the Gallo-Romans, conceived to be unskilful in arms and timid in the face of defeat. They were a distinct race, heroic and military, made for command and insistent upon the marks of respect assured by honorific distinctions."

c In the First Edition this paragraph ran thus: "If we see in the privileged order, which is the constant enemy of the Third Estate, that which is alone in fact observable there, viz. the children of this same Third Estate, how are we to describe the parricidal audacity with which the privileged hate, despise and oppress their brothers?"

But we are less concerned in this book with the civil rights of the Third Estate than with its relationship to the constitution. Let us see what part it plays in the States-General.

Who have been its so-called "Representatives"? Men who have been raised to the nobility or have received temporary privileges. These bogus deputies have not even been always freely elected by the People. In the States-General sometimes, and in the Provincial Estates almost always, the representation of the People is considered as inherent in the holder of certain offices.

The old aristocracy detests new nobles; it allows nobles to sit as such only when they can prove, as the phrase goes, "four generations and a hundred years." Thus it relegates the other nobles to the order of the Third Estate to which, obviously, they no longer belong.[7]

In law, however, all nobles are equal—those whose nobility dates from yesterday just as much as those who succeed for better or for worse in hiding their origins or their usurpation. In law all have the same privileges. Only *opinion* distinguishes between them. But if the Third Estate must endure a prejudice sanctioned by law, there is no reason why it should submit to a prejudice contrary to law.

Let them create as many noblemen as they like; it still remains certain that the moment any citizen is granted privileges against the common laws, he no longer forms part of the common order. His new interest is contrary to the general interest; he becomes incompetent to vote in the name of the People.

According to the same undeniable principle, those who merely hold temporary privileges must also be debarred from representing the Third Estate. Their

7 On this point, the nobility has sacrificed its ancient vanity to a better understanding of its interests. In the *Pays d'Election*, the nobility of the *bailliages* (bailiwicks) felt that it was impolitic to irritate the new nobles and so make them side with the Third Estate out of spite. [Note by S.E. Finer: The *bailliage*, which in some places was called a *sénechaussée*, was the subdivision of a province for judicial and administrative purposes.] The *Pays d'Etats* followed this maladroit rule. Experience showed it was mistaken. Thereupon the aristocracy rectified the position and admitted all those whose nobility is *hereditary*. Consequently many people who, in the *Pays d'Etats* and in the *Provincial Assemblies*, must sit only with the Third Estate are without any difficulty included in the order of the nobility in the *bailliages* and will sit with this order in the States-General. But, still, what is the point of this distinction between the nobles who can *transfer* their nobility to their children and those who allegedly cannot? If they cannot, it concerns only their children; but there is no question of admitting to our assemblies the children to whom their father has not yet transferred nobility. Our only concern is the father, and he has certainly acquired, what you say that he has not yet acquired for his children's generation: he, *personally*, is noble; admit his *person*, then, to vote the nobility.

interest, too, is in greater or lesser part opposed to the common interest; and although opinion assigns them to the Third Estate and the law does not mention them, the nature of things, stronger than both opinion and the law, sets them irresistibly apart from the common order.

It is objected that to remove from the Third Estate not only those with hereditary privileges, but even those with mere temporary ones, is to try, from sheer wantonness, to weaken that order by depriving it of its more enlightened, courageous and esteemed members.

The last thing I want to do is to diminish the strength or dignity of the Third Estate, since, in my mind, it is completely coincident with my idea of a nation. But can we, whatever our motives, arrange for truth to cease to be truth? If an army has the misfortune to be deserted by its best soldiers, are these the troops it entrusts with the defense of its camp? One cannot say it too often: any privilege runs contrary to common laws; hence, all those who enjoy privileges, without exception, constitute a separate class opposed to the Third Estate. At the same time, I must point out that this should not alarm the friends of the People. On the contrary, it takes us back to the higher national interest by showing the urgent necessity for immediately suppressing all temporary privileges[8] which split the Third Estate and may seem to oblige it to put its destiny in its enemies' hands. Besides, this remark must not be separated from the ensuing one: the abolition of privileges within the Third Estate does not mean the loss of immunities which some of its members enjoy. Such immunities are nothing but common rights and it was totally unjust to deprive the main part of the People of them. Thus, I am not calling for the loss of a right but for its restitution;[9] and should it be objected that the universalization of certain privileges—e.g. not balloting for militia service[10]—would make it impossible to satisfy various public needs, my answer is that any public need

8 Some municipal officials, the Procurators of the Royal Court of Rennes, etc., have already given the fine example of renouncing all exemptions and privileges that distinguished them from the common People.

9 It is the certain that common ownership of privileges is the best way to bring the orders closer together and to prepare the most important of all laws, the law changing the orders into *a single* nation.

10 I cannot help expressing surprise at seeing that noblemen are excused from balloting for militia service! Is this not to show open contempt for the only pretext for so many outmoded pretensions? What will you ask payment for, if not for *the blood shed for the King*? M.C— has stamped this old tune with ineffaceable ridicule by his quotation: "Was the people's blood mere water?" [Note by S.E. Finer: i.e. A.J.J. Cerutti. This was his riposte to the *Mémoire au Roi* of December 12, 1788.]

is the responsibility of everybody and not of a separate class of citizens, and that one must be as ill-acquainted with reasoning as with fairness if one cannot think of a more national means of constituting and maintaining whatever kind of army one wants to have.

Consequently, either because they were never elected at all; or because they were not elected by the full membership of the Third Estate of towns and rural areas who were entitled to representation; or because, owing to their privileges, they were not even eligible; the so-called deputies of the Third Estate who have sat until now in the States-General never had a real mandate from the People.[d]

Some occasionally express surprise at hearing complaints about a three-fold "aristocracy composed of the army, the Church and the law." They insist that this is only a figure of speech; yet the phrase must be understood strictly. If the States-General is the interpreter of the general will, and correspondingly has the right to make laws, it is this capacity, without doubt, that makes it a true aristocracy: whereas the States-General as we know it at present is simply a *clerico-nobili-judicial* assembly.

Add to this appalling truth the fact that, in one way or another, all departments of the executive have also fallen into the hands of the caste that provides the Church, the law and the army. As a result of a spirit of brotherhood or *comradeship*, nobles always prefer each other to the rest of the nation. The usurpation is total; in every sense of the word, they reign.

If you consult history in order to verify whether the facts agree or disagree with my description, you will discover, as I did, that it is a great mistake to believe that France is a monarchy. With the exception of a few years under Louis XI and under Richelieu and a few moments under Louis XIV when it was plain despotism, you will believe you are reading the history of a *Palace* aristocracy. It is not the King who reigns; it is the Court. The Court has made and the Court has unmade; the Court has appointed ministers and the Court has dismissed them; the Court has created posts and the Court has filled them ... And what is the Court but the head of this vast aristocracy which overruns every part of France, which seizes on everything through its members, which exercises everywhere every essential function in the whole administration? So that in its complaints the People has grown used to distinguishing between the monarch and those who exercise power. It has always considered the King as so certainly misled and so defenseless in the midst of the active and all-powerful Court, that it has never thought of blaming him for all the wrongs done in his name.

---

d This paragraph did not appear in the First Edition.

Finally, is it not enough simply to open our eyes to what is occurring around us at this very moment? What do we see? The aristocracy on its own, fighting simultaneously against reason, justice, the People, the minister and the King. The end of this terrible battle is still undecided. Can it still be said that the aristocracy is only a chimera! Let us sum up: to this very day, the Third Estate has never had genuine representatives in the States-General. Thus its political rights are null.

Chapter 3

What Does the Third Estate Want to Be? Something

It is wrong to judge the claims of the Third Estate from the isolated remarks of certain authors who are partially aware of the rights of man. The Third Estate is still very backward in this matter, not only by comparison with the insight of students of the social order, but also with that mass of common ideas which constitutes public opinion. The authentic requests of the Third Estate can only be adjudged through the formal demands which the great municipalities of the kingdom have addressed to the government.[e] What do we see therein? That

---

e These petitions were still flowing in as Sieyès was writing. They were a direct outcome of the declaration by the States-General of Paris, September 25, 1788, that the coming Estates General must convene according to the ancient forms of 1614. Necker sought to offset this declaration by re-convening the Notables and getting them to agree to increased representation for the Third Estate. Simultaneously the leaders of the 'national party' decided to bring pressure on the municipal authorities throughout France to flood the government with petitions demanding that the Third Estate's representation should equal that of the other two orders combined; and voting by heads instead of voting by orders. They found a model for their demands in the proceedings in Dauphiné where, from September 10–28, a consultative assembly had met at Romans to frame a constitution for the Provincial Estates. This assembly had re-convened in November 1788 to learn of the government's reactions to their proposals; whereupon Mounier, the president of that assembly, seized the opportunity to draft a letter to the King in which he demanded for the nation what had been proposed for the Estates of Dauphiné: viz. the representation of the Third Estate to be equal to that of the other two orders combined, and voting by head and not by order.

Thenceforward the 'national party' throughout the towns got the municipal authorities to draft petitions to the King demanding similar arrangements for the coming States-General. Their usual practice was to canvass the town's guilds and corporations and get them to accept these demands, and to present them to the municipal authorities (or, failing them, a town meeting) for adoption and transmission to the King. The capital town having set the example, the smaller towns tended to follow suit. Thus, after Dijon had petitioned (December 16, 1788),

the People wants to become *something*, and in fact, the least thing possible. It wants to have 1) genuine representatives in the States-General, i.e. deputies *drawn from its own ranks* and competent to interpret its wishes and defend its interests. But what good would it do the Third Estate to participate in the States-General if the interest opposed to its own were to preponderate there? It would simply sanction by its presence the oppression of which it would be the everlasting victim. Therefore, it most certainly cannot come and vote in the States-General unless its influence there *is at least equal to that of the privileged orders*. So it asks for 2) a number of representatives equal to that of the other two orders taken together. However, this equality of representation would become entirely illusory if each chamber voted separately. The Third Estate, therefore, asks for 3) the votes to be counted *by heads and not by orders*.[11] Such is the whole extent of the claims which appear to have so alarmed the privileged orders; and for this reason alone have these come round to believing that the reform of abuses has become indispensable.

The Third Estate's modest aim is to possess an equal influence in the States-General to that of the privileged orders. Once again, could it ask for less? And is it not clear that if its influence is less than equal, it cannot hope to come out of its political non-existence and become *something*?

11 By the *'Resultat du Conseil'* of December 27, the second claim has been *granted* without the third being mentioned and after the first had been refused. But is it not obvious that one cannot go without the others? They constitute a whole. To destroy one is to cancel all three. We shall say later whose function it is to pronounce on any matter concerning the constitution. [Note by S.E. Finer: After the Notables had rejected the proposal to make the Third Estate's representation equal to that of the other two orders combined, Necker dismissed them (December 12, 1788) and took the fight to the Royal Council. There, after prolonged argument, he got his way. The decisions were recorded, not as might have been expected by a law or decree, but by a communiqué with the laconic title: *Le Resultat du Conseil du 27 Decembre, 1788*. It ran: (1) The deputies to the forthcoming States-General will number at least one thousand. (2) This number will be made up, as far as possible, by reference to the population and the taxes paid in each *bailliage*. (3) The number of deputies of the Third Estate will be equal to that of the two other orders combined.]

16 other towns of Burgundy did likewise. The example of Rouen (November 29, 1788) was followed by 25 Norman towns. Egret quotes a gazette of the time as saying:

"It is known that the number of petitions from Provinces, towns, guilds and corporations demanding a representation for the Third Estate equal to the other two orders combined is enormous, and reputed to be more than 800, not counting those flowing in on all sides every day." J. Egret, *La Pré-Revolution Française* (Paris, 1962), p. 358.

However, the great pity of it all is that the three articles which constitute the claim of the Third Estate are not enough to give it the equal influence which it cannot effectively dispense with. To grant it no more than an equal number of representatives drawn from its own ranks will be useless: for the privileged orders will continue to exercise their dominating influence in the very sanctuary of the Third Estate. For who has places, posts and benefices to hand out? Who needs protection and who is powerful enough to grant it? This consideration alone is enough to make every friend of the People tremble.

And the non-privileged citizens who by their abilities appear most apt to defend their order's interests, are these not reared in a superstitious or obligatory respect for the nobility? How easily most men succumb to any habit that may prove useful to them! Men are always busy improving their lot; and when self-interest cannot make progress by honest methods, it employs bad ones. Among some ancient peoples, so we read, children were trained to expect their food only after they had participated in some strenuous or skillful exercise. That was the chosen method for teaching children to excel in such matters.[f] In our society, the most able portion of the Third Estate has to obtain its basic needs by practicing flattery and dedicating itself to the service of the powerful, and this kind of education is less honorable and less social but equally effective. That unhappy part of the nation has come to constitute a sort of enormous ante-room; ceaselessly noting what its masters are doing or saying, it is always ready to sacrifice everything to the fruits it anticipates from being lucky enough to find favor. When we observe such habits, how can we fail to fear that the qualities most appropriate to defend the national interest may be prostituted to defend prejudices? The boldest champions of aristocracy are to be found within the Third Estate, among the men endowed with wide intelligence but petty souls and who are as greedy for pelf, power and the caresses of the mighty as they are insensitive to the value of liberty.

Besides the empire of the aristocracy which disposes of everything in France and the feudal superstition which still further debases most minds, there remains the influence of property. Such an influence is natural and I do not condemn it; but you will agree that it is another factor that favors the privileged orders and that one can justifiably fear that it will lend them powerful support against the Third Estate. Municipalities have been too quick to believe that they could eliminate the influence of privileges by simply precluding privileged

f In the First Edition, the sentence reads thus: "Some ancient people whose name I forget, trained its children to practice violent and skilful exercises by giving them their food only after they had successfully applied them selves to such efforts."

persons from representing the People. In rural areas, and indeed everywhere, any fairly popular lord who so chooses can dispose of just as large a crowd of commoners as he wants. Work out the consequences and the after-effects of this primary influence, and then remain tranquil, if you can, about their effect on an assembly which, although you picture it as far removed from the first electoral colleges, is, for all that, no more than a combination of these.[g] The more one considers this matter, the more one perceives the inadequacy of the three claims of the Third Estate.

However, even as they stand, they have been violently attacked. Let us examine the pretexts for such spiteful hostility.

First claim of the Third Estate: That the representatives of the Third Estate be chosen solely from among citizens who really belong to the Third Estate.

We have already explained that really to belong to the Third Estate, one must either be untainted by privileges of any sort, or else relinquish them immediately and completely.

Those lawyers who have attained nobility through a door which for unknown reasons they have decided to close behind them[12] are determined to sit in the States-General. They tell themselves: "The nobility does not want us and we for our part, do not want the Third Estate. If only we could form a separate order, it would be wonderful; however, we cannot. What are we to do? Our only chance to is maintain the old abuse by which the Third Estate elected nobles. By doing this, we shall fulfill our desires without lowering our pretensions." All new nobles, whatever their origin, hastened to repeat in the same spirit that the Third Estate must be allowed to elect noblemen. The old nobility, which claims to be the true one, has not the same stake in maintaining the old abuse; but it knows how to take things into account. It thought: "We shall put our sons in the *House of Commons*, so that it is altogether an excellent idea to charge us with representing the Third Estate."

---

12 They say that they want to *better the future composition* of their *order*, and for that purpose, which leads to pride through humility since it presupposes that they used to be in *bad company*, they have taken the decision that legal offices may no longer go to any families except those which already possess them today. You remember what we said earlier on aristocratism thirsting for all powers.

---

g Sieyès is simply *assuming* that the coming States-General would be indirectly elected. He could not have known this since the Royal Letter of Convocation was not published until January 24, 1789. However, he had good reason for his assumption. The new Provincial Assemblies were indirectly elected. And, elsewhere Sieyès himself lays down a plan of indirect election for his own proposed Constituent Assembly.

Once one has made up one's mind, reasons for it, as we well know, are never wanting. "We must maintain the ancient *custom*," people said. An excellent custom which, intended to provide representation for the Third Estate, has positively excluded it from representation until this very day! The Third Estate has political rights as it has civil rights; and it alone must be able to exercise both.[13] What an idea—to *distinguish* between orders when it is to the advantage of the first two and the misfortune of the third, but to fuse them *together* as soon as it becomes useful to the first two and harmful to the nation! What a custom—by which the Church and the aristocracy can take over the chamber of the Third Estate! In all candor, would the privileged feel they were being represented if the Third Estate could invade the deputation of *their* orders?

In order to demonstrate the flaw in a principle, it is permissible to push its consequences as far as they can go. Using this method, I will argue thus: if the members of the three orders allowed themselves to elect whomsoever they pleased, the assembly might well end up consisting of members of a single order only. But who would admit—to take one example—that the clergy alone could represent the whole nation?

Let me go further: we have just assumed that all three estates chose their representatives from the membership of a single order. Let us now assume that the citizens all give their votes to a single individual. If this happened, is one to admit that a single individual can replace the States-General? The principle that leads to such absurd consequences is pernicious.

Another argument is that if electors are restricted in their choice they will not be completely free. I have two answers to this so-called difficulty. First, those who raise it are hypocrites, and I will prove it. Everyone knows how lords domineer over the peasants and others who live in the countryside; everyone knows the habitual and the potential tactics of their multifarious agents, including their law-officers. Hence any lord who cares to influence the primary election is generally sure to be sent as a deputy to the '*bailliage*', where it only remains to select a candidate from among the lords themselves or from those who have earned their most intimate trust. Is it then to preserve the People's freedom that you establish the possibility of abusing and betraying its trust? It is appalling to hear the sacred name of freedom profaned as a disguise for designs which are most adverse to it. Certainly, electors must be given the utmost freedom, and this is precisely why it is necessary to exclude from their deputation all the privileged classes who are too fond of overbearing the People.

13 This principle is of the utmost importance. It will be elaborated later.

My second answer is direct. In no circumstances can any freedom or right be unlimited. In all countries, the law prescribes certain qualifications without which one can be neither an elector nor eligible for election. For example, the law must decide the age under which one is incompetent to represent one's fellow-citizens. Thus, rightly or wrongly, women are everywhere excluded from mandates of this kind. It is unquestionable that tramps and beggars cannot be charged with the political confidence of nations. Would a servant, or any person under the domination of a master, or a non-naturalized foreigner, be permitted to appear among the representatives of the nation? Political liberty, therefore, has its limits, just as civil liberty has. The only question to answer is whether the non-eligibility of members of the privileged orders, which the Third Estate is asking for, is as vital as the other non-eligibilities I have just mentioned. Comparison runs completely in favor of this proposition; for the interests of a beggar or a foreigner might not conflict with the interest of the Third Estate, whereas nobles and clerics are, by their very status, supporters of the privileges which they themselves enjoy. Therefore, the restriction requested by the Third Estate is the most important of all the restrictions which the law, in accordance with equity and the nature of things, must lay down for the choice of representatives.

To emphasize this line of argument, I will make an assumption. Suppose that France is at war with England and that everything concerned with the hostilities is, at home, under the command of a Directory composed of national representatives. In such a case, I ask, would the provinces be allowed, on the pretext of not infringing their liberty, to choose members of the English cabinet as their deputies to the Directory? Yet the privileged classes are no less the enemies of the common order than are the English of the French in times of war. From among the illustrations which multiply and throng in my mind, I select another. If it were *desired to create* a general Diet of maritime nations in order to establish rules for the freedom and safety of navigation, do you believe that Genoa, Leghorn, Venice, etc., would choose their plenipotentiary ministers from among the Barbary pirates? Or do you believe that the law that would enable rich pirates to buy or bribe votes in Genoa, etc., would be a good one? I do not know whether this comparison is exaggerated, but I am satisfied that it makes clearer what I had to say; besides, I hope, as well as the next man, that since enlightenment cannot long remain ineffective, the aristocrats will cease some day to resemble the Algerian pirates of France.

In accord with these principles, we must not permit men of the Third Estate who are under the exclusive domination of members of the first two orders to be given the trust of the Commons. It is clear that their dependency makes them untrustworthy; unless they are formally excluded, the lords will not fail to use the influence which they can no longer use for themselves in favor of the men whom they control. Above all, beware, I beg you, of the multifarious agents of feudalism.[14] It is to the odious remnants of this barbaric system that we still owe the division of France, to her misfortune, into three mutually hostile orders. All would be lost if the lackeys of feudalism came to usurp the representation of the common order. Who does not know that servants are more harsh and bold to defend their masters' interests than the masters themselves? I know that this proscription covers many people since it concerns, in particular, all officers of feudal tribunals[15] and the like, but, in this instance, we must be governed by the logic of the situation.

---

14 These agents' innumerable depredations continue to desolate the countryside. It is just to say that the tail of the privileged order is as obnoxious as it is itself. The Treasury with its hundred arms does not press more heavily upon the People. Well! Is it not incredible that the aristocrats have dared to utilize all this suffering in order to insinuate that the real enemies of the People come from the Third Estate! As if the tools of feudalism, the men of all liveries and all denominations who live in dependence on the aristocracy, really belonged to the Third Estate! It is only too true that the most dangerous enemies of the People come from these classes which are divorced from the national interest, albeit not under the name of orders, and which the privileged hire for their service. France, Holland and everywhere else provide terrifying examples of the natural coalition between the lowest class of society and the privileged orders. Let us be frank; in every country in the world, the rabble belongs to the aristocracy.

15 Private courts! It is difficult to imagine anything more contrary to sound policy. The jurists are the ones to thank for having salvaged as much as they could from the rubble of feudal anarchy; for having clothed this gloomy structure in a similitude of legal form, and perhaps for having set some new traps inside it. One must have an odd idea of *property* to confound public posts with it and to see, with no sensation of surprise, the scepter of so monarchical a country broken into a thousand fragments and thieves turned into legitimate owners. [Note by S.E. Finer: In the First Edition, the note ended here]. Ought one not to mark how the undefined word *property* has come to shelter what is most opposed to genuine property—for instance, the right to harm others? However long the proprietorship may have lasted, how could it justify such a confusion? Public services, obviously, ought never to become the property of a private individual or be separated from sovereign duty. Let us leave that topic, then, and discuss the obvious usurpations of *common* liberty or property. Tell me: what is a *lord*, and why are *vassals* necessary? Do these metaphysical relationships (for I am not dealing with financial or material obligations) appertain to a sound political association? There is a definite possibility that the word *property* could shelter outright thefts, thefts of the sort that cannot fall under the statute of limitations. Indeed, I suppose that, in the absence of police, if Cartouche had more solidly established himself on a highway, he would have acquired a genuine right to collect a toll? If he had had time to sell this monopoly, quite common in ancient times, to a *bona fide* purchaser, would his

On this point, the Dauphiné has set a great example. We must follow it and declare that all tax agents and their guarantors, all administrators and the like, are ineligible for election by the Third Estate. As to those who farm lands which are owned by the first two orders, I consider them also, in their present state, as being too dependent to vote freely in favor of the common order. But may I not hope that some day the legislator will consent to be informed of the interests of agriculture, good citizenship and national prosperity and that he will at last cease to believe that harsh taxation and government are the same thing? Then he will not only permit but even encourage life-tenancies, and we will be able to consider these useful farmers as independent tenants who will then be clearly competent to defend the interests of the nation.[16]

Some people have supposed that they reinforce the difficulty of which we have just disposed by submitting that the Third Estate does not contain enough intelligent or courageous members and so forth competent to represent it, and that it has no option but to call on the leading figures of the aristocracy ... So ridiculous a statement deserves no answer. Look at the *available* classes in the Third Estate; and like everyone else I call "available" those classes where some

---

right have become more respectable in the hands of the purchaser? Why is restitution always considered as a less fair and more impossible action than theft? There is a third class of possessions which, although they were originally legal, can be deemed harmful to the commonwealth. It is not unreasonable that compensation should be paid in such cases but they must nevertheless be extinguished. *After* such a just and necessary political discrimination, be sure that we will all fall on our knees before the sacred name of *property*; and do not believe that the man who owns least is less interested in it than he who owns most; above all, do not believe that we attack genuine property when we discredit false property.

16 When an aristocrat wants to crack a joke at what he calls the pretensions of the Third Estate, he always affects to equate this order with his harness-maker, shoe-maker, etc.; he then chooses the language which he thinks most proper to inspire contempt for the men of whom he speaks. But why should the more humble activities dishonor the *order of the Third Estate* when they do not dishonor a *nation*? On the other hand, when the intention is to sow dissension within the Third Estate, no difficulty is experienced in distinguishing its different classes. Townsmen and country folk are incensed against each other; efforts are made to oppose the poor to the rich. If everything could be made public I could relate many pleasing strokes of refined hypocrisy! [Note by S.E. Finer: The text of the First Edition went straight from "distinguishing its different classes" to "In spite of an these efforts"] In spite of all these efforts, what divides men is not a difference in occupation or wealth or ability but a difference in interests. In the present case, there are only two interests: that of the privileged, and that of the non-privileged. All classes of the Third Estate are bound together by a common interest against the oppression of the privileged.

sort of affluence enables men to receive a liberal education, to train their minds and to take an interest in public affairs. Such classes have no interest other than that of the rest of the People. Judge whether they do not contain enough citizens who are educated, honest and worthy in all respects to represent the nation properly.

But then, it is argued, what if a '*bailliage*' insists on giving the mandate of the Third Estate only to a nobleman or an ecclesiastic? What if it has trust in only such a man?

I have already stated that there can be no freedom without limits and that, of all the qualifications that could be imposed on eligibility, the qualification the Third Estate requested was the most necessary. But let us give a direct answer. Supposing that one '*bailliage*' is determined to prejudice its own interests, does it follow that it must be allowed to prejudice the interest of others? If I alone am affected by the steps taken by my agent, a man may be content with simply saying to me: "Hard luck; but why did you make such a bad choice?" But, in the case in point, the deputies of a district are not merely the representatives of the '*bailliage*' which nominated them, they are also called upon to represent the whole body of citizens, to vote for the whole kingdom. One must therefore have a common rule and such qualifications, which, although they may displease some people, will reassure the whole of the nation against the whim of a few electors.

Second claim of the Third Estate: That its deputies be equal in number to those of the two privileged orders.

I cannot refrain from repeating once more that the timid inadequacy of this claim is an after-effect of times gone by. The towns of the kingdom have not given enough consideration to the progress of enlightenment or even of public opinion. They would have met with no greater difficulties by demanding two votes to one; but they might even have been hastily granted the very equality which some people are so loudly opposing today.

Furthermore, when we want to decide a question of this kind, we must not simply do what is only too common, and give our personal wish or our will or custom as valid reasons. It is necessary to argue from principles. Like civil rights, political rights derive from a person's capacity as a citizen. These legal rights are identical for every person, whether his property happens to be great or small. Any citizen who satisfies all the formal requirements for an elector has the right to be represented, and the extent of his representation cannot be a fraction of the extent of some other citizen's representation. The right to be represented is single and indivisible. All citizens enjoy it equally, just as they are all equally protected by the law which they have helped to make. How can one argue on the one hand, that the law is the expression of the general will, i.e. the majority, and on the other hand that ten individual wills can cancel out a thousand individual wills? Would one not thereby run the risk of permitting a minority to make the law? Which would obviously be contrary to the nature of things.

If these principles, certain though they may be, are too remote from common view, I will direct the reader's attention to a comparison which lies under his very nose. Is it not a fact that it seems fair to everybody[h] that the huge '*bailliage*' of Poitou should send more representatives to the States-General than the small '*bailliage*' of Gex? Why is that? Because, it is stated, the population and the contribution of Poitou are far more important than those of Gex. Thus it is admitted that there are principles according to which it is possible to determine the proportion of representatives. Should we take taxation as a basis? Although we have no exact information as to the amount of taxes paid by each order, it is obvious that the Third Estate pays more than one-half of the total.

With respect to population, everybody knows that the third order enjoys a vast numerical superiority over the first two. I have no better knowledge than anybody else as to the exact proportion; but, like anybody else, I can estimate:

1. The Clergy

There are 40,000 parishes including Chapels of Ease. This gives us immediately the total number of parish priests including priests in charge of Chapels of Ease	40,000
We can count one curate for every four parishes, on an average	10,000
There are as many Cathedrals as Dioceses; let us say that, on an average, there are 20 canons per Cathedral, including the 140 bishops and archbishops	2,800
We can assume, very roughly, that there are twice as many canons regular	5,600
After that, one should not assume that there are still as many ecclesiastics as there are Benefices, Abbeys, Priories and Chapels. Besides, it is common knowledge that the plurality of Benefices is not unheard of in France. Bishops and canons are at the same time abbots, priors and chaplains. To avoid counting the same people twice, I estimate at three thousand the number of Benefice holders who are not already included in the figures above	3,000

h First Edition: "it seems fair to everybody, except to the bishop of Nev., that …"

Finally, I assume that there are about three thousand ecclesiastics, in Holy orders of course, who have no Benefice of any kind	3,000[i]
We still have to count the monks and nuns whose numbers have been diminishing faster and faster in the past thirty years. I do not believe that they could be more than 17,000 nowadays	17,000
Total number of ecclesiastics	81,400

2. The Nobility

I know only one way of estimating the numbers of this order, viz. to take the province where the number is best known and to compare it with the rest of France. The province is Brittany, and I stress, in advance, it is richer in nobility than other provinces, either because nobles do not lose caste there or because their privileges are such as to keep the families at home. There are in Brittany 1,800 noble families. Actually, I will assume that there are 2,000 because some of them do not yet come to the Estates. If you say that the average family has five members, there are in Brittany 10,000 nobles of all ages and both sexes. The total population of Brittany is 2,300,000. This figure represents one-eleventh of the total French population. Therefore, if we multiply 10,000 by 11 we obtain the maximum figure of 110,000 nobles for the whole kingdom.

Therefore, in total, there are less than 200,000 privileged individuals of the first two orders.[17] Compare their number with the 25 or 26 million inhabitants, and draw your own conclusions.

17 I observe from the above that, by deducting monks and nuns but not convents from the total number of ecclesiastics, one can infer that we are left with about 70,000 men who are truly citizens, tax-payers and who qualify to be *electors*. In the nobility, if you remove women and children, not liable to taxation and not *electors*, there hardly remain 30 to 40,000 with the same qualifications; it follows that the clergy is, relatively to national representation, a much more sizable mass than the nobility. If I make this observation, it is precisely because it is opposed to the torrent of present prejudices. I will not bow before the idol; and when the Third Estate, swept by a blind animosity, applauds a decision by which the nobility receives twice as many representatives as the clergy, I tell the Third Estate that it consults neither reason, nor justice, nor its own interest. Will the public never be able to see otherwise than through the glass of current prejudices? What is the clergy? A body of agents in charge of the public services of education and worship. Change its internal administration; reform it to some extent; it still remains a necessary service in some form or other. This body is not an exclusive caste but is open to all citizens; this body is so constituted that it makes no financial calls on the state. Just calculate how

i In the First Edition, this figure was 2,000, bringing the total number of ecclesiastics to only 80,400.

Now, to reach the same solution on a basis of different but equally indisputable principles, let us bear in mind that the privileged classes are to the great body of citizens what exceptions are to the law. Any society must be governed by common laws and submitted to a common order. If exceptions are to exist, at least they ought to be rare; and they must never have the same weight and influence on the commonwealth as the common rule. It is absurd to oppose the interest of the privileged classes to the grand interest of the mass of the nation as if they were capable of counterbalancing each other. (We will explain this point at greater length in Chapter 6.) When, a few years hence, we look back on all the obstacles raised to the over-modest claim of the Third State, we shall be amazed at the inadequacy of the arguments used against it, and even more at the brazen effrontery of those who were bold enough to dig them up.

---

much it would cost the Royal Treasury to pay only the cures, and you will be terrified at the increase of taxes entailed by the squandering of Church property. Finally, this cannot avoid being a *corps*, because it is part of the administrative hierarchy. The nobility, on the contrary, is an exclusive caste, separated from the Third Estate which it despises. It is not a corps of public civil servants; its privileges are attached to the person independently of any function; nothing can justify its existence but the right of the stronger. Whereas the clergy loses privileges every day, the nobility keeps them; indeed, it increases them. Was it not yesterday that the ordinance appeared requiring *evidence* the produced to become a military officer, *evidence* not of ability or aptitude, but of *letters-patent of nobility*, thus excluding the Third Estate from the service! [Note by S.E. Finer: The regulation of May 22, 1781, prescribed that youths who desired to be nominated as sub-lieutenants in the infantry and cavalry without serving in the ranks, must prove four generations of nobility on their father's side]. It seems that the *Parlements* were originally created for the express purpose of supporting and strengthening the People against the tyranny of the barons, but they have seen fit to change their role; very recently and very quietly they made the nobility a perpetual gift of all seats of assessors and presiding magistrates, etc. [Note by S.E. Finer: The text of the First Edition went straight from "What do I say? It increases them" to "Has not the nobility just obtained …"] Has not the nobility just obtained, in the *Notables of 1787*, a ruling that precedence in the Provincial Assemblies and everywhere shall henceforth alternate between itself and the clergy; and, in getting this precedence shared, did it not effectively exclude the Third Estate from it, although the Third Estate had also been summoned by the Minister? By way of a consolation prize, the Third Estate was given the sole right to choose the President of the assembly—but from the membership of the first two orders! … Finally, which order is more to be feared by the Third Estate, the order which gets feebler day by day and of which, by the way, it constitutes nineteen-twentieths, or the order which, just when it seems that the privileged classes ought to move towards the common order, does the reverse and finds methods to become more and more distinct? When the *curés* enjoy their necessary and appropriate role among the clergy, the Third Estate will see how much more rewarding it would have been to reduce the influence of the nobility rather than that of the clergy.

The very persons who invoke the authority of facts against the Third Estate could, if they were honest, find in those facts the guide for their own conduct. The existence of a mere handful of loyal cities was enough to constitute, under Philip the Fair, a Chamber of Commons in the States-General.

Since that day, feudal servitude has disappeared and rural areas have provided a numerous population of *new citizens*. Towns have increased in number and size. Commerce and arts have, as it were, created new classes thronging with prosperous families of educated and civic-minded citizens. Why did not this two-fold increase, so much greater than the loyal cities' ancient contribution to the nation, encourage the same authority to create two new chambers in favor of the Third Estate? Justice and sound policy alike require it.

No-one dares act so unreasonably in respect of another kind of increase that has occurred in France, viz. the new provinces which have become united with her since the last States-General met. Nobody would dare to claim that these new provinces should have no representatives of their own over and above those who were in the States-General in 1614. But do not manufactures and the arts create new riches, new taxes and a new population just as much as territory does? Since this form of increase is easily comparable to that of territory why on earth should one refuse to accord it representatives over and above the number allotted to the States-General in 1614?

But I am trying to reason with people who are moved only by self-interest. Let us present them with an argument that might touch them more closely. Is it proper for the nobility of today to retain the language and attitudes which were characteristic of it in the gothic centuries? And is it proper for the Third Estate, at the end of the eighteenth century, to languish in the sad and cowardly customs of ancient servitude? If the Third Estate learns how to know itself and respect itself, the others will indeed respect it too. Reflect that the former ratio between the orders has been altered simultaneously on both sides. The Third Estate, which had been reduced to nothing, has re-acquired by its industry something of what had been seized from it by the offence of those in power. Instead of demanding that its rights be restored, it has consented to pay for them; they have not been given back but sold back. But, at last, in one way or the other, it can take possession of them. It must realize that today it represents a reality within the nation, whereas formerly it represented only a shadow; that, while this long transformation was taking place, the nobility has ceased to be a monstrous feudal power free to oppress as it willed; that now it is the nobility that is a shadow, and that this shadow is still trying to spread terror through a whole nation—but to no avail, unless our nation is willing to be thought the basest in the world.

Third and last claim of the Third Estate: That the States-General vote, not by orders, but by heads.

One can regard this question from three points of view: as apprehended by the Third Estate; as relating to the interests of the privileged classes; and in terms of sound principles. As far as the first of these is concerned, it would be pointless to add anything to what we have already said; clearly, the Third Estate considers that this claim is the necessary consequence of the two others.

The privileged classes fear the third order's possession of an influence equal to their own, and so declare it unconstitutional. This behavior is all the more striking as they have, until this moment, enjoyed a superiority of two against one without seeing anything unconstitutional in this unjust predominance. They feel passionately that they must retain a veto on everything that might conflict with their interests. I am not going to restate the arguments by which a score of writers have combated this pretension, and the argument of "the ancient procedures." I want to make one observation only. There are, beyond any doubt, abuses in France; these abuses are profitable to some persons: but they hardly ever benefit the Third Estate, and, on the contrary, it is to the Third Estate that they do most harm. Now I ask: in such circumstances is it possible to abolish any abuse so long as those who profit therefrom retain a veto? Justice would be powerless—everything would depend entirely upon the magnanimity of the privileged classes. Would this correspond to our idea of what constitutes social order?

If we now turn to considering this question apart from any individual interest, but according to the principles appropriate to illuminate it, i.e. the principles of the science of social order,[j] it strikes us in a new light. I maintain that it is impossible to accept the claim of the Third Estate or to defend the privileged classes without turning some sure and certain ideas upside down. Naturally, I do not accuse the loyal towns of the kingdom of intending this. They simply wanted to come closer to their rights by asking for at least an equilibrium between the two influences. Moreover, they have formulated some excellent truths, for it is obvious that one order's right of *veto* over the others is likely to bring everything to a standstill in a country where interests are so conflicting. It is quite certain that unless votes are counted by heads the true majority may be set aside, which would be the supreme difficulty, since it would render legislation null and void. Such truths are indisputable. But the true question is whether the orders, as now constituted, could unite to vote by heads? No, they could not. If one relies on true principle, they cannot vote *together* at all,

j Instead of "the science of social order", the First Edition reads "social science."

either by heads or by orders. Whatever the proportion arranged between them, it cannot achieve the intended aim: viz. to bind all representatives together by a *single* common will. This statement doubtless calls for elaboration and for proof. Allow me to postpone these until Chapter 6. I do not want to upset the moderate-minded, who always fret in case the truth should make its appearance at the wrong moment. I must first make them admit that, simply because of the privileged classes and nobody else, conditions are now such that it is time to come to a decision, and to proclaim what is true and just in its full strength.

Chapter 4

What the Government Has Attempted and what the Privileged Classes Propose on Behalf of the Third Estate

The government has not been prompted by considerations for which we need to feel gratitude, but by its own blunders; it has become convinced that it cannot remedy these without the willing assistance of the nation; and it has therefore reckoned that by offering the nation some concessions it could secure from it a blind consent to everything. This was M. de Calonne's intention in proposing the scheme for the Provincial Assemblies.[k]

---

k On August 20, 1786, Calonne, Controller General of Finance, faced with a yawning deficit, memorialised the King thus: "The only course left, the sole means for a final success in putting the finances in order, must be to revivify the entire state by reforming everything that is vicious in its constitution."

His two chief proposals were to replace the *vingtième* by a land tax levied on all landed property without distinction; and to secure this by having the citizens assess and apportion the taxes themselves. He proposed to effect this by establishing (outside the *Pays d'Etats* which already had their representative assemblies, viz. the Provincial Estates) new representative bodies called Provincial Assemblies. These bodies were to be elected by and consist of the landed proprietors. Each parish was to elect its own assembly; the parish assemblies would elect some of their members as delegates to a district assembly; and the district assemblies would do likewise to constitute the Provincial Assembly. There was to be no distinction between the orders: the sole qualification for electing or being elected was based on proprietorship. These Provincial Assemblies were to work under the administrative control of the Intendant and their chief task would be to apportion the new land tax. Fearing the opposition of the *Parlements* to his proposed reforms, Calonne summoned an assembly of Notables, hoping for their support for his proposals. He failed to get it, and after increasing friction between the Notables and himself, was dismissed on April 8, 1787, and replaced by his opponent, Brienne, on May I.

1. The Provincial Assemblies

Nobody who showed the faintest concern for the nation's interest could fail to be struck by the political incapacity of the Third Estate. The Minister even felt that the distinction of orders prejudiced all hope of success, and without any doubt, planned to abolish it later. At least, this is the spirit in which the first plan for the Provincial Assemblies seems to have been conceived and drafted. One does not need to read it very attentively to notice that it does not allow for the *personal* status of citizens. It deals only with their properties, i.e. their *real* status. It was as property-owner and not as priest, noble or commoner that one was to be convoked to these assemblies. These were interesting by virtue of their duties, but, far more importantly, by the way they were to be constituted; for through them a genuine national representation was established.

The plan distinguished four sorts of properties. First came the *seigneuries*. Their owners, whether nobles or commoners, ecclesiastics or laymen, were to constitute the first class. Ordinary properties, as opposed to *seigneuries*, were divided into three other classes. A more natural differentiation would have created only two classes, divided according to the kind of work carried on and to the balance of material interests; namely, country and town properties. In this last class one would have included, with the dwelling-houses, all the arts, manufactures, trades, etc. But it was probably thought that the time was not yet ripe to merge ordinary church properties within these two divisions, and so it was felt necessary to put the ordinary, i.e. non-manorial, properties of the Church in a separate class, viz. the second class. The third class contained the country properties, and the fourth the town properties.

Notice that since three of these kinds of properties could be owned indiscriminately by citizens of all three orders, three classes out of the four could have been composed indiscriminately of nobles, commoners and priests. The second class itself would have contained Knights of Malta, and even laymen, to represent hospitals, parish *manufactures*, etc.

It is natural to believe that, since public business would have been transacted in these assemblies irrespective of personal status, a community of interests between the three orders would soon have sprung up; that this would in due course have become the general interest; and that the nation would have wound up at the very point where all nations ought to begin, namely by being *one*.

A great many valuable points eluded the vaunted mind of the *Principal Minister*.[1] It was not that he was not clearly aware of the interest which he wanted to

1 The expression *Principal Minister* indicates that Sieyès is now talking of Brienne, not Ca-

serve, but that he did not understand the real value of what he was spoiling. He reintroduced the impolitic division of personal status; and although this single change called for a completely new plan, he was content to use the old one whenever it did not seem to clash with his purposes; and, afterwards, he kept expressing surprise at the numerous difficulties which arose, day after day, from the want of agreement. Above all, the nobility could not conceive how it could be expected to regenerate itself in assemblies in which genealogists had been forgotten. Its anxieties on this ground were pleasant to behold.[18]

Of all the mistakes made in the erection of this structure, the greatest was to start with the roof instead of with the natural foundations, namely free election by the People. However, the Minister, to make some sort of obeisance to the rights of the Third Estate, did at least announce that it would have as many representatives as the clergy and the nobility taken together. His plan is positive on that point. What became of it? The Third Estate was forced to choose its deputies from the members of the privileged classes. I know one of these assemblies where, out of 52 members, there is only one who has no privilege. This is how the cause of the Third Estate is served, even after a public announcement of the intention to do it justice.

18 See the Minutes of the Provincial Assemblies.

lonne. Calonne's title was Controller General of Finance. Brienne also held this title, but on August 26 was made Principal Minister.

In replacing Calonne, Brienne aimed at using his credit as a former Notable to push through such parts of Calonne's plans as he approved of. His first words to the Notables were to assure them that "he had sought to fulfil the functions of a Minister during the time he had been a Notable and would try to fulfil those of a Notable now that he was a Minister."

Qua Notable, with his fellows, Brienne had vigorously opposed Calonne's intention to suppress the distinction of orders in the new Provincial Assemblies. As Minister, he now proposed that the assemblies should be constituted by orders but with the proviso that the representation of the Third Estate should be double that of the other two orders combined. This concession was resisted by the Notables and in its final form the plan provided that the Third Estate's representation would be equal to that of the other two orders combined. An edict establishing the assemblies was promulgated June 1787, and the regulations made under it between June 23 and September 4, 1787. However, the elections were temporarily postponed. To start the assemblies up, the Crown nominated half of their membership, and these members then proceeded to co-opt the remainder. Everywhere the nobility or the clergy provided the presidents for these assemblies; and Lefebvre (*The Coming of the French Revolution*, New York 1961, p. 29) states that of the 341 members representing the Third Estate, 63 were nobles and 100 were privileged persons-not counting the bourgeois who owned manors or lawyers who were acting as agents for lords of the manor.

2. The Notables

The Notables fell short of the expectations of both the Ministers.[m] Nothing could depict them more truly than M.C—'s excellent stroke of the pen:

> The King called them around him twice to consult with them in the interests of the Throne and of the Nation. What did the Notables do in 1787? They defended their privileges against the Throne. What did the Notables do in 1788? They defended their *privileges* against the Nation.[n]

The reason is that, instead of consulting men notable for their privileges, one should have consulted men notable for their enlightenment. The merest private individual would not make the same mistake if he needed advice about his own business or that of people he is genuinely concerned about.

M. Necker deluded himself. But could he foresee that the same men who had voted in favor of granting an equal number of seats to the Third Estate in the Provincial Assemblies would abandon that policy of equality in respect of

---

m Calonne decided to convene the Notables in the hope of securing their support against the obstruction he anticipated from the *Parlements*. The Notables met on February 22, 1787. They comprised (according to the *Procès Verbal* of the Assembly of Notables, Paris, 1788) 14 prelates; 36 lay magnates; 7 Princes of the Blood; 37 magistrates of the Parlements; 12 Councillors of State and intendants; 12 representatives of the Provincial Estates; and 26 officers of the municipal corporations. Of the latter only three were commoners. The assembly was aristocratic and privileged in the extreme.

Calonne quarrelled with the Notables and was dismissed on April 8, 1787. His successor, Brienne, had not much greater success and dismissed the Notables on May 25, 1787. Thereupon he plunged into his long struggle with the *Parlements*, described in the chronological summary at the beginning of the volume.

Necker succeeded Brienne on August 24, 1788. His plan was to rely on the forthcoming States-General which Brienne had been forced to convene. His policy was challenged, however, by the Paris *Parlement's* pronouncement on September 25, 1788, that the States-General must meet according to its ancient form. Necker wanted the Third Estate to have a representation equal to that of the other two orders combined. To offset the *Parlement's* declaration he therefore re-convened the Notables, on October 5, 1788, hoping that they would advise in this sense.

As Sieyès implies, Necker had good reason to hope that they would do so; for, under Brienne, they had conceded equality of representation for the Third Estate in the Provincial Assemblies. But Necker was completely deceived. Led pre-eminently by a bloc of totally intransigent prelates, magistrates of the *Parlements* and Councillors of State, the Notables rejected equal representation for the Third Estate by 111 votes to 33.

n 'M. C—' is A.J.J. Cerutti, author of a well-known polemic, the *Memoire pour le Peuple Français* (1788).

the State-General? Well, however that may be, the public made no mistake. It expressed continued distaste for a plan whose outcome it foresaw and from which it expected, on the most optimistic assumptions, a dilatoriness which would injure the nation. This seems to be the right place to explain some of the motives which prompted the majority of the latest *Notables*. But why anticipate the judgment of history? It will come all too quickly for men who were placed in the most favorable circumstances, and empowered to dictate to a great nation all that was just, beautiful and good, yet preferred to prostitute this superb occasion to their miserable corporate interest and so give posterity a further example of the power of prejudice over public spirit.

The efforts of the government, it is clear, produced nothing of worth to the Third Estate.

3. Patriotic Writers of the First Two Orders

It is noteworthy that the cause of the Third Estate should have been defended more eagerly and forcibly by ecclesiastical and noble writers than by the non-privileged classes themselves.

In this torpidity of the Third Estate I see nothing but the habitual silence and fear which are common among the oppressed, and it provides additional proof of how real that oppression is. Is it possible to make any serious study of the principles and purpose of society without being sickened to the very soul by the monstrous partiality of human institutions! I am not surprised that the first two orders should have produced the earliest defenders of justice and humanity; for if *ability* is the fruit of a long and dedicated application of the intellect, and if members of the Third Estate are for hundreds of reasons bound to distinguish themselves in this respect, the *comprehension* of civic morality will arise more frequently among those whose social position affords them a conspectus of the major inter-relationships of society and whose early ambitions are less commonly cut short. It must be admitted there are sciences which depend as much on the soul as on the mind. When the nation achieves its freedom it will remember with gratitude the patriotic writers of the first two orders who were the first to abjure archaic errors and who preferred the principles of universal justice to the murderous conspiracies of corporate interest against the interest of the nation. Until those public honors are conferred upon them, may they be pleased to accept the homage of a citizen whose soul is consumed for his country and who worships all efforts which help her rise from the rubble of feudalism!

The first two orders are unquestionably interested in reinstating the third in its rights. But let us not dissimulate; the guarantee of public liberty lies only where real power lies. We can be free only with the People and by the People.

If a consideration of such magnitude is too much for the frivolity and narrow egotism of the majority of Frenchmen, these must at least be impressed by the changes in public opinion. Day by day, the influence of reason spreads further, increasingly necessitating the restitution of the rights that have been usurped. Sooner or later, every class will have to withdraw inside the boundaries of the social contract, the contract which concerns everyone, and binds all the associates one to the other.[19] Will this result in reaping its countless advantages, or in sacrificing them to despotism? This is the real question. During the long night of feudal barbarism, it was possible to destroy the true relations between men, to turn all concepts upside down, and to corrupt all justice; but, as day dawns, so gothic absurdities must fly and the remnants of ancient ferocity collapse and disappear. This is quite certain. But shall we merely be substituting one evil for another, or will social order, in all its beauty, take the place of former chaos? Will the changes we are about to experience be the bitter fruit of a civil war, disastrous in all respects for the three orders and profitable only to ministerial power; or will they be the natural, anticipated and well-controlled consequence of a simple and just outlook, of a happy cooperation favored by the weight of circumstances and sincerely promoted by all the classes concerned?

4. Promise to Bear Taxes Equally

The Notables have formally expressed the wish that all three orders should bear similar taxes,[o] but this was not what they were asked to advise upon. They were asked how to convoke the States-General, not what should be the subject of its deliberations.[p] Therefore, we must look upon that wish just as we do upon

19 It is impossible to understand the social contract otherwise than as binding the associates together. It is a wrong and dangerous idea to consider it as a contract between a people and its government. The nation cannot enter into a contract with its mandatories; it is the body that *authorizes* them to exercise its powers.

o After rejecting the proposal to grant equal representation to the Third Estate the Notables recorded their wish for complete equality between the orders in respect of public taxation (November 1788).

p Another reference to the second session of the Notables (that convened by Necker in October 1788). The intention was to efface the impression made by the Paris *Parlement's* pronouncement that the coming States-General must meet according to its ancient forms and hence that no concessions were to be made to the Third Estate. Necker explained his policy thus: "It seemed to me absolutely necessary, to offset the viewpoint expressed by the first *Parlement* of the Realm by sonie commanding opinion and I proposed to the King that those expressed by the peers, the *Parlement* and, finally, by so many private associations and individuals, all of whom hasten to agree today that the richer must pay as much as the poorer.[q]

We cannot dissemble: so novel a cooperation has frightened some of the public. Undoubtedly, some have said, it is good and praiseworthy to pledge oneself to submit loyally to a fair distribution of taxes once the law has so decided. But (they ask) what is the origin of so novel a zeal, of so much agreement, of so much haste on the part of the second order? Was it its hope that by offering a voluntary surrender it could avoid the necessity for making it a legal act of justice? Is its excessive zeal to anticipate the work of the States-General aimed at making the latter unnecessary? I will not accuse the nobility of having told the King: "Sire, you need the States-General only to restore your finances: well! We offer to pay as much as the Third Estate; see whether this surplus could not deliver you from an assembly which worries us even more than it does you." No, it is impossible to take this view.

More likely, one suspects, the nobility is trying to hoodwink the Third Estate at the price of a kind of anticipation of justice, in order to divert it from its current demands and so distract it from its need to be *something* in the States-General. The nobility seems to be saying to the Third Estate: "What are you demanding? Do you want us to pay as much as you do? That is just and we shall do so. But let things proceed as in the past when you were nothing and we were everything and when it was so easy for us to pay only as much as we chose." How useful it would be to the privileged classes, if, for a forced renunciation, they were able to purchase the retention of all the old abuses and the hope of even increasing them! If all that is required to strike this excellent bargain is to raise a little enthusiasm among the People, do you think that it will be difficult to beguile and even placate it, by telling it that its burden will be eased, and by pouring into its ears *words* like equality, honor, fraternity ...?

To this the Third Estate can retort: "It is high time that you, like us, bore the burden of a tax which is far more useful to you than to us. You correctly foresaw that this monstrous iniquity could not last any longer. If we are free

---

he should consult the Notables of his kingdom on this important matter." But Sieyès's strictures as to the competence of the assembly are exact. The summons of October 5, 1788, specified that the Notables were to reassemble "exclusively (*uniquement*) to discuss the most regular and appropriate method of going about setting up the States-General." (Quoted, Egret, *La Pré-Revolution Française*, Paris 1962, p. 339.)

q The First Edition went on: "If taxes had been what they ought to be, i.e. voluntary contributions by the tax-payers, one feels that the Third Estate would surely have been unwilling to appear more generous than the other orders."

to give what we choose, we clearly cannot, must not, and will not[r] give any more than you. Having made up our minds on this, we are virtually unmoved by these acts of renunciation which you keep vaunting as the rarest fruit of the *generosity* and the honor of the *French Knights*.[20] Yes, you will pay; not out of generosity, however, but out of justice; not because you consent to do so, but because you have to. We expect you to submit to the common laws, not to offer a token of insulting pity for an order which you have treated mercilessly for so long. But it is for the States-General to discuss this matter; today's question is how to constitute it properly. If the Third Estate is not represented in the States-General, the voice of the nation will be mute in that assembly, and none of its acts will be valid. Even if you were to find ways of rectifying everything without our participation we will not allow anyone to dispose of us without our consent. A long and lamentable experience prevents us from believing in the soundness of the best of laws when this comes merely as a *gift of the strongest*."

---

20 I confess my inability to agree with those who attach so much importance to the privileged classes' renunciation of their pecuniary exemptions. The Third Estate does not seem to realize that, since consent to taxes is constitutionally required from itself just as much as from the others, all it has to do is to declare that it will bear no tax that is not borne by all three orders.

Nor am I satisfied with the manner in which this renunciation (over-solicited, anyway) was made in most *bailliages*, notwithstanding the show of gratitude in the newspapers and gazettes. These state that the nobility "reserves the sacred rights of property ... the prerogatives attaching to it ... and the distinctions that are essential to a monarchy." It is surprising that the Third Estate did not retort, first, to the notion that '*the sacred rights of property must be reserved*': that the whole nation had the same interest in doing that, but that it could not see against whom the clause was directed; that if orders wanted to be considered individually, history would probably tell them which of the three had most reason to mistrust the others; and that, briefly, it can only consider as a gratuitous insult what amounts to saying: "We will pay taxes provided that you do not steal from us." Next: what are these '*prerogatives attaching*' to a part of the nation, which the nation has never granted? Prerogatives which one would even cease to esteem if their origin were known to be something other than the *right of the sword*. Lastly, even more incomprehensibly, where are we to find those '*distinctions essential to the monarchy*', distinctions in the absence of which, presumably, a monarchy could not exist? No distinction, to our knowledge, not even the right to travel in the King's coaches, seems to be important enough to allow it to be said that, without it, monarchy *must* cease to exist.

---

r "must not, and will not" did not appear in the First Edition.

The privileged classes never tire of saying that once the orders renounce their financial exemptions all is equal between them. If all is equal, what have they to fear from the demands of the Third Estate? Do they imagine that it wants to damage itself by attacking a common interest? If all is equal, why then all the efforts to stop the Third Estate emerging from its political incapacity?

But, may I ask, where is the miraculous power that insures France against the possibility of any abuse of *any sort* simply because the nobility pays its fair share of a tax? Alternatively if abuses or disorders still persist, then how can all be equal between those who profit and those who suffer from them?

All is equal indeed! Was it in a spirit of equality, forsooth! that the Third Estate was ignominiously excluded from all offices and posts of any distinction? Was it the spirit of equality that made the Third Estate pay excess taxes so as to create the enormous quantity of resources of every kind for the exclusive use of what is called the *poor nobility*?

In all dealings between a privileged man and a commoner, is it not certain that the latter has no redress against oppression, since if he is bold enough to take legal action he has to appeal to members of the privileged classes? They alone dispose of authority and is not their first reaction to regard the commoner's law-suit as insubordination?

Why are the police agents so terrified when they act against a man of the privileged classes, even when they catch him red-handed, while they maltreat a pauper who is merely a suspect?

For whose benefit are all the judicial privileges, attributions, evocations, letters-patent of suspension and the like, with which to discourage or ruin the contending party? Can the non-privileged Third Estate dispose of these?

Which class of citizens are most exposed to personal humiliations from tax agents and the petty officials of every branch of the bureaucracy? The members of the Third Estate—that is, of course, the real Third Estate, i.e. the Third Estate which enjoys no exemptions.[s]

Why do the privileged nearly always escape the penalty for the most horrible of crimes? And why is public order thus robbed of its most effective examples?

With what ridiculous and ferocious contempt do you dare to relegate the criminal of the first two orders to the third, in order, so you proclaim, to *degrade*

---

s Many bourgeois enjoyed fiscal privileges. For instance, *taille* was not paid by such persons as university students, military officers or civil servants. Again, the only class of persons charged with the *corvée* and with balloting for military service was the peasantry.

him and, apparently, to render him, in such company, *liable* to be executed! What would you say if the legislator, before punishing some scoundrel of the Third Estate, proposed to rid his order of him by giving him letters-patent of nobility?[t]

The law lays down different penalties for the privileged classes and for the non-privileged. It appears to take a fond interest in a noble criminal and to seek to honor him right up to the scaffold. To this abominable distinction which, fundamentally, only potential criminals could wish to retain, is linked, as we know, a sentence of attainder for the entire family of the wretch who is executed without benefit of privilege. The law is responsible for this atrocity; and you would refuse to change it! If the *duty* is the same for everybody, and if the *infraction* is the same, why should the *penalty* be different? Remember: as things now stand, whenever you punish a privileged man you honor him but punish the nation which has already suffered enough from his crime.

I put it to you: cast but the most superficial glance over society and still repeat that all will be equal from the moment the nobility renounces its financial exemptions! Some men are only sensitive about money; their senses are literally paralyzed at anything connected with liberty, honor or equality before the law, in short by all social rights apart from money; they cannot conceive of people worrying about anything except one crown more or one crown less. But it is not for the vile that I am writing this book.

How justify the exclusive privilege of carrying arms, even in peace-time, irrespective of any military function and without wearing the uniform of that profession? If the privileged man arms himself to defend his life, his property and his honor, why is a man of the Third Estate any less interested in protecting his life and his property? Is he less sensitive about honor? Who would dare argue that the law is so much more vigilant on his behalf that it therefore *excuses* him from arming for self-defense?

---

t The nobility benefited by virtue of certain distinctions which, in this and the following paragraphs, Sieyès holds up to ridicule. For instance, the noble enjoyed title, rank and certain honors such as the right to appear at Court. He also enjoyed certain judicial exemptions, e.g. the right to be adjudged by his peers in the *Parlement*; also, certain financial exemptions such as exemption from the duty to pay the *taille*. Within his manor he enjoyed rights of jurisdiction and to a limited extent certain financial rights. And he enjoyed the privilege of bearing arms. On the other hand he had certain obligations. If condemned for a crime he lost his nobility '*par déchéance*'. If he lived 'ignobly' he might lose his nobility '*par dérogeance*'; and ignobly could mean (there were many local variations) simply plying a trade. For Sieyès such 'obligations' were, understandably, even more insulting to the Third Estate than the privileges and exemptions.

If all is equal, why the voluminous collections of laws benefiting the nobility? Have you perchance discovered how to favor one order without damaging the others? You know full well that this discriminatory legislation turns the nobility into a race apart, born to rule, and everybody else into a nation of helots, destined to serve. Yet you dare lie to your conscience and try to bemuse the nation by clamoring that "all is equal."[21]

Finally, even those laws which you think are the most general and impartial are themselves accessory to the privileges. Look at the spirit in which they are drafted; trace out their consequences. For whom do they appear to be made? For the privileged classes. Against whom? Against the nation ...

And so the People is to be content and to forget about all this because the nobility (forsooth!) *agrees* to pay, like the People! Future generations are to close their eyes to the enlightenment of their day and settle down quietly to a state of oppression which the present generation can no longer endure! But let us leave this inexhaustible topic, it does nothing but rouse indignation.[22]

All taxes peculiar to the Third Estate must be abolished. This is indubitable. What an odd country, where the citizens who profit most from the commonwealth contribute least to it! Where there are taxes which it is shameful to bear and which the legislator himself styles 'degrading'! To think only in terms of wholesomeness, what kind of society is it where you *lose caste* if you work? Where to consume is honorable but to produce is vile? Where laborious occupations are called *base*? As if anything but vice could be base, and as if this baseness of vice, the only true one, could be found mostly among those who work![u]

---

21 "I would like somebody to show me where to find the numerous privileges which people complain that we enjoy," said an aristocrat. You had better say "where they are not," answered a friend of the People. Everything about the privileged person smacks of privilege; even the way he asks questions, which would be considered extraordinary on the part of a simple citizen; even the self-assured tone with which he raises issues, so obviously solved in the depth of his soul. But, even if all privileges were reduced to one alone, I would still find it insufferable. Do you not realize that it would multiply, just like the number of privileged persons?

22 However, I deal here only with the inequality of *civil* rights; in the last two chapters, I will put forward sound views on the monstrous inequality of political rights.

---

u If the noble ceased to live 'nobly' he lost his nobility by '*dérogeance*'. But the rule varied from district to district. In Normandy, nobility lapsed if the noble no longer had enough money to support his rank, but in other places the '*dérogeance*' was temporary. The noble entered commerce, made his fortune and then supplicated the King to have his '*dérogeance*' cancelled. Again, certain trades and vocations were open to the nobility, e.g. overseas trading, wholesaling, iron- and glass manufacturing.

Finally, words such as '*taille*',[23] '*franc-fief*', '*ustensiles*'[v] etc., must be banned from the political vocabulary for ever and the legislator must no longer take a stupid pleasure in repelling the foreigners who have been prevented from bringing their capital and skills to us by these derogatory distinctions.

But whilst I can foresee this and the thousand other advantages which a well-constituted assembly must bring to the nation, I see, as yet, nothing that promises the Third Estate an acceptable constitution. Its claims are no nearer to being granted. The privileged classes persist in defending all their

---

23 It is proper to remark that the suppression of the *taille* will be to the financial advantage of the privileged if, as seems likely, it is not replaced by anything other than a general tax. The privileged classes will pay less and here is the proof [Note by S.E. Finer: *Taille*, the most important of the taxes, varied in form and onerousness from province to province. It took two main forms. *Taille personelle* was based on the status of the tax-payer and was paid by members of the Third Estate who had not been granted exemption from it. In practice it fell exclusively on the poor and the peasantry. *Taille réelle*, however, was based on property irrespective of the status of the owner.]:

1. In places where the *taille* is personal, it is well known that, basically, the tax is paid by the land-lord only. Therefore, if you substitute for the *taille* a tax bearing equally on all properties, even on those on which *taille* is not liable to be levied today, you clearly relieve the mass of properties that bear the *taille* to-day of the whole proportion of the replacement tax that will be paid by the properties which are to-day exempt from *taille*. As leased lands pay the biggest share of *taille*, it is certain that the greatest part of the relief will be to the benefit of the whole class of these estates. And since they mostly belong to the privileged classes, I am therefore right in saying that the privileged will pay less tax. 2. In places where the *taille* is based on real property, rural properties will be relieved of all that part of the replacement tax that will fall on noble properties. This commutation will be made irrespective of the personal status of the owners. Since we do not know to which order of citizens most noble lands and most rural properties belong, we cannot apportion the special advantages or disadvantages that will accrue to the nobility from the suppression of the *taille*.

The wealthy lords have calculated correctly that the abolition of the *taille*, *franc-fief*, etc., would facilitate transfers among their vassals and increase the value of the property, and consequently that it promises them new financial benefits. It is certainly wrong that the *taille* should be levied on the farmers; but, if it were levied under another name on the landlords themselves for all the properties which they *let*, it would be a perfectly sound tax, in so far as it would discourage small-holders from abandoning the management of their property, and it would play the part of a prohibitive tax or of a fine levied on large, but idle, landlords.

---

v The *franc-fief* was a tax which a commoner had to pay on his purchasing a fief, i.e. a manor. *Ustensiles* was the duty to billet troops in passage and was usually commuted for a cash payment.

advantages. Irrespective of the number of their representatives they still want to constitute two separate chambers, i.e. they want two votes out of three, and they also insist that each chamber shall have the right of veto. An excellent way to make all reform impossible! This deadlock might suit the taste of the first two orders. But can the Third Estate get much pleasure out of it? Evidently, it is not for the Third Estate to repeat the nice witticism of the Farmer-General: "Why change? We are so well off."

5. Middle Course Proposed by Friends Common to the Privileged Classes and to the Government

What the government fears above all other things is a deliberative procedure which, by bringing all public business to a standstill, would hold up the subventions it is waiting for.[w] If agreement could be reached on meeting the deficit, however, it would hardly give anything else a thought; the orders could quarrel as much as and long as they wanted. Indeed, the less progress they make, the more the government might hope to recover its arbitrary power. It is this idea that underlies a proposed means of reconciliation which is beginning to be canvassed everywhere and which would be as helpful to the privileged orders and the government as it would be fatal for the Third Estate. The proposal is that the subventions and all subjects connected with taxation should be by individual vote; but, after that, it is suggested that the orders should withdraw into their separate chambers as into impregnable fortresses,[x] where the Commons would debate to no avail, the privileged orders pleasure themselves without fear, while the Minister would remain their master. But who can believe that the Third Estate would fall into such an obvious trap? The vote on the subventions must be the final debate of the States-General; this will make it necessary to agree beforehand on a general procedure for all the debates; and we must hope that the procedure adopted will be one that enables the assembly to make use of all its enlightenment and of all its wisdom.[24]

6. It Is Proposed to Imitate the English Constitution

Within the nobility, different interests have had time to emerge. It is not far from being divided into two parties. All those who belong to the most distinguished three or four hundred families sigh for an upper chamber on the

---

24 See Vues sur les Moyens d'Exécution, etc., pp. 87 to 91.

---

w The First Edition read: "... a procedure which would kill all public business."

x This was Necker's view. Cf. Lefebvre, *The Coming of the French Revolution* (New York, 1961), p. 50.

English model; their pride is sustained by the hope of ceasing to be merged with the general mass of the gentlefolk. Hence the High Nobility would gladly agree to thrusting the rest of the nobility down into the House of the Commons along with the generality of the citizens.

The Third Estate must suspect a system which aims at nothing less than filling its own chamber with people whose interest is so contrary to the common interest; of a system which would soon cause the Third Estate to revert to its old impotence, to be once again a victim of oppression. From this point of view, there is a real difference between France and England. In England, the only aristocrats who have privileges are those on whom the constitution confers part of the legislative power.[25] All other citizens share the same interest; there are no privileges to divide them into separate orders. Therefore, if in France we want to merge the three orders into one, we must first abolish all privileges of all kinds. The nobleman and the priest must have no interest other than the common interest, and by law they must enjoy only the rights of ordinary citizens. Failing these conditions, though you may unite the three orders under the same name, they will continue to constitute three heterogeneous substances unable to amalgamate. No-one can accuse me of defending the distinction between orders which I regard as the most noxious of all inventions directed against the social good. I know only one misfortune which could be worse: to merge the orders *nominally* while leaving them separated *in fact* by the maintenance of privileges. Such an action would consecrate for ever the triumph of the orders over the nation. Public welfare requires that there should be some place wherein the common interest of society is kept pure and unalloyed. On this view, which is the only sound view, the only national view, the Third Estate must never consent to the admission of several orders to a so-called House of the Commons because the idea of a Commons composed of different orders is grotesque. One may say that it is a contradiction in terms.

---

25 The Lords of the Upper Chamber do not even constitute a separate order. In England, there is only one order, the nation. The member of the House of Lords is a superior mandatory appointed by law to exercise part of the legislative power and all the higher judicial functions. He is not privileged by right of caste irrespective of public functions, for the brothers of a lord do not share the privileges of the eldest. It is true that these high functions are attached to birth, or rather to primogeniture; this is a tribute paid to the feudalism that was still so preponderant a hundred years ago; it is an institution that is both gothic and ridiculous, for if kings became hereditary to avoid the civil disturbances that their election might cause, there is no reason to be afraid of anything of the sort in nominating a mere lord.

The Third Estate's resistance will be supported by the lesser nobility which will never agree to exchange its privileges for benefits that would accrue to somebody else. Indeed, look at the way in which the lower nobility protests against the aristocracy of the Barons in Languedoc.[y] Men generally like to reduce to equality all that is above them; they then prove themselves 'philosophers'. This word only becomes odious to them from the moment when they discover the same principle operating among their inferiors.

However, the plan of bicameralism attracts so many supporters in this country that there is real occasion for alarm. The differences which we have just mentioned are real; never will a nation sliced into orders have anything in common with a nation which is *a whole*. With such different materials, how can you hope to build in France a similar political structure to England's?

Do you propose to admit part of your first two orders to the lower chamber? First, teach us how to make a Commons of several orders. As we have just shown, the Commons cannot be anything other than a body of citizens who enjoy the same civil and political rights. It is sheer mockery to use the word otherwise, to act as if it were possible to form a Commons by making citizens with unequal civil and political privileges sit in the same room. You will never find so strange a combination in England. Furthermore, it will not take long for that portion of the nobility which is to be introduced into your so-called House of the Commons to take possession of most of the seats. The Third Estate would soon lose its real representatives, and we would go back to the former state of affairs in which the nobility was everything and the nation nothing.

To avoid such drawbacks, why not reserve the second chamber exclusively for the Third Estate? In that case you would not alter your present condition. Indeed, by uniting the two privileged orders, you simply make matters worse: this alliance strengthens them as against the common order, while it weakens all the orders collectively as against the government. And this government is well aware that, between two separated nations, it will always be called in to lay down the law.

Furthermore, I still fail to see how this new arrangement brings you any closer to the English constitution. You legitimize and consecrate the distinctiveness of the privileged order; you separate its interests from those of the nation for all time; and you perpetuate the hatred, if not indeed civil war, which

y Languedoc was one of the *Pays d'Etats*. At this moment it was in turmoil over proposals to reform its ancient Provincial Estates. While the bourgeois protested at being represented by newly created nobles and by municipal officers, the lesser nobility protested at the rule that the only nobles entitled to sit in the delegation of the order of nobility were those who possessed baronies.

destroys the tranquility of any nation divided into those who are the privileged and those who are not. In England, things are just the reverse. There all the interests of the nation are united in the House of Commons. The Lords themselves are careful not to oppose the common interest because this is also their own interest and above all that of their brothers, their children and their whole family, who belong by right to the Commons. Yet some are bold enough to compare the Upper House of England with a chamber which in France is to unite the clergy and the nobility! However you disguise it, you cannot avoid certain evils which are an essential part of it. If it is to consist of genuine representatives of the clergy and the nobility of the whole kingdom, you will, as already stated, separate for ever the two interests and renounce all hope of establishing *one* nation. If it is to be a House of Lords, you can either fill it with deputies elected by a certain number of the most distinguished families, or, to deviate even less from your English model, you can simply make the Peerage an hereditary or at least life-term privilege. All such proposals merely serve to multiply the difficulties; they all entail a House of Commons that would be hybrid and therefore preposterous. Moreover, when it pleases the King of England to create a peer, he is not obliged to pick him from a single class of citizens; this is another difference which completely upsets our own views on nobility.

I have one last point to make; it springs naturally from the conception of an Upper House composed of hereditary or life members. Such persons certainly cannot in any way be representatives of the nation, yet they would none the less exercise its powers. Frankly, now, is it impossible to imagine circumstances in which it might prove highly awkward to summon the Commons? If so, scores of reasons could easily be found to postpone it from one date to another, until time finally became so pressing that the Upper House would be conveniently invited to give prior consent to a loan, or a law, etc. I leave the rest to the reader's imagination. It would be amusing indeed if we ended up again with that *Plenary Court*[z] to which we gave such a hostile reception not so long ago!

---

z There were two main institutional checks on the despotism of the French monarchy in the eighteenth century. One consisted of the ancient Provincial Estates in those provinces (*Pays d'Etats*) where they still persisted. The other consisted of the *Parlements*. These *Parlements* were courts of law of great antiquity. As judicial bodies they served mainly as courts of appeal from inferior courts; but they also possessed certain administrative functions, viz. the right to 'register' royal edicts and decrees. They had successfully expanded this right into a right to 'verify' whether such edicts were in accord with the 'fundamental laws of the kingdom' and, if they thought they were not, to remonstrate against them and even refuse registration. The King's response would then be to order the registration in a *lit de justice* at which he was personally present and, if the *Parlement* refused to acknowledge the validity of

I feel that one must be allowed to dislike a measure which could lead us to the very precipice we thought we had avoided for ever. Assuredly, we need neither a *royal* chamber, nor a *feudal* chamber.

Let me just add, before passing from this topic, that I have attacked the distinction between *chambers* only in so far as it would mean a distinction between *orders*. Separate these two ideas, and I will be the first to ask for three chambers equal on all points, each of them composed of one-third of the grand national deputation. All that would need to be added to this new scheme would be to adopt the method indicated on pages 89 and 90 of *Vues sur les Moyens d'Exécution*, etc., i.e. for decisions to be taken by simple majority of heads whenever the three chambers were in disagreement with one another.

---

his action, to break their resistance by exiling them to some remote place by issuing *lettres de cachet*. These *Parlements*, of which there were thirteen, were nests of aristocratic privilege. Magistrates became ennobled on acquiring their post and this nobility was hereditary. Thus was formed the *noblesse de robe*, which enjoyed the fiscal privileges common to all the nobility. Recruitment to the *Parlement* was by hereditary descent or by co-option. By this time many *Parlements* were openly fighting against the admission of commoners and some, e.g. those of Rennes, Rouen and Grenoble, refused to admit any person who could not prove four generations of nobility. Throughout the eighteenth century, the *Parlements* had fought a running battle with the monarchy. They had defeated the reforming efforts of Machault, of Turgot and of Necker. In 1771, Louis XV had abolished them, at the hand of his celebrated Minister Maupéou; but the youthful Louis XVI had restored them. It was the conviction that these courts would obstruct his efforts at reform that led Calonne to seek to by-pass them by convening the Notables in February 1787. As already explained in the chronological summary, Calonne and his successor, Brienne, failed to get the Notables' support and Brienne was compelled to take his proposed reforms to the Paris *Parlement*, thereupon provoking the clash of Crown *versus Parlement*. Finally, on May 8, Brienne attempted to repeat the famous '*coup de Maupéou*'. He enforced the registration of decrees which abrogated the *Parlement's* right to register and verify those decrees and edicts which applied to the whole kingdom. Henceforth this right was to inhere in a *Cour Plénière*. This would consist of the senior judges of the Paris *Parlement* and the president and one other magistrate from each of the provincial *Parlements*; of the Princes of the Blood; and, for the rest, of peers, government officials and leading representatives of the Church, the army and the bureaucracy. Brienne's coup was greeted by a howl of rage throughout France. The provincial *Parlements* declared their solidarity with the Paris *Parlement*. Riots broke out. In checking royal absolutism and demanding the recall of the States-General the Paris *Parlement* appeared to be acting in the interests of the nation as a whole. On July 5, Brienne gave way. He simultaneously suspended the decree creating the *Cour Plénière* and announced that the States-General would be convened. Brienne resigned on August 25, 1788, and his successor, Necker, lost no time in recalling the Paris *Parlement*, which met in Paris on September 23, 1788.

7. A Spirit of Imitation Is not a Fit Guide for Us

We would not put so much faith in English institutions if our own political knowledge was of longer standing or more prevalent. In this respect the French nation consists of men who are either too young or too old. These two age-groups, which are so closely related in many other respects, share an inability to act otherwise than by imitation. The young try to copy; the old can but repeat. The old stick to their own ingrained habits. The young ape the practices of others. This is as far as their capacity can take them.

We should not therefore be surprised to see a nation which has only just had its eyes opened, turn towards the English constitution and accept it as a model in every detail. What we need at this moment is some able writer to enlighten us on the two following questions: Is the English constitution good in itself? If so, would it be suitable for France?[26]

I am afraid that this much vaunted masterpiece cannot survive any impartial examination which is based on the principles of the true political order. We should then recognize, perhaps, that it is much more a product of chance and circumstance than of enlightenment. Its Upper House obviously bears the marks of the Revolution of 1688. We have already made the point that it can hardly be regarded as anything but a monument to gothic superstition.

Look at the national representation! See how imperfect it is in every respect, as the English themselves admit! And yet a good representation is essential for a good legislature.

How sound is the principle which inspires the notion of dividing the legislative power into three parts, of which only one is supposed to speak in the name of the nation? If the lords and the King are not the representatives of the nation, they should have no share in legislative power; for none but the nation can will for the nation and consequently legislate for the nation. But no parts of the legislative body are competent to vote in the name of the nation unless they have received a mandate from it. Yet where is the mandate when there is no free general election?

I do not deny that the English constitution is an astonishing work for its time. Nevertheless, although people are always ready to sneer at a Frenchman who does not prostrate himself before it, I am bold enough to say that I do not find in it the simplicity of good order, but rather a framework of precautions against

---

26 Since this book first appeared, an excellent work has been published that fulfills almost completely the wish I was expressing here. It is the *'Examen du Gouvernement d'Angleterre, comparé aux Constitutions des Etats-Unis'*, a pamphlet of 291 pages.

disorder.[27] And since all political institutions are linked together, since every effect is in its turn the origin of a series of causes and effects which can be followed as far as the mind will carry, it is not extraordinary that good minds should have thought it very profound. Furthermore it is natural that the most complicated contraptions should precede the true advances in the social arts as in all others: and their triumph likewise will be to produce great effect by simple means.

It would be wrong to prefer the English constitution merely because it has lasted for a hundred years and seems likely to last for centuries to come. As far as human institutions are concerned, is there a single one that does not last for a very long time, however bad it is? Does not despotism last? Does it not seem endless throughout most of the world?

A better test is to look at *results*. When you compare the English with their neighbors on the Continent in this respect, it is difficult to feel that they do not possess something better. However incomplete it may be, they do at least have a constitution, whereas we have nothing at all. The difference is vast. It is not surprising that it should make itself manifest in the results. But, surely, it is a mistake to attribute all that is good in England to the power of the constitution alone.

There is an obvious example of one particular law which is better than anything in the constitution itself, viz. trial by *jury*, which is the true safeguard of individual liberty wherever in the world people want to be free. This is the only legal procedure that can protect people against the abuses of the judiciary which are so frequent and so formidable wherever one is not tried by one's own peers. Under this procedure, all that freedom demands is due precaution against any illegal orders emanating from the government. This calls for either a good constitution, which England has not, or such circumstances as will prevent the head of the executive from resorting to force in support of his own arbitrary decisions. Obviously England is the only nation

27 In England the right to govern is the object of an endless struggle between the administration and the aristocrats of the opposition. The nation and the King are, virtually, no more than spectators. The King's policy always consists in taking the stronger side. The nation fears both sides equally; and so, if it is to be secure, the struggle must go on. It therefore supports the weaker side to prevent it from being completely crushed. But if the People decided not to let the management of its affairs become a prize in this gladiatorial combat, and chose to look after itself through genuine representatives, can one really believe that the importance now attributed to a *balance* of powers would not disappear with the circumstances that have created it?

which can afford not to have land forces of a size dangerous to her citizens, and is consequently the only nation able to be free without a good constitution.

This consideration should suffice to dampen our passion for imitating our neighbors. Let us rather look at our own needs; they are closer to us; they will be a better source of inspiration.[aa] If you try to naturalize the English constitution in your own country, you will quite certainly, and with the greatest ease, secure all of its defects. The reason is that these defects will serve the purposes of the one solitary power from whom you have anything to fear. The question is—will you receive its advantages as well? This is more problematical, for in this case you have to encounter the opposition of this power, whose purpose is to thwart you. After all, why do we think so much of this exotic constitution? Apparently, because it comes close to the principles of the good society. But if ideal models of the beautiful and the good exist to guide us, and if, moreover, we are unable to say that the ideal model of society is less well known to us now than it was to the English in 1688, how then can we disregard the true good and be satisfied with imitating its copy? Let us rise at once to the challenge of setting up ourselves as an example to the nations.

It is argued that no people has done better than the English. Even if that were so, must the products of political art at the end of the eighteenth century be no better than those of the seventeenth? The English proved equal to the enlightenment of their time; let us not prove unequal to the enlightenment of ours.[bb] Above all, let us not be discouraged because we find nothing in history that can be adapted to our present situation. The true science of society does not date back very far. Men were building cottages for many a year before they were able to build palaces. Surely it is obvious that the advance of social architecture had to be even slower; for this art, the most important of all, could obviously never expect to receive the slightest encouragement from the hands of despots and aristocrats.[cc]

---

aa The First Edition read: "Let us rather look at our own needs and our own social relationships. This constitution which we keep envying is not good because it is English. It is good because, despite its very real defects, it offers precious advantages. If you attempt to naturalise ..."

bb The First Edition read: "... to the enlightenment of ours. That is the best kind of imitation, the worthiest way of following in the footsteps of the good examples. Above all ..."

cc The First Edition read: "... before they were able to build palaces. Social architecture had good reasons for being slower in its advance than the many arts that can perfectly well coexist with despotism."

Chapter 5

What Ought to Have Been Done? Basic Principles

"In morals, nothing can replace simple and natural means. But the more time man has wasted in failures, the more he dreads the thought of beginning afresh; as if it were not always better to make a fresh start and complete the task, than to lie at the merry of events and to depend on factitious resources with which one would begin again and yet again, and yet accomplish nothing."

In every free nation, and every nation ought to be free, there is only one way of settling disputes about the constitution. One must not call upon Notables, but upon the nation itself. If we have no constitution, it must be made, and only the nation has the right to make it. If we do have a constitution, as some people obstinately maintain, and if, as they allege, it divides the National Assembly into three deputations of three orders of citizens, nobody can fail to notice, at all events, that one of these orders is protesting so vigorously that nothing can be done until its claim is decided. Now, who has the right to judge in such a matter?

A question of this nature could only seem unimportant to those who disparage just and natural methods of handling social affairs and put their trust in the factitious qualities, usually rather undesirable and devious, on which the reputations of so-called statesmen, the alleged "leading politicians," are based. As for us, we shall not deviate from the moral rule; morality must determine all the relationships which bind men to each other, both in their private interests and in their common or social interest. Morality must point out the way for us; and, after all, only morality can do so. We must always go back to basic principles for they are more cogent than all the achievements of genius.

We shall never understand social machinery unless we examine a society as though it were an ordinary machine. It is necessary to consider each part of it separately, and then link them all together in the mind in due order, to see how they fit together and hear the general harmony that necessarily follows. We need not embark on so extensive a task here. But, since one must always be clear, and since one is not clear unless one expounds from first principles, we shall at least ask the reader to distinguish three periods in the making of a political society, and these distinctions will pave the way for such explanation as is necessary.

In the first period, we assume a fairly considerable number of isolated individuals who wish to unite; by this fact alone, they already constitute a nation: they enjoy all the rights of a nation and it only remains for them to exercise them. This first period is characterized by the activity of the *individual* wills. The association is their work; they are the origin of all power.

The second period is characterized by the action of the *common* will. The associates want to give consistency to their union; they want to fulfill its aim. They therefore discuss and agree amongst themselves on public needs and on ways of satisfying them. We see that power, then, belongs to the community. Individual wills still constitute its origin and form its essential components; but, taken separately, they would be powerless. Power exists only in the aggregate. The community needs a common will; without *singleness* of will it could not succeed in being a willing and acting body. It is certain, also, that this body has no rights other than such as derive from the common will.

But let us leap the lapse of time. The associates are now too numerous and occupy too large an area to exercise their common will easily by themselves. What do they do? They separate out whatever is necessary to attend to and satisfy public requirements; and they put a few of their number in charge of exercising this portion of the national will, that is to say this portion of power. We have now reached the third period, the period of *government by proxy*. Let us point out a few facts: 1) The community does not cast aside its right to will: this is inalienable; it can only delegate the exercise of that right. This principle is elaborated elsewhere. 2) Nor can it delegate the full exercise of it. It delegates only that portion of its total power which is needed to maintain order. In this matter, no more is surrendered than necessary. 3) Therefore, it does not rest with the body of delegates to alter the limits of the power that has been entrusted to them. Obviously such a competence would be self-contradictory.

I distinguish the third period from the second in that it is no longer the *real* common will which is in operation, but a *representative* common will. It has two ineffaceable characteristics which we must repeat. 1) This will which resides in the body of representatives is neither complete nor unlimited; it is a mere portion of the grand, common, national will. 2) The delegates do not exercise it as a right inherent in themselves, but as a right pertaining to other people; the common will is confided to them in trust.

For the moment I put aside a mass of problems which this discussion naturally gives rise to, and go straight on. What is meant by the political constitution of a society? And what is its exact relationship to the nation itself?

It is impossible to create a body for any purpose without giving it the organization, procedures and laws appropriate for it to fulfill its intended functions. This is called the *constitution* of this body. Obviously, the body cannot exist without it. Therefore, it is equally obvious that every government must have its constitution; and what is true for the government in general is true for each of its components. Thus the Assembly of Representatives which is entrusted with the legislative power, i.e. the exercise of the common will, exists only in the form which the nation has chosen to give it. It is nothing outside the articles of its constitution; only through its constitution can it act, conduct its proceedings and govern.

In addition to this need to organize the government so as to permit it to exist and to act, the nation's interest also requires that the delegated public power shall never be able to injure those who have delegated it. Hence, a multiplicity of political safeguards have been worked into the constitution: regulations imposed on the government, failure to observe which would render the exercise of power illegal.[28]

One senses therefore the double necessity of subjecting the government to precise procedures, both internal and external to it, to ensure both its ability to fulfill and its impotence to deviate from the purpose for which it was established.

But who will tell us for what purpose and in whose interest a constitution could have been given to the *nation* itself? The nation is prior to everything. It is the source of everything. Its will is always legal; indeed it is the law itself. Prior to and above the nation, there is only *natural* law. If we want to formulate a clear idea of that sequence of *positive* laws which can emanate exclusively from the will of the nation, the first are the *constitutional* laws. These are of two kinds: some determine the organization and the functions of the *legislative* body; the others determine the organization and the functions of the various *executive* bodies. These laws are called *fundamental*, not in the sense that they could become independent of the national will, but because the bodies to which they grant existence and means of action cannot modify them. Neither aspect of the constitution is the creation of the constituted power, but of the constituent power. No type of delegated power can in any way alter the conditions of its delegation. In this sense, and in this sense alone, are constitutional laws *fundamental*. Those which establish the legislative body are *founded* by the national will before any constitution has been established; they form the first stage of the constitution. Those which establish the executive bodies must similarly be the *ad hoc* product of a representative will. Thus all the parts of a government are interrelated and, in the last analysis, depend on the nation. We merely put forward this idea in passing, but it is none the less correct.

---

28 When the constitution is simple and well-framed, safeguards are few; in the countries where it is complicated and, to be frank, ill-comprehended, safeguards multiply *ad infinitum*. They provide a subject for study. The constitution itself becomes the butt of political scientists and what ought to be the essence of it, i.e. its internal organization, is lost to view, behind the scaffolding of mere accessories.

Following from this, it is easy to conceive how the laws properly so-called, i.e. the laws which protect civil rights and interpret the common interest, are the work of the legislative body composed and functioning according to the terms of its constitution. Although we mention these laws *after* the constitutional laws, they are, nevertheless, the more important, for they are the *end* to which the constitution is only the *means*. They can be divided into two groups: immediate or protective laws, and mediate or guiding laws. But this is not the place to develop this analysis.[29]

We have seen how the constitution had its origin in the second period. Clearly this constitution relates only to the government. It would be ridiculous to suppose that the nation itself could be constricted by the procedures or the constitution to which it had subjected its mandatory's. If its becoming a nation had depended upon a *positive* act, it never would have existed. The nation owes its existence to *natural* law alone. The government, on the contrary, can only be a product of *positive* law. Every attribute of the nation springs from the simple fact that it exists. No act of will on its part can give it greater or lesser rights than those it already enjoys. Even in its first period, it enjoys all the rights of a nation. In its second period, it exercises them. In its third, it appoints representative to exercise those rights which are necessary for the preservation and good order of the community. To deviate from this sequence of simple ideas is simply to fall into one absurdity after another.

The power exercised by the government has substance only in so far as it is constitutional; it is legal only in so far as it is based on the prescribed laws. The national will, on the contrary, never needs anything but its own existence to be legal. It is the source of all legality.

Not only is the nation not subject to a constitution, but it *cannot* be and it *must not* be; which is tantamount to saying that it is not.

It *cannot* be. From whom indeed could it have received positive form? Is there a prior authority which could have told a multitude of individuals: "I put you together under such and such laws; you will form a nation on the conditions I prescribe." We are not speaking here of brigandage or domination, but of a legitimate, that is to say voluntary and free, association.

Can it be said that a nation, by a primary act of will which is completely untrammeled by any procedure, can bind itself to express its will thereafter only in certain determined ways? In the first place, a nation can neither alienate nor waive its right to will; and whatever its decisions, it cannot lose the right

29 Let us only say that the best way of being misunderstood is to confound all parts of the social order under the name "constitution."

to alter them as soon as its interest requires. Secondly, with whom would this nation have entered into such a contract? I see how it can *bind* its members, its mandatory's, and all those who belong to it; but can it in any sense impose on itself duties towards itself? What is a contract with oneself? Since both parties are the same will, they are obviously always able to free themselves from the purported engagement.

Even if it could, a nation *must* not subject itself to the shackles of a defined procedure. That would put it in danger of losing its liberty for ever, for tyranny, under the pretext of giving the People a constitution, would only need a momentary success to bind it so closely by procedural rules that it would lose the ability to express its own will, and, consequently, to shake off the yoke of despotism. We must conceive the nations of the world as being like men living outside society or "in a state of nature," as it is called. The exercise of their will is free and independent of any civil form. Existing only within the natural order, their will can take full effect provided it bears the *natural* characteristics of a will. The manner in which a nation exercises its will does not matter; the point is that it does exercise it; any procedure is adequate, and its will is always the supreme law. To imagine a legitimate society, we assumed that the purely natural *individual* will had enough moral power to form the association; how then can we refuse to recognize a similar power in the equally natural *common* will? A nation is always in a state of nature and, amidst so many dangers, it can never have too many possible methods of expressing its will. Let us not be afraid of repeating it: a nation is independent of any procedures; and no matter how it exercises its will, the mere fact of its doing so puts an end to positive law, because it is the source and the supreme master of positive law.

But there is even stronger proof that our principles are correct, though further arguments are really superfluous.

A nation must not and cannot identify itself with constitutional forms, for as soon as a conflict arises between different parts of that constitution, what will become of a nation organized by the very constitution that is in dispute? Mark how important it is, socially, that citizens shall be able to look to some department of the executive to provide an authoritative solution for their private litigation. In the same way, the various branches of the executive must be at liberty, in a free nation,[dd] to appeal to the legislative body for a decision whenever they meet unforeseen difficulties. But if the legislative body itself—the very basis of the constitution—is in a state of disruption, who then will be the supreme judge? For without one, order must give way to anarchy.

---

dd The words "in a free nation" did not appear in the First Edition.

How can one believe that a constituted body may itself decide on its own constitution? One or more component parts of a corporate body are of no consequence individually. Power belongs only to the whole. As soon as a part protests, the whole ceases to exist; if non-existent, then how can it pass judgment?[30] From this it follows that the constitution of a country would cease to exist at the slightest difficulty arising between its component parts, if it were not that the nation existed independently of any rule and any constitutional form.

In the light of these explanations, we can answer the question we asked ourselves. The component parts of what you believe to be the French constitution are quite obviously at loggerheads. Whose task is it to decide? It is the nation's, independent as it necessarily is of any positive forms. Even if the nation enjoyed regular States-General, this constituted body would be incompetent to decide on a dispute concerning its own constitution. It would be a *petitio principii*, a vicious circle.

The *ordinary* representatives of a nation are charged with the exercise, under the constitution, of that portion of the common will which is necessary to maintain a good social administration. Their power is confined to governmental affairs.

Extraordinary representatives will have whatever new powers the nation chooses to give them. Since a large nation cannot physically assemble when extraordinary circumstances make this necessary, it must entrust extraordinary representatives with the necessary powers on such occasions. If it could meet and express its will before your eyes, would you dare to dispute it on the ground that it did so by one procedure rather than another? Here reality is everything, the form is nothing.

A body of extraordinary representatives takes the place of the assembly of the nation. It does not, of course, need to be in charge of the *whole* of the national will; it needs only special powers, and those only in rare cases; but it is in the same position as the nation itself in respect of *independence* from any constitutional forms. It is not necessary in this case to take many precautions to prevent abuse of power; these representatives are appointed as deputies for just one purpose, and only for a limited time. I maintain that they are not bound by the constitutional forms on which they have to decide. 1) It

30 In England, it is said that the House of Commons represents the nation. This is not so. Perhaps I have already said so, in which case I repeat that if the Commons alone represented the whole of the national will, they alone would constitute the whole legislative body. The constitution having decided that they are only *one* component out of *three*, it is necessary to regard the King and the Lords as being representatives of the nation as well.

would be self-contradictory since these forms are in dispute; it is the task of the representatives to settle them. 2) They have nothing to do with the class of matters for which definitive forms have already been settled. 3) They are a substitute for the whole nation in the course of framing its constitution. They are as independent as the nation would be in that period. They need only to will as individuals in the state of nature would will; whatever the manner in which they were appointed as deputies, whatever their method of holding meetings or debates, and bearing in mind that they are acting on an extraordinary mandate from the people (and how could the nation that mandates them be unaware of it), their common will has the same value as the common will of the nation itself.

I am not saying that a nation cannot give the aforesaid new mandate to its ordinary representatives. Identical people can certainly take part in different bodies and can exercise in turn, by virtue of special mandates, functions which, given their nature, must not be merged together. But it remains true that an extraordinary representative body is different from the ordinary legislature. They are distinct authorities. The latter can move only according to prescribed forms and conditions. The former is not subjected to any procedure whatsoever: it meets and debates as the nation itself would do if we assumed a nation consisting of a tiny population that wanted to give its government a constitution. These distinctions are not idle. All the principles that we have recited are essential to social order; social order would be incomplete if there could arise a single case in which it was impossible to point to rules of conduct suitable to meet all needs.[31]

---

31 These principles clearly decide the issue now being raised in England between Messrs. Pitt and Fox. [Note by S.E. Finer: In November 1788, George III became insane. Thereupon his Prime Minister, Pitt, proposed that the Prince of Wales should become Regent, but under certain restrictions laid down by statute. Fox and Burke, the opposition leaders, insisted that the Prince succeeded automatically and to the full plenitude of royal power once the King's incapacity was established. They argued further that in the event of such incapacity a statute such as Pitt had proposed was an impossibility, since the necessary royal consent could not be forthcoming. From this imbroglio Parliament was suddenly rescued (February 1789) by the King's return to sanity.] Mr. Fox is wrong not to want the *nation* to appoint as Regent *whoever* it chooses and *however* it pleases. Where the law is silent, the nation alone can decide. Mr. Pitt is wrong to want the matter to be decided upon by Parliament. Parliament is incomplete, and indeed non-existent, since the King who is the third part of it is unable to exercise his will. The two Houses can draw up a bill, but they cannot *enact* it. I take this word in the sense that usage gives it nowadays. It is necessary therefore to ask the nation to appoint extraordinary representatives. But this will not happen. The time is ripe for a good constitution, but neither the Opposition nor

It is time now to come back to the title of this chapter. *What ought to have been done* amidst all the difficulties and disputes about the coming States-General? Should we have convened Notables? No. Should we have let the nation and its interests languish? No. Should we have exercised diplomacy upon the interested parties to persuade them all to compromise? No. We should have resorted to the extreme measure of calling an extraordinary representative body. It is the nation that ought to have been consulted.

Let us answer two questions which still remain. Where is the nation to be found? Whose function is it to consult the nation?

1) Where is the nation to be found? Where it is; in the 40,000 parishes which embrace the whole territory, all its inhabitants and every element of the commonwealth; indisputably, the nation lies there. A geographical division would have been chosen so that '*arrondissements*' of 20 to 30 parishes could easily form and elect first deputies. Along similar lines, '*arrondissements*' would have formed provinces; and the provinces would have sent to the capital authentic extraordinary representatives with special powers to decide upon the constitution of the States-General.

You object that this procedure would have entailed too much delay? Surely no more than the succession of expedients which have simply led to further confusion. Besides, it was not a question of saving time, but of adopting workable measures to achieve the aim. Had people been willing and able to stick to true principles, more could have been done for the nation in four months than the progress of enlightenment and public opinion, powerful none the less as I believe it to be, could do in half a century.

But, if the *majority* of the citizens had nominated extraordinary representatives, what would have happened, you may ask, to the distinction between the three orders? What would have become of privileges? They would have become what they deserve to be. The principles which I have just recited are certainties. Abandon the hope of having social order, or else accept these principles. The nation is always free to amend its constitution. Above all, it cannot absolve itself from the responsibility of giving certainty to a disputed constitution. Everybody agrees on that today; cannot you see, then, that the nation could not interfere

---

the Ministry feel like having one. People cling to the rules they are used to; however vicious these may be, they prefer them to the finest social order. Have you ever known a decrepit old man find compensation for his own death in the sight of the fresh and vigorous young man who is ready to take his place? It is a law of nature that political bodies, just like all living bodies, defend themselves in an effort to hold their own, right to the very end.

if it were itself merely a participant in the dispute? A body subjected to constitutional forms cannot take any decision outside the scope of its constitution. It cannot give itself another one. It becomes null and void from the moment when it moves, speaks or acts in any other than the prescribed forms. Even if the States-General were already in session, it would therefore be incompetent to decide upon the constitution. Such a right belongs only to the nation which, we continue to reiterate, is independent of any procedure and any qualifications.

As is obvious, the privileged classes have good reasons for befogging the concepts and principles which relate to this matter. They are boldly prepared today to uphold the opposite of the views they were advocating six months ago. At that time there was a single outcry in France: we had no constitution and we asked for one to be made. Today, we not only have a constitution but, if we are to believe the privileged classes, one which contains two excellent and unchallengeable provisions. The first is the *division* of the citizens *into orders*; the second is the *equality of influence* of each order in the formation of the national will. We have already sufficiently proved that even if both these elements were indeed comprised in our constitution, the nation would always be free to change them. It remains to examine more particularly the nature of this *equality* of influence that they seek to attribute to each order in the formation of the national will. We shall see that such an idea is impossibly absurd and that no nation could possibly include anything of the kind in its constitution.

A political society cannot be anything but the whole body of the associates. A nation cannot decide not to be the nation, or to be so only in a certain fashion: for that would be saying that it is not the nation in any other fashion. Similarly, a nation cannot decree that its common will shall cease to be its common will. It is sad to have to state facts which may appear so simple as to be silly, until one thinks of the conclusions they entail. It follows that no nation has ever been able to decree that the rights inherent in the common will, i.e. in the majority, should pass into the hands of the minority. The common will cannot destroy itself. It cannot change the nature of things, nor arrange that the opinion of the minority shall be the opinion of the majority. Clearly such a regulation would not be a legal or a moral act: it would be lunacy.

Consequently if it be claimed that under the French constitution two hundred thousand individuals out of twenty-six million citizens constitute two-thirds of the common will, only one comment is possible: it is a claim that two and two make five.

The sole elements of the common will are individual wills. One can neither deny the greatest number the right to play their part, nor decide that these ten wills are equivalent to only one while another ten wills amount to thirty. These are contradictions in terms, pure absurdities.

If for the slightest moment one loses sight of this self-evident principle that the common will is the opinion of the majority and not of the minority, there is no point in carrying on the discussion. One might just as well decide that the will of a single man is to be called the majority and that we no longer need States-General or national will at all. For, if the will of a nobleman can be worth as much as ten wills, why should not the will of a minister be worth as much as a hundred? a million? twenty-six million? On the basis of this reasoning, all the national deputies may as well be sent home and every demand of the People suppressed.

Is it necessary to insist further on the logical deduction from these principles? It is a certainty that among the national representatives, whether ordinary or extraordinary, influence must be proportionate to the number of citizens who have the *right* to be represented. If it is to accomplish its task, the representative body must always be the substitute for the nation itself. It must partake of the same *nature*, the same *proportions* and the same *rules*.

To conclude: these principles are all self-consistent and prove: a) only an extraordinary representative body can establish or amend the constitution; b) this constituent representative body must be set up without regard to the distinction between orders.

2) Whose function is it to consult the nation? If the constitution provides for a legislature, each of its component parts would have the right to consult the nation, just as litigants are always allowed to appeal to the courts; or, rather, because the interpreters of a will are obliged to consult with those who appointed them to seek explanations about their mandate or to give notice of circumstances requiring new powers. But for almost two centuries we have been without representatives—even assuming that we had them at that time. Since we have none, who is going to take their place vis-à-vis the nation? Who is going to inform the People of the need for extraordinary representatives? This question will embarrass only those who attach to the word 'convening' the hotchpotch of English ideas. We are not talking here of the royal *prerogative*, but of the simple and natural meaning of 'convening'. This word embraces: *notice* as to the national necessity and *designation* of a common meeting place. Well then, when the preservation of the motherland harries every citizen, is time to be wasted inquiring who has the *right* to convene the assembly? Ask, rather: who has not such a right? It is the sacred *duty* of all those who can do something about it. *A fortiori*, the executive is qualified to do it; for it is in a better position than private individuals to give notice to the whole nation, to

designate the place of the assembly and to sweep aside all the obstructions of corporate interests. The Prince indubitably, in so far as he is the first citizen, has a greater interest than anyone else in convoking the People. He may not be competent to decide on the constitution, but it is impossible to say that he is incompetent to bring such a decision about.

So it is not difficult to answer the question, "what ought to have been done?". The nation ought to have been convened, so as to send to the capital extraordinary representatives with a special mandate to frame the constitution for the ordinary National Assembly. I would have objected to such representatives having the power to sit in the ordinary assembly as well. This ordinary assembly would be operating under the constitution which they had themselves drawn up in their previous capacity; hence my fear lest, instead of confining themselves to the national interest alone, they might pay too much attention to the body of which they were about to become members. In politics, it is the mingling and confusion of powers that constantly make it impossible to establish social order anywhere in the world; by the same token, the moment it is decided to separate what ought to be distinct, the great problem of organizing a human society for the general welfare of its members will be successfully solved.

Why, it may be asked, do I linger so long over *what ought to have been done*? Is not the past over and done with? To this I reply: first, that the knowledge of what ought to have been done may help us to know what must be done. Secondly, it is never unimportant to expound the correct principles of one's topic, particularly when it is so new to most minds. And, finally, the truths expounded in this chapter may conduce to a better understanding of those in the one that follows.

Chapter 6

What Remains to Be Done: Development of Certain Principles

Gone is the day when the three orders were moved by the single thought of defending themselves against ministerial despotism and were ready to unite against their common enemy.[ee] Today, however, the nation cannot turn

ee Up to September 25, 1788, aristocracy, clergy, *Parlements* and Provincial Estates had formed common front with the middle classes against the King and his Ministers. The Paris *Parlement's* declaration of September 25, that the coming States-General must meet according to the ancient forms, "completely changed the whole controversy," as Mallet du Pan observed. King, despotism and constitution are now minor questions. The war is between the Third Estate and the other two orders. This judgement is one which all modern historians have accepted.

circumstances to advantage or take the slightest step towards social order without the Third Estate deriving some side-benefits thereby. Despite this, when the great municipalities of the realm claimed the merest fraction of the People's political rights the sight was enough to make the pride of the first two orders rebel. Just what did these privileged orders want, these orders which in this connection are so eager to defend their own superfluity and so quick to prevent the Third Estate from obtaining its basic needs? Did they expect the vaunted regeneration[ff] to be for themselves alone? Did they want to utilize the ever-suffering People as some blind instrument with which to enhance and consecrate their own aristocracy?

What words will future generations use when they learn of the ferocity with which the second order of the state and the first order of the clergy combated every demand of the municipalities?[gg] Will they be able to credit the secret conspiracies and open plotting, the fake alarms,[32] the perfidiousness of the

32 It is really too ludicrous to see the bulk of the nobility trying to denounce as rebellion against royal authority measures which they profoundly fear to be favorable to despotism. They deny that the Third Estate has any spirit and they can only account for its courage by referring to what they call the maneuvers of the Minister himself; but they are not afraid of painting this pathetic order of the Third Estate as a collection of *rebels* against the King. What the nobles say to each other is: "Nothing is more dangerous to freedom than the language of the Third Estate; it sounds a bit too much like asking: 'Sire, do with us as you

ff *'Regeneration'* had become a vogue-word at this time. Thus Louis XVI, explaining his decision, July 6, 1788, to convene the States-General, spoke of "The great enterprise I have undertaken for the *regeneration* of the Kingdom and the re-establishment of good order in all its parts" (Egret, *La Pré-Revolution Française*, Paris 1962, p. 307). Likewise Necker, in his *apologia* (*Sur l'administration de M. Necker par lui même*, 1791), wrote of "the great enterprise that would ensure a general regeneration, viz. the meeting of the States-General." (Egret, *La Pré-Revolution Française*, Paris 1962, p. 325.)

gg The "demands of the municipalities" were flowing in at the very time the Notables were meeting, at Necker's summons, to decide on the representation of the Third Estate in the coming States-General. Sieyès is here referring to the activity in this assembly of Notables. The "second order" is of course the nobility and the first order the clergy. Egret (*La Pré-Revolution Française*, Paris 1962, pp. 340–341) has pointed out that the opposition to the increased representation of the Third Estate was led by an intransigent bloc of eleven prelates, thirty-seven magistrates of the *Parlements* and twelve Councillors of State and that this bloc easily carried the majority of the Notables with them. They were vigorously opposed by a minority of twenty-four mayors and five representatives of Provincial Estates who were there to represent the interests of the Third Estate. To them must be added seven sympathetic nobles and three clerics. Egret notes in particular that "as a whole the high Clergy closed their ears to moderation" (*La Pré-Revolution Française*, Paris 1962, p. 342).

stratagems in which the defenders of the People were ensnared? Nothing of this will be omitted from the records which patriotic authors are faithfully preparing for posterity. In them they will discover how *nobly* the magnates of France conducted themselves—despite circumstances that ought to have inspired even the most brazen egotists with some sparks of patriotism. How could princes of the reigning dynasty bring themselves to take sides in a controversy between the different orders of the nation? How could they have allowed certain despicable authors to spew forth the ridiculous and yet outrageous calumnies which cram the incredible *Mémoire* published under their name?[hh]

Some people complain of the violence of one or two writers of the Third Estate. What does the attitude of an isolated individual amount to? Nothing. The only truly authentic steps taken by the Third Estate were the petitions

---

please, provided you do not let the aristocrats devour us.'" But they simultaneously tell the King: "Look out, the People is after your throne!; it plans to overthrow the monarchy." In such a state of mind, why should they not themselves rouse the populace, with its blind and superstitious submission to whatever impulses the aristocracy chooses to transmit to it?

They would thus provide themselves with a pretext for saying: "Here is your precious Third Estate!" But, everywhere, honest folk will answer: "Here are the precious aristocrats! Without an aristocracy, how easily we could become, at this very moment, the first nation of the world, that is to say, the most free and the most happy!"

---

hh Defeated in all his efforts to get the Notables to pronounce in favor of increased representation for the Third Estate, Necker prorogued the assembly on December 12, 1788. On the same day, five Princes of the Blood, viz. the Prince de Conti, and the Counts of Artois, Condé, Bourbon and Enghien, submitted their *Mémoire au Roi*. This document repeated all the arguments used in the Notables against conceding the Third Estate a representation equal to the other two orders combined; it warned the King against a "system of deliberate insubordination and contempt for the laws of the state" which had been caused by the "effervescence of opinions"; it expressed fears for the future of property rights and the inequality of wealth; and it deprecated the proposals to suppress feudal rights. It begged the King "not to sacrifice and humiliate this brave, ancient and respected nobility which has shed so much blood for the country"; a sentiment which provoked the famous riposte of Cerutti, "I suppose the people's blood was so much water?"

The *Mémoire* concluded with the contemptuous words: "Therefore let the Third Estate desist from its attacks on the rights of the first two orders. These rights are not less ancient than the Monarchy, and are equally as unalterable. Let the Third Estate confine itself to seeking to reduce taxation with which it may be overburdened. In such an event, the first two orders, recognising in the Third Estate citizens who are dear to them, may from generosity of mind consent to renouncing their fiscal privileges and bear the burden of public taxation in equal measure."

of the municipalities and of some of the *Pays d'Etats*. Compare those to the equally authentic steps taken by the Princes against the People, although the People had carefully refrained from attacking the Princes. How modest and moderate the first are! And how violent and profoundly unjust the second!

In vain will the Third Estate await restitution of its *political* rights and the plenitude of its *civil* rights from the consensus of the orders.[ii] The fear of seeing abuses reformed alarms the aristocrats more than the desire for liberty inspires them. Between liberty and a few odious privileges, they have chosen the latter. The soul of the privileged has become identified with the favors of servitude. They are afraid now of the States-General for which they were lately so ardent. Everything goes well with them. They have no complaints, except for the spirit of innovation. They no longer require anything: fear has provided a constitution for them.

The Third Estate must now see the direction in which both thought and action are moving, and realize that its sole hope lies in its own intelligence and courage. Reason and justice are on its side; the least it must do is to assure itself of their full support. No, it is too late to work for the conciliation of all parties. What sort of an agreement could one hope for between the energy of the oppressed and the rage of the oppressors? They have dared utter the word *secession*. With it they have threatened both King and People. Heavens! How fortunate it would be for the nation if so desirable a secession could be perpetuated! How easy it would be to do without the privileged! How difficult it will be to induce them to become citizens!

The aristocrats who led the attack did not realize that they were making an enormous blunder by drawing attention to certain questions. Among a people used to servitude, truth can be left to sleep; but if you attract the attention of the People, if you tell it to choose between truth and error, its mind clings to truth as naturally as healthy eyes turn towards the light. And, light, in morals, cannot spread to any extent without, willy-nilly, leading to equity; for, in morals, truths are connected to rights, because the knowledge of rights arouses consciousness of them, and the consciousness of one's rights winds up, deep in the soul, the spring of liberty which is never completely broken among Europeans. One would have to be blind not to see that our nation has happily seized upon some of these fecund principles that point the way to all that is good, just and useful. It is impossible to ignore them or simply contemplate them in sterile indifference. In these new circumstances, the oppressed classes are naturally the most impressed by the need to put things right; they have acquired most

ii The First Edition said "Corporations."

interest in reinstating Justice among men—Justice, that prime virtue, long exiled from this world. It is consequently for the Third Estate to play the leading role in the advance towards national recovery. The Third Estate must, moreover, recognize the danger that unless it improves its status it cannot simply remain as it is. The circumstances do not permit of this faint-hearted calculation. Not to go forwards is to go backwards. Unless you want to proscribe this mass of iniquitous and anti-social privileges, you must decide to recognize and justify them. Yet the blood boils at the mere thought that it is possible to give *legal recognition*, at the close of the eighteenth century, to the abominable fruits of abominable feudalism. There was an epoch, and alas a long one, when the melancholy incapacity of the Third Estate warranted the regrets and the tears of patriots. But if it became its own executioner; if, just when it was able to act, it voluntarily condemned itself to contempt and opprobrium; with what emotions, with what epithets, ought we to brand it? One may weep for the weak; but one must despise the coward. Then cast aside this vision of undiluted woe; it is quite impossible, for it assumes that twenty-five million men have touched the lowest depths of infamy.

While the aristocrats talk of their honor but pursue their self-interest, the Third Estate, i.e. the nation, will develop its virtue, for if corporate interest is egotism, national interest is virtue. It will suffer the nobles to nourish their expiring vanity on the pleasure of abusing the Third Estate with the most insulting words in the vocabulary of feudalism. The nobles will repeat such words as *commoners, peasants* and *villeins*, forgetting that these terms, no matter in what sense one means them, either do not describe the Third Estate as it is today or are common to the three orders; forgetting also that, when these words did make sense, ninety-nine per cent of their own number were unquestionably *commoners, peasants* and *villeins*, and that the others, necessarily, were brigands. In vain do the privileged classes close their eyes to the revolution which time and events have effected: it is real for all that. There was once a time when the Third Estate was in bondage and the nobility was everything. Now the Third Estate is everything and nobility is only a word. But under cover of this word, however, and based solely on the strength of false opinion, a new and intolerable aristocracy has established itself; and the People has every reason not to want any aristocrats.[33]

33 '*No aristocracy*' ought to become a kind of rallying-cry for all the friends of the nation and of good order. The aristocrats will think that they can retort by crying: '*No democracy*'. But we will repeat '*No democracy*' with them and *against* them. These gentlemen do not realize that representatives are not democrats; that since real democracy is impossible amongst

In this situation, what remains to be done by the Third Estate if it wants to take possession of its political rights in a way that will serve the nation? There are two methods of achieving this aim.

By the first method the Third Estate must meet separately; it must not cooperate with either the nobility or the clergy and it must not vote with them either by *orders* or by *heads*. Mark the enormous discrepancy between the assembly of the Third Estate and those of the other two orders. The former represents twenty-five million people and deliberates over the interests of the nation. The other two, even if they join together, derive their powers from only about two hundred thousand individuals and consider nothing but their own privileges. It is alleged that the Third Estate cannot form the *States-General* by itself. So much the better! It will form a National Assembly.[34][jj] Such

---

such a large population, it is foolish to presume it or to appear to fear it; but that false democracy, alas, is all too possible; that it resides in a caste which claims by right of birth (or some such ridiculous qualification), and independently of the mandate of the People, the *powers* that the body of the citizens would exercise in a real democracy. This false democracy, with all the ills which it trails in its wake, exists in the country which is said and is believed to be monarchical, but where a privileged caste has assigned to itself the monopoly of government, power and place. Here is the feudal democracy you have to dread, which relentlessly inculcates false fears in order to maintain its powerful influence, which hides its inability to do good under the name of '*Corps intermédiare*' and its power to do evil under the imposing authority of the aristocrat Montesquieu. It should be obvious to whoever cares to think about it, that a caste of aristocrats, even if it is flattered by the most stupid kind of prejudice, is as opposed to the authority of the Monarch as it is to the interest of the People.

34 There are great advantages in having legislative power exercised by three bodies or chambers rather than by a single one. Yet it is highly unreasonable to compose these three chambers of three *orders* which are hostile to one another. The true middle course, therefore, consists in separating into three equal parts the representatives of the Third Estate. Arranged thus you will find a common authority, a common interest and a common purpose. I address this remark to those who are fond of the idea of *a system of checks and balances between the branches of the legislative power* and who imagine that nothing can be better in this respect than the English constitution. Cannot one welcome the good without adopting the bad? Besides, as we said earlier, the English have only one order, or rather none at all: so that if we composed our legislative checks and balances out of different *orders*, the system would still be (we cannot repeat this too often) infinitely more vicious than that of our neighbors. It is very important that research should take place into the principles on which legislatures should be constituted, bearing in mind that one

---

jj Which is precisely what it did on June 17, 1789. Forced to meet separately from the two privileged orders in the States-General, the Third Estate proceeded (June 10) to verify the

important advice must be justified by showing that it is firmly based on the very essence of sound principle.

I maintain that the deputies of the clergy and of the nobility have nothing in common with national representatives, that no alliance is possible between the three orders in the States-General and that they are not only unable to vote *in common*, but neither by *orders* nor by *heads*. At the end of the third chapter, we promised to provide evidence of the truth of this statement which all well-meaning readers must be quick to publicize.

A maxim of universal law lays down that '*no default is greater than default of power*'. It is public knowledge that the nobility is not deputed by either the clergy or the Third Estate and that the clergy holds no mandate from either the nobles or the commoners. Each order is in fact a separate nation which is no more competent to interfere in the affairs of the other orders than the States-General of Holland or the Council of Venice are to vote in the debates of the English Parliament. An agent can commit only his principals and a representative can speak only for those whom he represents.[35] If the truth of this be doubted then any recourse to first principles and to rationality must be abandoned.

It follows logically from this that it is perfectly pointless to try to determine the ratio or *proportion* in which each order should participate in the making

---

must never derogate from the *common* interest, but, contrariwise, assure it by achieving an appropriate balance between the great forces which are its essential elements. We shall deal with this question elsewhere.

35 We must, nevertheless, beware of asking for meetings of all three orders in each '*bailliage*' for the purpose of electing all deputies in common. This scheme appears to solve our difficulty; but, I think for my part that it is extremely dangerous so long as equality of *political* rights has not been established. The Third Estate must never consent to any step by which it would be compelled to recognize and sanction the *distinction* between the orders and the absurd triumph of the minority over the overwhelming majority. This imprudent behavior would be as harmful to its own and the national interest as it would be contrary to the most elementary rules of sound policy and arithmetic.

---

names and powers of all deputies to the States-General, beginning with the privileged orders. The latter were invited to join in this task but the only persons to do so were a few of the lower clergy. On June 17, the Third Estate and these clerics adopted by 490 votes to 90 the title of *National Assembly*, and from this time no longer passed "resolutions" as heretofore; but "decrees." Also, this assembly took to itself, without permission from the Crown, the right to recast the constitution. This claim was underlined when on July 9, 1789, the assembly changed its name once more, this time to "Constituent Assembly."

of the general will.[kk] This will cannot be *one* as long as you retain three orders and three representations. At the very most, these three assemblies could meet together to pass the same resolution, just as three allied nations can express the same wish. But they will never be *one* nation, *one* representation, *one* common will.

I am aware that these truths, undisputable as they are, tend to stir up difficulties in a state that was not founded on the basis of reason and political fair-dealing. But what do you expect! If the house you live in still stands up, that is because it is shored up. It is kept upright by a ragged forest of crude supports, erected with no more sense of design than was necessary to prop up each bit that looked like falling down. Unless it is reconstructed, you must reconcile yourself to living from day to day (as the saying goes), worrying and fearful for the moment when it will finally crush you in its ruins. The elements of social order are all interconnected. To neglect some is to endanger the others. A disorderly start makes itself felt by its consequences. The succession of events is inevitable. Ah me! If injustice and illogicality yielded the same profit as reason and fair-dealing, what advantage would lie with the latter?

You retort that, if the Third Estate meets separately, not as one of the three so-called *General Estates*, but as the National Assembly, it will be no more competent to vote for the clergy and the nobility than are these two orders to deliberate for the People. First, recollect what we have just said, that the representatives of the Third Estate unquestionably possess the mandate of the twenty-five or twenty-six million people who compose the nation, with the exception of about two hundred thousand nobles and priests. This is quite enough to entitle them to assume the title of National Assembly. They will then find no difficulty in deliberating for the entire nation, minus a trivial two hundred thousand heads.

On this assumption, the clergy could continue to hold assemblies about the "free donation,"[ll] and the nobility could select some means or other of offering

kk Though the general demand of the municipalities was to make the representation of the Third Estate equal to that of the other two orders combined, certain publicists were advocating different proportions. Thus Target (*Les Etats Généraux convoquées par Louis XVI* ...) advocated that the Third Estate should have three-fifths of the total representatives. Rabaut St. Etienne proposed that it should have five-eighths of the total (*A la nation française*). In the text Sieyès condemns all such exercises as useless, since all proceed from a false premise.

ll The Gallican Church, represented by a periodical assembly and possessing its own administrative, judicial and financial system, was subject to none of the ordinary taxes but granted on its own authority a '*don gratuit*' or 'free donation'.

its subsidy to the King; and, to prevent the arrangements of these two orders from imposing too heavy a burden on the Third Estate, the latter would open with a clear and unequivocal announcement that it would pay no tax that was not equally borne by the other two orders. It would only vote the subsidy on these terms; and though voted, it would not be collected from the People if the clergy and the nobility were seen to abstain from paying their shares on any pretext whatsoever.

In spite of appearances, such an arrangement might be as good as any other as a piecemeal method of restoring social unity to the nation. It would at least provide an immediate remedy for the danger that threatens this country. The People was bound to take fright at the sight of two privileged bodies, with perhaps a third part-privileged one, making ready under the name of States-General to decide its lot and destine it to a fate as immutable as it would be wretched. Nothing could be more proper than to dispel the anxieties of twenty-five million people; when one goes so far as to talk of a constitution, one must prove by one's principles and behavior that one knows and respects the first elements of it.

It is an established fact that the deputies of the clergy and the nobility are not the representatives of the nation; therefore, they are incompetent to vote for the nation.

If they are nevertheless allowed to discuss matters of general interest, what will be the outcome?

1) If votes are taken by *order*, it must follow that twenty-five million citizens cannot make any decision for the general interest if this displeases a couple of hundred thousand privileged individuals; or, to put it another way, that the wills of over one hundred people are to be vetoed and nullified by the will of one person alone.
2) If votes are counted by *heads* and divided equally between privileged and non-privileged, it still remains true that the wills of two hundred thousand people can cancel those of twenty-five million, since both have an equal number of representatives. Is it not outrageous to form an assembly in such a way that it can vote in the interest of the minority? Is this not an *anti*-assembly?

In the previous chapter we demonstrated that the *common* will can be discovered only in the opinion of the majority. This lies beyond question. It follows that in France the representatives of the Third Estate are the authentic trustees of the national will. They may speak then, without error, in the name of the whole nation. For, even supposing that the privileged orders always voted unanimously together against the Third Estate, they would still be incapable of outweighing the majority of the Third Estate in votes taken when this order was deliberating. For, each deputy of the Third Estate votes—according to the figure decided upon—for about fifty thousand persons; therefore all we need is a decision that a majority shall be deemed to consist of half the votes of the Third Estate *plus* five. In this way the unanimous vote of two hundred thousand nobles and priests would be covered by these five votes, and would so become irrelevant. Notice that in this supposition I have temporarily ignored the fact that deputies of the first two orders are not the representatives of the nation. Notice also my willing admission that, as members of a genuine national assembly (though disposing of no greater influence than they have a right to), they would steadily oppose the wishes of the majority. Even in such a case, their opinion would be swallowed up in the vote of the minority.

Enough has been said on this point, therefore, to demonstrate the Third Estate's obligation to form a national assembly on its own and to justify in the name of reason and fair-play its claim to deliberate and vote for the whole nation without any exception whatsoever.

I know that such principles will be distasteful even to those members of the Third Estate who are best at defending its interests. This does not matter, provided they agree that I started from correct principles and thereafter proceeded by sound logic alone. Let us add that, if the Third Estate parts company with the first two orders, it cannot be accused of *seceding*; this rash word and the meaning that it implies must be left to those who first used it. For the majority never separates from the whole; this would be a contradiction in terms because it would imply that it separates from itself. Only the minority is in the position of refusing to submit to the will of the majority and, consequently, of seceding.

However, in showing the Third Estate the full extent of its resources, or rather its rights, it is no intention of ours to get it to push them to the limit.

I pointed out earlier that the Third Estate had two methods of obtaining its rightful place in the political order. If the first, which I have just described, seems a little too abrupt; if it is felt that the public must have time to accustom itself to liberty; if it is believed that the most obvious national rights still need, if they are disputed by even the smallest number, some kind of legal pronouncement that, so to speak, establishes them and gives them a final sanction; I am willing to concur. Let us then appeal to the tribunal of the nation which is the only competent judge in any disputes about the constitution. This is the second method open to the Third Estate.

At this point we have to recall all that was said in the previous chapter about the need to *constitute* the body of ordinary representatives as well as on the need to commit this great work to the care of an extraordinary deputation given *ad hoc* special powers.

Nobody can deny that in the coming States-General the Chamber of the Third Estate will be fully competent to convoke the kingdom in *extraordinary representation*. Therefore, it is preeminently the duty of the Third Estate to explain the falsity of France's constitution to the citizenry. It is its duty to expostulate that since the States-General is composed of several orders, it must necessarily be ill-organized and incapable of fulfilling its national tasks; at the same time it is its duty to demonstrate the need to provide an extraordinary deputation with special powers to determine, by clearly defined laws, the constitutional forms of the legislature.

Until then, the order of the Third Estate will suspend, not of course its preparatory proceedings, but the exercise of its actual power; it will take no definitive decisions; it will wait for the nation to pass judgment in the great contention between the three orders. Such a course, I admit, is the most straightforward, the most magnanimous, and, therefore, the best suited to the dignity of the Third Estate.

The Third Estate can therefore view itself in either of two ways. The first is to regard itself simply as *an order*; in that case, it agrees not to shake off completely the prejudices of archaic barbarism; it recognizes two other orders in the state, without however attributing to them more influence than is compatible with the nature of things; and it shows all possible regard for them by consenting to doubt its own rights until the supreme arbiter has made its decision.

From the second point of view, the Third Estate is the *nation*. In this capacity, its representatives constitute the whole National Assembly and are seized of all its powers. As they alone are the trustees of the general will, they do not need to consult those who mandated them about a dispute that does not exist. If they have to ask for a constitution, it is with one accord; they are always ready to submit to the laws that the nation may please to give them, but they do not have to appeal to the nation on any problem arising out of the plurality of orders.[mm] For them, there is only one order, which is the same as saying that there is none; since for the nation there can be only the nation.

The appointment of an *extraordinary* deputation, or at least the granting of special powers, as explained above, to settle the great problem of the constitution ahead of everything else, is therefore the true means of ending the present dissension and avoiding possible disturbances within the nation. Even

mm In the First Edition, the paragraph ended here.

if these disturbances gave no cause for alarm such a step would still be necessary because, disturbance or no disturbance, we have to know where our political rights lie and take possession of them. This will be seen to be more pressing when we realize that political rights are the sole guarantee of our civil rights and our personal freedom. I invite the reader to think this over.

This is the point at which I would end my *mémoire* on the Third Estate if I had wanted to do nothing but canvass courses of action ... However, my other object was to explain certain principles. I therefore take leave to pursue the interests of the Third Estate beyond this point and up to the public discussion which is likely to arise over the true *composition* of a *National Assembly*.

When the extraordinary representatives frame the constitution of the legislative body, will they continue to respect the odious and impolitic distinction between orders?[nn] I do not intend to discuss either their agenda or their authority, only the laws governing the personnel of the deputations. In addition to citizens, are they to include priests and nobles in a capacity other than that of citizens? Above all, are these priests and nobles to be allowed separate and superior rights by reason of this special capacity? These are great issues on which I cannot do less than expound the true principles.[oo]

Our first task is to obtain a clear understanding of the *object* or *aim* of the representative assembly of a nation; this *object* cannot be different from that which the nation itself would propose if it could assemble and confer in any one place.

What is the will of a nation? It is the resultant of the individual wills, just as the nation is the aggregate of the individuals that compose it. It is impossible to imagine a legitimate association whose object would not be the common security, the common liberty and, finally, the common welfare. Of course, each private individual also has his own personal aims; he thinks: "Protected by the common security, I shall quietly pursue my own personal plans, I shall pursue happiness in my own way, sure of coming up against no legal obstacles other than those prescribed by society for the common interest in which I have a share and with which my private interest has concluded such a useful alliance."

But who can possibly imagine the general assembly containing a member so insane as to declare: "You are not meeting here to deliberate on our common affairs, but to attend to the private interests of myself and a small clique I have formed with a few others here"?

---

nn The First Edition went straight on from "the composition of a National Assembly" to "I do not intend to discuss."

oo The First Edition read "... the laws governing the personnel of the deputations."

To say that the associates meet to decide on matters of *common* concern, is to explain the sole motive that could induce individuals to enter into association. It expresses one of those self-evident truths which are so simple that any attempt at proof merely weakens them. The object of the assembly then, is: matters of common concern.[pp]

For our present purposes, it is worth demonstrating how every member of a National Assembly helps, through his individual will, to shape the common will which can move in only one direction: that of the public interest.

First of all, let us examine this political activity or mechanism on the basis of the most advantageous hypothesis: let us assume that the public spirit is so strong that it allows only activity in the common interest to be manifested in the assembly. Prodigies of this sort have been rare in the history of this world and none of them has lasted long. Only an imperfect knowledge of mankind would lead one to associate the fate of society with the efforts of virtue. At a time when public morals are in decay, when everybody seems actuated by self-interest, it is necessary—I repeat it—that, even during such ages, the assembly of a nation should be so constituted as to insulate each personal interest it contains, and ensure that the will of its majority is always consistent with the general good. Such a result is insured if the constitution enjoys support.

Three types of interest can be discerned in a man: 1) the interest in respect of which all citizens[qq] are alike; this demonstrates the exact extent of the common interest: 2) the interest whereby an individual allies himself to a few others; this is corporate interest: finally, 3) the interest whereby everyone stands apart, thinking of himself only; this is personal interest.

The interest whereby a man concurs with all his co-associates is obviously the *objective* of everybody's will and that of the common assembly. Each voter may bring to the assembly his two other interests; let it be so. But the first, i.e. personal interest, is not dangerous since it is insulated. To each man his own. In its diversity lies its own cure.[rr]

Thus the major difficulty springs from the interest by which a citizen allies himself with just a few others. This type of interest leads to conspiracy and collusion; through it anti-social schemes are plotted; through it the most formidable enemies of the People mobilize themselves. History teems with examples of such misfortunes.

pp This last sentence did not appear in the First Edition.

qq The First Edition read: "... the interest of all men in equality."

rr In the First Edition, this paragraph read: "Personal interest must have no influence. And it has none in fact; in its diversity lies its own cure."

It is not therefore surprising that social order inflexibly requires that no citizens must be allowed to organize themselves in *guilds*, and even insists on public officials (necessarily the only persons allowed to form a genuine *corps*) renouncing the right to sit in the legislature as long as they hold office.

In this and in no other way can the common interest be made to dominate private interests.

Only on these terms can we be satisfied of the possibility of founding human associations for the general advantage of all the associates, and, consequently, understand what makes political societies legitimate.

By this route and no other can we find the solution to our problem, and understand how, in a national assembly, private interests are bound to remain insulated, and the will of the majority always conform to the general good.

When we reflect upon these principles, we are driven to realize that we must so plan the constitution of the representative assembly that it cannot possibly develop an *esprit de corps* of its own and so degenerate into an aristocracy. Hence the fundamental maxims, developed at sufficient length elsewhere,[36] that the body of representatives must be renewed by one-third every year; that when deputies complete their term they must be ineligible for re-election until enough time has elapsed to allow the greatest possible number of citizen the opportunity to participate in public affairs. For how could these remain public if they could come to be regarded as the peculiar property of a limited number of families ...?

But when, instead of conforming to these clear and unquestionable first principles, the legislator does the very opposite; when he himself creates corporations within the nation; when he recognizes all those that establish themselves; when he sanctions them with his own authority; and when finally he dares to call upon the largest, most privileged and consequently most deadly ones to share, under the name of *orders*, in the national representation; then this illustrates the evil principle at work, depraving, ruining and disordering all human relationships. To complete and consolidate the social disorder, all that remains is to give these terrifying guilds an effective preponderance over the great body of the nation; and we might accuse the legislator of having done just such a thing in France, were it not more natural to attribute most of the evils that distress this superb kingdom to the blind course of circumstance or to the ignorance and the ferocity of our predecessors.

We know the true *object* of a National Assembly. Such an assembly is not set up to regulate the private affairs of individual citizens. It only regards these

36 See Vues sur les Moyens d'Exécution, etc., sect. III.

in the mass and from the point of view of the *common* interest. Let us draw from this the natural consequence that the right to be *represented* is enjoyed by citizens only by virtue of the qualities they share in common, not those that differentiate them from one another.

Advantages which differentiate citizens from one another lie outside their capacity as citizens. Inequalities of wealth or ability are like inequalities of age, sex, size, color, etc. In no way do they alter the nature of the *equality* of citizenship; the rights inherent in citizenship cannot attach to differences. Of course, these *special* advantages are protected by the law; but the legislator has no right to create advantages of this kind, to give privileges to some citizens and refuse the same privileges to others. The law grants nothing. It protects what exists until what exists begins to be harmful to the common interest. These are the only limits set to personal freedom. I picture the law as being in the centre of a huge globe; all citizens, without exception, stand equidistant from it on the surface and occupy equal positions there; all are equally dependent on the law, all present it with their liberty and their property to be protected; and this is what I call the *common rights* of citizens, the rights in respect of which they are all alike. All these individuals communicate with one another, transact business, enter into contracts together, always under the common guarantee of the law. If, in this general movement, somebody wishes to rule over the person of his neighbor or usurp his neighbor's property, the common law puts down such an outrage; but it does not prevent anyone, according to his natural or acquired capacities, according to more or less favorable accidents, from increasing his property with all that a prosperous fortune or a more productive labor can add to it, nor from being able, without *expanding beyond* his legal position, to rise or to create for himself the type of happiness most suited to his taste and most worthy of envy. The law, by protecting the common rights of every citizen, protects each citizen in all that he can become up to that point when his efforts tend to prove harmful to the rights of others.[37ss]

37 I decline to undertake to answer the windy platitudes, sometimes ludicrous by their absurdity but always so contemptible by their intention, which petty persons continue to recite so ridiculously about the fearsome word '*equality*'. These malign puerilities will prove short-lived and, after their day is over, writers will feel ashamed to have used their pens to refute such feeble nonsense that the very persons who are proud of it today will stand amazed and will scornfully cry: "Does this writer think we are all idiots!"

ss The First Edition said: "... until that point when what he wishes to be tends to harm the common interest."

If I harp too long on the same ideas, it is because my time is too limited to reduce them to their most simple form; besides, in formulating concepts which are over-frequently forgotten, it is inadvisable to be too concise.

Interests whereby citizens are alike, therefore, are the only ones which they can administer in common, the only ones by which and in the name of which they can claim political rights, i.e. an active part in the making of the social law; and the only ones, consequently, which qualify a citizen *to be represented.*

It follows that if one has a right to elect deputies or to be elected oneself, it is not because one is *privileged*, but because one is a *citizen.* I reiterate that everything that pertains to the citizens, both common advantages and special advantages, provided these are not against the law, has a right to protection; but since social unity is attainable only through common characteristics, a right to legislate inheres only in the common capacity. Hence corporate interest, far from weighing with legislators, can only raise their suspicions; it will always be as opposed to the purpose of a body of representatives as it is divorced from its mission.

These principles apply still more rigorously in the case of the *privileged orders.* By privileged, I mean any man who stands outside common rights, either because he claims freedom *in every respect* from subjection to the common laws, or because he claims *exclusive* rights. We have sufficiently proved elsewhere that any privilege is by its nature unjust, hateful and opposed to the social contract. A privileged class is to the nation what special advantages are to the citizen; like them, it is *not entitled to be represented.* This understates the case: a privileged class is to the nation what *harmful* special advantages are to the citizen; the legislator fulfills his duty by suppressing them. This parallel is affected by a last difference: a special advantage, though harmful to other persons, at least benefits the man who possesses it, but a privileged class is a plague for the nation which suffers, it. Thus, to reach an exact comparison, one is obliged to consider the privileged class in a nation as one would some horrible disease eating the living flesh on the body of some unfortunate man. It needs a disguise: disguise it then under all the *honorific* distinctions that you can summon up.

Thus a privileged class is noxious, not simply because of its *esprit de corps*, but because it exists at all. The more successful it has been in obtaining favors, which necessarily run counter to the general liberty, the greater the need to bar it from the National Assembly. A privileged man *could be represented,* but only in his capacity as a citizen; but, in him, this capacity has been destroyed. He stands outside citizenship. He is the enemy of common rights. To give him the right to be represented would be a manifest contradiction in the law. The nation could only submit to it through an act of servitude, and this we refuse to assume.

When we demonstrated that a member of the executive could be neither an elector nor eligible for election, we did not, for that reason, cease to regard him as a genuine citizen; he remains one, like everyone else, by virtue of his individual rights; and the necessary and honorable functions that set him apart, far from destroying his citizenship and far from harming other people's citizenship, exist, on the contrary, to serve the rights of citizenship. If it is none the less necessary to suspend the exercise of his political rights, what can be said of those who, despising common rights, have created such a special position for themselves that they have become divorced from the nation? Or of those men whose very existence amounts to perpetual warfare against the great body of the People? There can be no argument but that such people have renounced the right to qualify as citizens, and they must be excluded from the right to be electors or to be eligible for election even more surely than any foreigner would be, since the foreigner's avowed interest might well not be opposed to yours.

Let us summaries: it is a matter of principle that all those who stand outside the common quality of citizen must have no share in political rights. The legislature of a nation can be entrusted only with care of the general interest. But if instead of some simple distinction which the law hardly notices there exist persons whose privileges make them enemies of the common order, they must be positively excluded. As long as their odious privileges last, they can be neither electors nor eligible.

I realize that such principles are going to seem *extravagant* to most readers. Truth must seem as strange to prejudice as prejudice does to truth. Everything is relative. But grant that my principles are certainties and my consequences properly deduced, and that is all I ask.

"Still," it will be said, "things like these are absolutely *impracticable* in these days." That is why I do not take it upon myself to put them into practice. My own role is that of every patriotic writer: to proclaim the truth. Others will either approximate to it as their ability or circumstances allow, or deviate from it because of their dishonesty; and then we shall have to put up with what we cannot prevent. If everybody's though ran true, the greatest changes could be effected without difficulty as soon as they held out hope of public advantage. What better can I do than help with all my power to spread the truth that paves the way? It may be badly received to begin with; but, little by little, minds accustom themselves to it, a public opinion takes shape, until at the end action is taken on principles that were at first decried as imbecilities. In respect of nearly every class of prejudice, had writers not been willing to be thought *foolish*, the world today would be much the less *wise*.

Everywhere I go, I meet those persons who in their moderation would like to break up the truth or proclaim it only bit by bit. I suspect their understanding when they argue in this way. They underestimate the difference between the obligations imposed on the administrator and those imposed upon the philosopher. The former progresses as best he can; and provided that he does not leave the right road, he deserves nothing but praise. But the philosopher must have opened the road to its very end. Unless he has reached it, he cannot guarantee that it really is the road that leads to this end.

If, on plea of caution, he claims to stop me whenever or however seems good to him, how can I be certain that he is a good guide? Reason has no room for blind trust.

It seems that those who prefer to utter only one word at a time really want and hope thereby to surprise and entrap the enemy. I do not want to enter into a discussion as to whether plain dealing is not always the most artful, even between private individuals; but surely, the arts of concealment and all those subtleties of behavior that we accept as the fruit of human experience are complete idiocy in national affairs, which are conducted overtly by a host of substantial and well-informed interests. Here the true means of making headway is not to conceal from the enemy what he knows just as well as we do, but to convince the majority of the citizens that their cause is just.

It is false to suppose that if the truth is divided and fragmented, the bits and pieces can thereby be fed the more easily into the mind. Not at all! Usually what is required is a powerful jolt. Truth requires every particle of its light to produce those vivid impressions that grave it for ever on the soul and evoke a passionate *interest* for everything recognized as beautiful, useful and true. Mark that in the physical world light does not proceed from the direct ray but from reflections; in the moral world it springs from the relationships between, and the sum total of, the truths pertaining to one's topic. Short of this sum total, nobody feels sufficiently informed. And the man who thinks he has the truth is often obliged to abandon this belief as he ponders the matter more deeply.

How poor an idea must one have of the progress of reason to believe that an entire nation can remain permanently blind to its true interests and that the most beneficial truths, known only to a small handful of people, must never see the light until a clever administrator requires them to forward his efforts! First, this view is false, because it is impossible to act upon. Secondly, it is bad; for who does not know that truth can only slowly penetrate a mass as enormous as a nation? There will always be all too much time wasted. The man who is troubled by the truth must be given time to get used to it; the young who receive it eagerly must be given time to become something; and the old must be given time to be no longer anything. In short, must we wait till harvest time before we sow?

What is more, reason abhors mystery. It can work powerfully only by spreading widely. Only by striking everywhere can it strike true because that is how public opinion arises, and to public opinion must probably be attributed most of the changes that have proved beneficial to peoples. It is the one force alone that can be of use to a free nation.

You retort that minds are not yet prepared to listen to me, that I am going to shock many people? Necessarily so! The most useful truth to proclaim is not the one which people have nearly reached or the one they are on the point of welcoming. No, it is precisely because a truth is going to upset more prejudices and more vested interests, that it proves the more necessary to spread it abroad.

Not enough attention is paid to the fact that the prejudice which needs most careful handling is the one that is mingled with sincerity; that the most dangerous vested interest to arouse is the one to which sincerity lends the full force of the feeling that justice is on its side. We must deprive the enemies of the nation of this borrowed strength. We must enlighten them, and thereby condemn them to the *debilitating* consciousness of their insincerity.

The moderate-minded persons, to whom these reflections are addressed, will cease to fear for the fate of truths which they deem premature as soon as they cease to confuse the measured and cautious conduct of the administrator —who would certainly spoil everything if he did not take opposition into account—with the freedom of the philosopher. Difficulties only serve to stimulate the philosopher. He is not called upon to exercise diplomacy. His duty is to introduce sound social principles in direct proportion to the number of minds that are corroded by feudal barbarism.

When the philosopher is driving a road, he is concerned with *errors*; to make progress he must destroy them without pity. The administrator follows in his footsteps. He meets with the *interests*, more difficult to encounter, I admit. Here a new talent is required, different from the meditations of the theorist, but, make no mistake, even more foreign to the art of certain ministers who think they are administrators simply because they are certainly not philosophers.

On the other side, it is only fair to admit that the speculations of the philosophers do not always deserve to be contemptuously relegated to the category of pure fancies. If opinion can succeed in imposing laws on the legislators themselves, then the men who can influence the shaping of this opinion are not indeed as useless or as idle as so many people who never had any influence on anything are wont to claim.

Talkers who lack ideas—and there are a few of this sort—drone on and on with nonsense about what they call the importance of practice and the uselessness or the perils of theory. Only one point need be made in reply: imagine any sequence of the most wise, useful and excellent *facts* possible.

Well! do you believe that there is no corresponding theoretical sequence of ideas or truths that exactly corresponds to your practical sequence of facts? If you are a rational creature, this sequence of ideas will follow you, or, to be more correct, it will precede you. What is theory, pray, but this corresponding theoretical sequence of truths which you are unable to see until they are put into *practice* but which, nevertheless, someone must have seen unless we are to assume that people had been acting without knowing what they were doing. Those who clutter conversation with the gibberish that I have just mentioned do not operate either on the practical or the theoretical plane, really. Why do they not pursue the wiser and more *practical* course of receiving enlightenment from the one, if their intelligence permits; or, at the least, deriving profit from the other by keeping quiet about what they can, privately, excuse themselves for not comprehending?

Let us now return to our theme.

One final objection is that the privileged, though they may have no right to concern the common will with their privileges, must at least enjoy the political right of representation in their capacity of citizens, like the rest of society does.

However, I have already shown that in becoming privileged they have become the actual enemies of the common interest. Consequently they cannot be charged with providing for it.

To this I would also add that they are at liberty to re-enter the real nation by purging themselves of their unjust privileges, and therefore it is by their own act that they are precluded from exercising political rights. And, finally, their true rights, which are the only ones that can be the concern of the National Assembly, are common both to them *and* the deputies of the assembly. They can therefore reassure themselves with the thought[tt] that the deputies cannot harm these interests without injuring themselves.

It is therefore quite certain that only non-privileged members are competent to be electors to, or deputies in, the National Assembly. The will of the Third Estate will always be good for the generality of citizens; that of the privileged would always be bad for it, unless, neglecting their own interests, they were prepared to vote as simple citizens. But this is the same as voting like the Third Estate itself. Therefore the Third Estate is adequate for everything that can be

tt First Edition: "so they can find consolation in the thought that ..."

hoped for from a National Assembly. It follows that the Third Estate, alone, can procure all the promised benefits of the States-General.

Perhaps you may think that in the last resort the privileged classes can regard themselves as a separate nation and so demand a distinct and independent representation. I myself advanced this as a tentative hypothesis. But it is inadmissible. It is anticipated in the first chapter of this book where I showed that the privileged orders never were and never could be a separate nation. They exist and can do so only at the expense of the real nation. What nation would bear such a burden willingly?

Justice and reason cannot yield to private convenience. Do not ask what is the appropriate place for a privileged class in the social order. It is like deciding on the appropriate place in the body of a sick man for a malignant tumor that torments him and drains his strength. It must be *neutralized*. The health of the body and the free play of its organs must be restored so as to prevent the formation of one of these malignancies which infect and poison the very essence of life itself.[uu]

But the word has gone round: you are not yet fit enough to be healthy! And to this aphorism of aristocratic wisdom, you give credence, like a pack of Orientals solacing themselves with fatalism. Sick as you are then, so remain!

---

uu The First Edition ended at this point.

CHAPTER 2

Reasoned Exposition of the Rights of Man and Citizen[a]

Preliminary Remarks

There are two ways to present important truths to men. The first is to dictate them as if they were so many articles of faith, to burden memory rather than reason. Many persons argue that the law must always take this route. Even if so, a declaration of the rights of the citizen is not an elaboration of the law, but an elaboration of principles. The second way of communicating the truth depends upon recognizing its essential characteristics: reason and evidence. Reason alone allows us to know what we truly know. I believe that in the eighteenth century, this is way the representatives of the French must address their constituents.

There are also two ways of being clear. The first entails editing from one's subject everything that requires attention, everything that transcends the trivial things that everybody already knows. Nothing is simpler and, for a large number of readers, easier than proceeding in this fashion. However, if one desires to treat the subject as its nature requires, to describe what is proper to it and what is not, a different approach is necessary. This approach demands that the reader pay attention.

In any case, the reader will find at the end of this brief work a series of principles written to appeal to the current taste for declarations of rights that are already known, designed, as it were, for the many citizens who are not accustomed to thinking about the relationships of men in society.

a Sieyès's 'Reconnaissance et exposition raisonnée des Droits de l'Homme et du Citoyen' was delivered before the National Assembly on July 21, 1789 and published the subsequent day by the printing press of the national assembly. This translation is based on a later, revised version, in which Sieyès added five articles (see note g). The most comprehensive original French version, with an extended introduction and 42 articles, can be found in *Œuvres de Sieyes*, ed. Marcel Dorigny (Paris, 1989), vol. 2, no. 9.

 | DOI: 10.1163/9789004273993_004

Reasoned Analysis of the Rights of Man and Citizen

The representatives of the French nation, united in the National Assembly, recognize that their mandates impose upon them the special obligation of reforming the constitution of the state.

They will, consequently, act as a constituting power. And yet, since the existing Assembly does not precisely meet all the requirements for the exercise of such a power, they declare that while the constitution that they are going to give the nation is provisionally obligatory, it will only become definitive after a new constituent power, convened specifically for this purpose, will provide it with the sanction necessitated by a rigorous application of principles.

The representatives of the French nation, acting in the capacity of *constituent power*, believe that the purpose of every society and thus of every political constitution is to make manifest, broaden and protect the rights of man and citizen.

Therefore, it is their judgment that they must annunciate these rights, that a reasoned presentation of them in the form of a preamble must precede the constitution, that all political constitutions, without exception, must be preceded by the goals or objectives that all must strive to attain.[b]

Consequently, the representatives of the French nation solemnly and formally recognize and consecrate the following declaration of the rights of man and citizen. By his nature, man is subject to needs; but, by his nature, he also possesses the means to satisfy them.

The Needs of Man and the Means of Their Satisfaction[c]

Throughout his life, he seeks well-being. To this end, nature has provided him with intelligence, a will, and strength: intelligence that he might know, a will that he might choose and strength to execute the decision of his will.

Thus well-being is man's goal: his mental and physical faculties are his personal means to this goal, and with them he will be able to claim or procure for himself all the objects and means external to himself that he requires.

How He thereby Controls Nature

Placed in the middle of nature, man harvests her gifts. He selects them, causes them to multiply, improves them through his work. At the same time, he learns

b This section is reproduced almost verbatim in the preamble of the Declaration of the Rights of Man and Citizen.

c This sentence and the headlines that follow—omitted in Goldstein's version—were originally printed as marginalia.

to anticipate and avoid what can bring him harm; he protects himself, as it were, from nature with the forces he has received from her. Indeed, he dares to enter into combat with her and, what with the unceasing development of his abilities, his power, whose development knows no limits, is seen increasingly bending all the forces of nature to his needs.

How He Sets them against His Own Kind

Placed in the midst of his fellows, man is affected by a multitude of new relationships. He necessarily views other individuals either as means or obstacles. Nothing then is more important for him than his relations with his fellows.

If men saw in one another only reciprocal means of gaining happiness they would live peacefully upon the earth and march together in security toward their common goal.

However, if they look upon one another as obstacles, the situation is quite different; soon they are let with nothing but the choice between flight or unending struggle, and the human species shows itself to have been an enormous mistake on the part of nature.

Two Kinds of Interpersonal Relations

Thus there are two kinds of human relationships: those born out of a state of war that arise from force alone, and those that arise freely out of mutual utility.

Unlawful Relations

The relationships whose origin can be traced entirely to force are evil and illegitimate. Two men, both being equally men, possess, to an equal degree, all the rights inherent in the nature of man.

Equality of Rights

Thus every man is proprietor of his person, or no one is. Every man has the right to utilize his capacities, or no one does. Individual means have been tied by nature to individual needs. Consequently, he who is confronted with needs must be able to use his capacities freely to meet them. This is not only a right but a duty.

Inequality of Means

It is true that a great inequality of means exists among men. Nature creates the strong and the weak. She gives intelligence to some and refuses it to others. It follows that they will be unequal in energy and output, in what they consume or enjoy, but it in no way follows that any inequality of rights exists among them.

Since all men possess an equal right that is derived from the same source, it follows that he who would infringe upon the rights of another transcends the limits of his own right, that the right of each man must be respected by the right of every other man, that this right and this duty are unable not to be reciprocal.

Thus, the right of the weak over the strong is identical to that of the strong over the weak. When the strong succeeds in oppressing the weak, he produces an effect without producing an obligation. Far from imposing a new duty on the weak, he revives in him the natural and eternal duty of resisting oppression.

Thus it is an eternal truth that cannot be too often repeated: the act by which the strong subjugates the weak can never become a right; on the other hand, the act by which the weak liberates himself from the domination of the strong is always a right, always an imperious obligation that he owes to himself. Consequently, only the relationships that can legitimately bind men to one another merit attention, that is, only those relationships that result from a legitimate commitment on their part.

Lawful Relations

Any such commitment is a product of the free will of those responsible. Thus, unless it be based on a free, voluntary and reciprocal contract on the part of the co-associates, there is no legitimate association.

Will as the Principle of All Duties

Since every man is so constituted as to will his own good, he may enter into contract with his fellows, and he will do this if he judges that it is to his own advantage. It has been noted above that men can do much to further the well-being of one another.

Civil Society Follows from Natural Law

Thus a society established on the basis of reciprocal utility truly follows from the natural means given to man to enable him to attain his goal. Hence this union is a gain and not a sacrifice, and society should be regarded as a successor, as a complementary development to the natural order. Even if man were not unconsciously led to society in a very real and powerful way by all his natural faculties, his reason alone would have guided him to this end.

The Purpose of Social Association

The reason for uniting in society is to procure well-being. We have stated that man constantly seeks this goal; when he joined with his fellows, he certainly did not intend to give it up. Thus, the end of society is not the degradation of men, but rather their perfection, their ennoblement.

Thus society neither weakens nor reduces the individual talents that each person brings into the association to use for his own well-being. On the contrary, it increases them, multiplies them by a more extensive development of his intellectual and physical powers. It increases them still further by the invaluable addition of public works and assistance such that a tax subsequently paid to the state by a citizen is only a kind of reimbursement that represents but an infinitesimal fraction of the profit and benefits he has gained from society.

Consequently, society does not establish an unjust inequality of right alongside the natural inequality of means; instead, it protects the equality of rights against the natural, but harmful, influence of unequal means. Law then is not made to weaken the weak and strengthen the strong; on the contrary, its purpose is to protect the weak from the assaults of the strong. Since all citizens find protection beneath its beneficent shield, it guarantees each of them the plentitude of his rights.

Civil Society Increases Liberty

It follows that man does not sacrifice pat of his liberty on entering society. Even when independent of its restraints, no one possessed the right to harm another. This principle is universally valid: liberty does not include the right to harm.

Far from reducing individual liberty, society extends and assures its deployment. It removes a great number of obstacles and dangers to which liberty was too exposed when defended only by individual strength, and guarantees it by the all-powerful protection of the entire association.

Hence, since both the physical and intellectual capacities of man are augmented in society, since, at the same time, he has freed himself from the worries that once accompanied their exercise, it is true to say that liberty is more complete in society than it could ever have been in what is called the state of nature. Liberty is exercised on what is one's own and on things held in common.

Kinds of Property

Property of one's person is the most basic of rights. From this fundamental right is derived the property of act and the property of work, for work is nothing else but the useful exercise of one's faculties and, as such, obviously proceeds from property in oneself and one's actions.

Similarly, property in external objects, or real property is only a consequence, an extension of personal property. The air we breathe, the water we drink, the fruit we eat are all transformed into our substance as a result of the voluntary or involuntary work of our bodies.

Through similar operations, although more dependent on the will, I appropriate an object that I need that does not belong to anyone else by means of my work which modifies it and prepares it for my use. My work was my own; it still is. The object in which I invested it was as much mine as it was everyone's. As a matter of fact, it belonged more to me than to the others since I had over it the right of first occupant. These conditions are enough for me to make this object my exclusive property.

Then, by the force of a general convention, society adds a kind of legal sanction to it; and this last act must be presumed in order to provide the word property with all the richness that we are accustomed to giving it in our civilized world.

Landed properties are the most important kind of real property. As they now stand, they related less to personal, than to social need. Their theory is different, and this is not the place to develop it.

The Extent of Liberty

He is free who has the assurance of not being disturbed in the exercise of his personal property and the use of his real property. Thus, every citizen has the right to come and go as he wishes; to think, speak, write, print and publish; to work, produce, save, transport, exchange and consume, etc.

Its Limits

The limits on individual liberty begin only where it stats to infringe upon the liberty of another. The identification and demarcation of these limits falls into the province of the law. Outside the law, everything for everyone is free, since the reason for uniting in society is not only to further the liberty of one or several individuals, but the liberty of all. A society in which one man would be more or less free than another would assuredly be dreadfully organized, no longer free and in need of immediate reconstitution.

The Relation between Rights and Duties

On first view, it seems that he who enters into a contract loses some of his liberty. However, it would be more exact to say that at the moment he makes a contract, far from having his liberty restricted, he exercises it as he sees fit, for every contract is an exchange where each party prefers what he receives to what he gives.

Undoubtedly, he must fulfill the obligations of the agreement as long as it is in effect; what he has engaged is no longer his own. Moreover, as we have observed, liberty never extends to the point of harming another. In shot, although the limits within which one exercised one's liberty have been modified, the liberty itself remains no less than it was if the new state of affairs is simply the result of one's own choice.

Guarantee of Liberty

In vain would one declare that liberty is the unalienable right of every citizen; in vain would the law impose penalties on those who violate it, if there did not exist a force capable of protecting one's rights and executing the law.

Liberty can only be preserved if the force whose task it is to defend it is more powerful than the forces that could be used to attack it. No right is completely guaranteed unless the force that protects it is adequate to the task at hand.

In a large society, individual liberty has three redoubtable enemies.

Of these, the least dangerous are ill-intentioned citizens. No more than ordinary measures are required for them to be kept in check. If, in this respect, justice has not always been done, the fault is due not to the absence of sufficient force, but to bad laws and a poorly constituted judiciary. Neither problem is beyond remedy.

Individual liberty has much more to fear from the officials charged with the deployment of the public's force.[d] Single agents, entire departments, the government as a whole may cease to respect the rights of the citizenry.

Long experience demonstrates that nations are not aware enough of this kind of danger.

Is there any sight worse than that of an official turning against his fellow citizens the weapons or the power that he had received so that they might be protected; who would commit a crime against himself and against his country by daring to change the means that had been given to him for the defense of all into instruments of oppression!

A good constitution is the only defense that nations and citizens have to protect them against calamities of this kind.

Finally, liberty can be attacked by a foreign enemy. Hence the need for an army. It is clear that this army has nothing to do with domestic affairs, that it was created only for dealing abroad. Indeed, were it possible for a people to live in isolation, or were it to become impossible for other nations to attack them, they would obviously have no need for an army.

Domestic peace and tranquility truly necessitate the existence of a coercive force, but its nature is not that of the military. If law and order within a country, as well as the force required to maintain both, can be established without any

d On this in more detail, see text 6 ('Second Thermidorian Intervention').

army, where one does exist, it is extremely important that the domestic force be so independent from it that there is absolutely no relationship between them.

Hence it is manifest that soldiers must never be deployed against citizens, that the force required to maintain order within a state must be organized in such a way that under no possible circumstance would it be necessary to have recourse to the military, unless it is against a foreign enemy.

Further Advantages of the Civil Society

The advantages that come from society are not limited to the effective and complete protection of individual liberty. Over and above this, the citizens have a right to all the benefits that result from the association.

These benefits will increase as society profits from the enlightenment that will come to the public with time, experience and reflection. The most essential and most important of all the arts is that of producing from society every possible advantage for society. An association organized for the greatest good of all will be the masterpiece of intellect and virtue.

No one is unaware of the enormous benefits that the members of society reap from public works and properties, etc.

Everyone knows that those citizens who, because of unfortunate circumstances, are incapable of providing for their own needs, may legitimately claim assistance from their fellow citizens, etc.

No one denies that there is nothing better for the intellectual and physical development of humankind than a good system of public education and instruction, etc. It is well known that the relations to foreign countries are determined by interests which should be strictly controlled by society.[e]

But it is not in the declaration of rights that a list of everything that a wise constitution can procure for its citizens needs be found. It is enough to say that the citizens as a whole have a right to everything the state can do for them.

Public Means of Society

The ends of society thus noted, it is clear that the public means to these ends must be proportional to them, that they must increase with an increase in national wealth and prosperity.

e This sentence is omitted in Goldstein's version.

Public Power Contains all Powers

All these means which include persons and things are to be called the public establishment in order to better emphasize its origin and purpose. The public establishment is a body politic that, like the body of man, has needs and means, and thus must be organized in essentially the same way. It must be given the faculty of willing and the faculty of acting.

The legislative power represents the former of these two faculties, the executive power the latter.

The government is often confused with the action or exercise of both power, but this word, more precisely defined, refers specifically to the executive power or its action. Nothing is more common than hearing that one must govern according to the law—which proves that the power of making the law is distinct from the government as such.

The government is subdivided into several branches. The analysis of this subdivision belongs to the constitution.

What a Constitution Is

The constitution itself embraces, at one and the same time, the formation and internal organization of the different public powers, their necessary interaction and mutual independence and, finally, the barriers with which it is wise to surround them so that, while always remaining productive, they can never become dangerous.

Such is the real sense of the word constitution. It refers to all the public powers and to the separation between them. It is not the nation that is constituted, but its political establishment. The nation is the sum total of all the associates governed by, and obedient to, the law that is the work of their will; all are equal in rights, free to communicate among themselves and enter into their respective commitments. On the other hand, those who govern, by this fact alone, form a political body created by society. But every body needs to be organized, delineated etc., or, in other words, needs to be constituted.

Thus, to repeat, the constitution of a people is, and can only be, the constitution of its government and of the power entrusted with giving laws as much to the people as to the government.

Constituent Power und Constituted Powers

Above all, a constitution presupposes a constituent power. The powers that are included in the public establishment are all subject to laws, rules or procedures that they do not have the right to change. Since the constituted powers were unable to constitute themselves, they are unable to change their own constitution. Similarly, they can do nothing about the constitutions of the other powers. The constituent power is supreme in this respect. It is not limited in advance to any specific constitution. The nation here exercises the greatest and most important of its powers; it must be free from every constraint, every procedural formality but that which it decides to adopt.

However, it is not necessary for the members of society to exercise the constituent power individually; they can give their confidence to representatives who will assemble only for this purpose without being able to exercise any of the powers they constitute.[f] But it is for the first chapter of the constitution to set forth the means for forming and reforming all its pats.

The Difference between Civil and Political Rights

To this point, we have only considered the natural and civil rights of citizens. It remains for us to treat their political rights.

The difference between these two kinds of rights lies in the fact that natural and civil rights are those for the defense and development of which society was formed; and political rights are those by which society is formed. For linguistic clarity, it is better to call the former passive rights and the latter active ones.

Active and Passive Citizenship

Every inhabitant of a country must enjoy the rights of a passive citizen: each man has a right to the protection of his person, his property, his liberty, etc., but all men do not have a right to play an active role in setting up the various public powers; they are not all active citizens. Women, at least at present, children, foreigners, those who contribute nothing to support the public establishment must not have an active influence on the direction of the state. All can benefit from the advantages of society, but only those who contribute to the public establishment are the real stockholders in the great business of society. They alone are genuinely active citizens, the authentic members of the association.

Political Equality

The equality of political rights is a fundamental principle and, like that of civil rights, is inviolable. Any inequality of political rights would soon result in privileges, that is, in either dispensation from a common obligation or in an

f According to Sieyès, the functions of constitutionmaking and lawmaking (legislation) should be strictly distinguished from one another, both personally and institutionally. See Chapter V of text 1 ('What is the Third Estate?').

exclusive right to a common good. Hence every privilege is unjust, odious and in opposition to the purpose for which society was formed. Since the law serves everyone, since the law is the work of a common will, it must concern itself only with the common interest.

The Unity of the Common Good

One society can only have one general interest. No order would be possible if several opposing interests were supposed to be realized. The existence of society necessarily entails the agreement of its members on means and ends.

Association as the Result of a United Will

A political association is the result of the unanimous will of the associates.

The Establishment of Public Powers as the Result of the Majority's Will

Its public establishment is the result of the will of a majority of its members, for it is apparent that since unanimity is difficult to obtain even from a small number of men, it becomes utterly impossible in a society made up of several million individuals. Society has its ends; consequently, it is necessary that the means available for arriving at these ends be adopted. It is necessary then to be satisfied with a decision of a majority.

However, it is worthwhile pointing out that even here there is a kind of mediated unanimity, for those who unanimously wanted to unite so that they might enjoy all the advantages of society unanimously will all the means necessary for obtaining these advantages. Only the choice of which means depends on the majority, and all those whose will is to be expressed agree in advance always to abide by its decisions. Hence there exist two areas where the rights of unanimity are rightfully replaced by the majority. Thus the will of the majority forms the general will.

All Empowerment and Authorization Proceeds from the People

Every public power, without exception, is an emanation of the general will; all come from the people, that is to say, from the nation. These two terms must be synonymous.

An Official Duty Is not a Possession, but a Responsibility

A public official, whatever his office, does not exercise a power that belongs to him. The power is everyone's; he is the person to whom it has been confided. The power could not be alienated for the will is inalienable, persons are inalienable, the right to think, will and act for oneself is inalienable. We do no more than entrust the exercise of it to persons in whom we have confidence—and the essential attribute of this confidence is that it is free.

The Exercise of an Office Is a Duty, not a Privilege

Consequently, to believe that a public position can ever become the property of a person is a grave error. To believe that the exercise of public authority is a right is a grave error. It is a duty. The only distinction between a nation's officials and the rest of its citizens is that the former have more duties. In stating this truth we have no intention of belittling the character of public servants. The origin of, and the justification for, the respect that we show to men in authority stems precisely from our knowledge that they are discharging heavy responsibilities and thus are serving others. However, neither respect nor esteem arise when we are confronted by men who are distinguished only by their rights, that is, who force us to become aware that their interest is personal, not general.

This is the end of the exposition of the rights of man and citizen that we wished to offer to the French nation and that we formulated for ourself to help guide us during the work on the constitution that lies ahead. However so that these rights be better known and more easily remembered by everyone to whom they pertain, the essence of our analysis is presented below in simplified form for the benefit of every class of citizen.

First Article

Every society is the result of an agreement into which all of its members freely enter.

Article II

The goal of a political society can only be the greatest good for everyone.

Article III

Every man is proprietor of his person. This property is inalienable.

Article IV

Every man is free to exercise his personal faculties as he sees fit, without, however, infringing upon the rights of another.

Article V

Thus no one need justify his thoughts or his feelings; every man has the right to speak or be silent: he may publish his thoughts or feelings as he sees fit. Each person is free to write, print or have printed what he wishes, unless this infringes upon the rights of another. Every writer may sell his works, or have them marketed; he may freely use the mail or any other means available for their distribution without every having to fear a breach of trust. Letters in particular arc to be considered sacred by every person who comes between the writer and the person to whom he has written.

Article VI

Every citizen is free to determine for himself how his labor, his skills and his capital will be used. No kind of work may be forbidden him. He may make what he wishes as he wishes; he may warehouse or transport every variety of merchandise which he may sell on either the retail or wholesale market. No individual, no group has the right to restrict these activities, still less to prohibit them. The law alone can establish the limits of this liberty, of any liberty.

Article VII

Every man may come or go, enter or leave, as and when he chooses.

He may indeed leave and re-enter the kingdom whenever and as he chooses.

Article VIII

Every man may use his property and his assets as he thinks appropriate.

Article IX

The liberty, property and security of citizens depend upon society's providing them with a guarantee capable of withstanding any attack.

Article X

Thus, the law must have at its disposal a force capable of repressing those individual citizens who would attack the rights of others.

Article XI

Thus, all persons who are responsible for the execution of the law, all persons who exercise any other facet of authority or public power, must be rendered incapable of interfering with the liberty of the citizenry.

Article XII

Thus, the legal force responsible for domestic law and order must establish and secure one and the other to such a degree that there never arises any need to seek the dangerous assistance of the military.

Article XIII

The military was only created for, only exists for, and only acts in, the domain of foreign affairs. Thus soldiers must never be deployed against citizens. They may only be used against a foreign enemy.

Article XIV

All citizens are equally subject to the law. No citizen is obliged to obey any authority but that of the law.

Article XV

The law is concerned only with the common interest. Therefore it may grant no privilege to anyone; should privileges exist, whatever their origin, they must be abolished without delay.

Article XVI

If men are not equal in means, that is, in wealth, intellect or strength etc., it does not follow that their rights are not equal. Before the law, each man is worth as much as another; the law protects them all without distinction.

Article XVII

No man is more free than another. None has a greater right to his property than another has to his. All must be equally protected, equally secure.

Article XVIII

Since all citizens are equally bound by the law, it must impose equal penalties on the guilty.

Article XIX

Any citizen who is summoned or apprehended in the name of the law must obey immediately. Resistance is criminal.

Article XX

No one is to be called to justice, apprehended or imprisoned except in those cases addressed by the law and according to the procedures that it has established.

Article XXI

Any arbitrary or illegal order is null and void. The person or persons who sought it or signed it are guilty. Those who transmitted it, executed it or had it executed are guilty. All must be punished.

Article XXII

Citizens victimized by such orders have the right to repel violence with violence.

Article XXIII

Every citizen has the right to see justice done without any delay, and this as much for his person as his property.

Article XXIV

Every citizen has a right to the common benefits that result from living in society.

Article XXV

Every citizen who is powerless to provide for his needs has a right to assistance from his fellow citizens.

Article XXVI

The law can only be the expression of the general will. For a large population, it must be the work of a body of representatives chosen for a short period of time either directly or indirectly by all the citizens who are capable and have an interest in the commonweal. These two qualities must be clearly and positively determined by the constitution.

Article XXVII

No one is obliged to pay any tax except those that have been freely established by the representatives of the nation.

Article XXVIII

All public authority comes from the people; its only purpose is the interest of the people.

Article XXIX

The constitution of public authorities must be such that while assuring that they are always operative and always able to meet their objective, they can never deviate from it to the detriment of the interest of society.

Article XXX

A public office can never become the property of those who occupy it; office is not a right, but a duty.

Article XXXI[g]

Public office is a function of public need. The number of offices must be rigorously limited to what is necessary. It is especially absurd that there exist functionless offices in a state.

Article XXXII

No citizen may be excluded from any office because of what an idiot prejudice has labeled inadequate descent. In every kind of public service, the most capable persons are to receive preference.

Article XXXIII

Since, at present, all service should receive remuneration and does receive remuneration, it follows that only the need for compensation or the need for charity justifies applying for pensions drawn on the public treasury.

Article XXXIV

Monetary compensation supposes distinguished or lengthy service to the country by men without wealth who can no longer be productively employed.

Article XXXV

As for public charity, it is clear that it must only be distributed to those persons who are truly unable to provide for their needs; and this word is to be understood as referring to real needs, not the needs of vanity, for tax payers never intended to deprive themselves—sometimes of a part of what they truly require—so that a pensioner of the state live in luxury. Moreover, it is necessary that charitable assistance cease as soon as the disabilities that justified it come to an end.

Article XXXVI

Public officials in every branch of government will be held responsible for their conduct and breaches of trust. Only the king is exempt from this law. His person is always sacred and inviolable.[h]

g [Note by M.A. Goldstein] This article and the four that follow were not included in the first edition of Sieyès's Declaration, but were added later in 1789.

h [Note by M.A. Goldstein] The two sentences establishing the inviolability of the king are not included in all versions of the Declaration.

Article XXXVII

A people always has the right to review and reform its constitution. Indeed, whatever the need, it is worthwhile to establish fixed dates when this revision will occur.

CHAPTER 3

Controversy between Mr. Paine and M. Emmanuel Sieyès[a]

From Mr. Thomas Paine to M. Emmanuel Sieyès

Paris, 8 July 1791

Sir,

During my preparations for a journey to England, I read in the *Moniteur* of Wednesday last a letter, in which you give to all true Republicans a challenge upon the subject of Government, and offer yourself for the defence of what is called "Monarchic Opinion" against the "Republican System."[b]

I accept your challenge with pleasure, and have such confidence in the superiority of the Republican System over that nullity of a System called Monarchy, that I engage myself not to exceed the extent of fifty pages in my part of the controversy, though I leave to you the liberty of taking whatever latitude you please.

My respect for your moral and literary character will be a sufficient assurance to you for my candour in our discussion; but, though I propose to conduct myself in it with as much seriousness as good faith, I ought to mention, that I do not preclude myself from the liberty of ridiculing, as they deserve, any monarchical absurdities which may occasionally present themselves to my mind.

I do not mean by Republicanism that which bears the name in Holland, or in some Italian States. I consider it simply as a Government by Representation; a Government founded upon the principles of the 'Declaration of Rights;' principles with which many parts of the French Constitution are at variance. The French and the American Declarations of Rights are but one and the same

a With the exception of Sieyès's name (originally spelled "Syeyes"), we adhere to the spelling of the original version of this text, which has been published in the *European Magazine and London Review* (1791).

b This text was not translated and reprinted in the *The European Magazine and London Review*. A French version of Sieyès's text from 6 July 'Note de Sieyès dans le Moniteur du 6 juillet 1791' can be found in *Œuvres de Sieyes*, ed. Marcel Dorigny (Paris, 1989), vol. 2, No. 29 (first of two texts).

 | DOI: 10.1163/9789004273993_005

thing in principles, and almost in expressions; and this is the republicanism which I undertake to defend against what is called Monarchy and Aristocracy.

I observe with pleasure, that we are already agreed upon one point—*the extreme danger of a Civil List of thirty millions.*[c] I cannot conceive the reason why one part of the Government should be supported with such extravagant profusion, while the other receives scarcely sufficient for its plainest wants.

This disproportion, at once dangerous and dishonourable, furnishes to one the means of corruption, and places the other in a situation to be corrupted. In America, we make but little difference, in this respect, between the legislative and the executive parts of Government; but the first is much better treated than in France.

But, however I may consider the subject, of which you, Sir, have proposed the discussion, I am anxious that you should have no doubt of my entire respect for yourself. I should also add, that I am not the personal enemy of Kings; on the contrary, no person can be more sincere than myself, in wishing to see them in the happy and honourable state of plain individuals. But I am the declared, open, and intrepid enemy of that which is called Monarchy, and I am so on account of principles which nothing can alter or corrupt;—my predilection for humanity, my anxiety for the dignity and honour of the human species, my disgust at seeing men directed by infants and governed by brutes, and the horror inspired by all the evils which Monarchy has scattered over the earth; and by the misery, the exactions, the wars and the massacres with which it has wounded humanity.

In short, it is against the *whole hell of Monarchy* that I have declared war.

(Signed) Thomas Paine

The Explanatory Note of M. Sieyès, in Answer to the Letter of Mr. Paine, and to Several Other Provocations of the Same Sort

Mr. Thomas Paine is one of those men who have contributed the most to establish the liberty of America. His ardent love of humanity and his hatred of every sort of tyranny, have induced him to take up in England the defence

c In the French constitutional monarchy, the *liste civile* defined the budget that was at the disposal of the king in his capacity as the head of parliament. The National Assembly set the *liste civile* at 25 million Livres. Paine presumably refers to the plans of the *amis de la liste civile* to raise this budget to 30 million Livres.

of the French Revolution, against the *amphigorical* declamation of Mr. Burke.[d] His work has been translated into our language, under the title of *Des Droits de l'Homme*, and is universally known.[e]

What French Patriot is there, who has not already, from the bottom of his heart, thanked this foreigner for having strengthened our cause by all the powers of his reason and his reputation? It is with pleasure that I observe an opportunity of offering him the tribute of my gratitude and my profound esteem for the truly philosophical application of talents so distinguished as his own.

Mr. Paine supposed that I have given him a challenge, and he accepts it. I have not given any challenge; but I shall he very glad to afford to so able an author an opportunity of giving the world some further truths.

Mr. Paine declares himself to be the open enemy of Monarchical Government. I merely say, that a Republican form of Government appears to me to be insufficient for liberty. After an avowal so positive on both sides, nothing seems to remain for us but to produce our proofs, the public being entirely ready to decide between us. But unfortunately abstract questions, those especially that relate to a science, the very language of which is scarcely yet fixed, require to be prepared for investigation by a sort of preliminary convention. Before we begin a contest, to be carried on at least under the standard of philosophy, it is necessary that we should be understood. Mr. Paine is so conscious of this necessity, that he begins by giving definitions. "I do not understand," says he, "by Republicanism that which bears the name in Holland, and some States of Italy."

When he wrote thus, this author was, no doubt, aware that I, on my part, do not undertake to defend either the Ottoman or the —Monarchy. In order to be reasonable in this discussion, and certainly we both desire to be so, we ought to begin by rejecting all examples. In point of social order, Mr. Paine cannot be[1] less pleased than I am with the models which history offers us. The question between us then depends upon simple theory. Mr. Paine defends his Republic, such as he understands it; I defend Monarchy, such as I have conceived it.

"In short," says Mr. Paine, "it is against the whole Hell of Monarchy that I have declared war." I intreat him to believe, that, in this undertaking, I would be his second, and not his adversary. I do not adopt the interest of the whole

---

1 [Note by the European Magazine]: "Here we have presumed, upon the sense of the context, to make an alternation in the original, which appears to have been misprinted."

---

d Sieyès polemicizes against Burke's *Reflections on the Revolution in France* (1789).

e Thomas Paine, 'Rights of Man' (1791/92), in *Political Writings*, ed. Bruce Kuklick (Cambridge, 1989), pp. 159–173.

Hell of Republics. The one is as real as the other, and avails just as much. It is impossible that either Mr. Paine or myself should ever take the part of any sort of Hell.

"By Republicanism," says Mr. Paine, "I understand merely a Government by Representation." I have had some difficulty in conceiving, why it should be endeavoured to confound two notions so distinct as those of a representative system and republicanism; and I hope for some attention to my answer.

It is only since the event of the 21st of June last, that this Republican Party has been perceived. What is their object? Can they be ignorant, that the plan of representation which the National Assembly has presented to France, though imperfect in some of its parts, is, notwithstanding, the purest and the best which has hitherto appeared in the world? What then is the object of those who desire a Republic, when they define it to be simply a Government by Representation?—What! does this Party, so lately formed, already endeavour to array itself with the honour of demanding, representative administration against the National Assembly itself? Will they seriously undertake to persuade men, that in all this there are but two opinions, that of the Republicans, who wish for a representation, and that of the National Assembly, who do not? It is impossible to impute to M. M. the new Republicans such a chimera; or, that they should hope for such a blind docility on the part of the public and posterity.

When I speak of political representation, I go further than Mr. Paine. I maintain that every social constitution of which representation is not the essence, is a false constitution. Whether a Monarchy or not, every association, the members of which do not all at once vacate their common administration, has but to chuse between representatives and masters, between despotism and a legitimate Government. There may be varieties in the manner of classing the representatives, and in their internal regulations; and none of the different forms may be able to attribute to itself exclusively the true, essential, and distinctive character of all good government. We are not to imitate those who say—Observe, I understand by a Republic, a good Government; and by Monarchy, a bad one: take that ground, and defend yourself. It is not to a man of abilities, like Mr. Paine, that it is necessary to give a caution against such language.

Whatever dispute may arise upon the different sorts of representations; however it may be enquired, for instance, whether it is wise to employ exactly the same method in the executive and the legislative order; or whatever other questions of this sort may be produced; it does not at all follow, that upon these gradations and shades depends the difference between Republicans and Monarchicans.

All these debates are, or will be, common to partisans of both systems, and they will be equally so in either hypothesis of a good or a bad representation.

In fact, whether our established proxies shall be well or ill chosen, or well or ill established, it will remain to be known what shall be their correlation, and how you will dispose them amongst themselves, for the best distribution and greatest facility of public operation.

In one word, it will still remain to be known, whether you will have a Republic or a Monarchy; because, of themselves, the republican and monarchic forms will apply either to a good or bad constitution, to a good or bad government. It is not, therefore, the character of a true representation, that it must bear the distinguishing attributes which mark republicans.[f]

Here, in my opinion, are the two principal points, by which the difference of the two systems may be recognized.

Make all political action, that which you please, to call the Executive Power, center in a Council of Execution appointed by the people or by the National Assembly, and you have formed a Republic.

Place, on the contrary, at the head of the departments which you call ministerial, and which ought to be better divided, responsible chiefs, independent of one another, but depending, as to their ministerial existence, upon an individual of superior rank, in whom is represented the stable unity of Government, or, what is the same, of National Monarchy; let this individual be authorized to chuse and dismiss, in the name of the people, these first executive chiefs, and to exercise some other functions useful to the public interest, but his irresponsibility for which cannot be dangerous, and you have formed a Monarchy.

It appears that the question depends entirely upon the manner of *crowning* the Government. What the Monarchists would do by individual unity, the Republicans would do by a collective body. I do not accuse the last of failing to perceive the necessity of unity in action, and I do not deny that it may be possible to establish this unity in a Senate, or superior Council of Execution. But I believe, that it would be ill-constituted under a multitude of Reports of Committees; and that, in order to preserve all the advantages of which the unity of action is capable, it should not be separated from individual unity.

Thus, in our system, the Government is composed of a first Monarch, the Elector and irresponsible, in whose name act six Monarchs, named by him and responsible. After these are the Directories of the Departments.

---

f In Sieyès, two meanings of this concept have to be distinguished: in a narrow sense, *système représentatif* denotes a system of political representation based on elections; in a broader sense it means the organization of society by means oft he division of labor. On the latter sense, see text 4 ('Of the Gains of Liberty') in this compilation.

In the other, a Senate or Council, named by the Departments or by the Legislative Assembly, would be in the first degree of execution; then the Administration of the Departments.

Those who aim at investing an image with abstract notions, may figure a monarchical Government as ending in a point, and a republican Government in a platform. But the advantages which we attribute to one form rather than the other, are so important, that they cannot be conveyed by a simple image. I do not give the exposition of them; this is not the place; but I am not unwilling to repeat, that in the two points here mentioned consist the distinctive characters of the two systems; that is to say, the difference which there is between an individual responsible decision, withheld by an irresponsible electing will, and a decision by a majority discharged of all legal responsibility. The consequences will be deduced elsewhere.

The Republicans and we may, moreover, differ upon many great questions referring to social regulation, though there may be no reason to acknowledge any new difference between Republicanism and Monarchism. For example: several combinations may be imagined in the election of the Council or Senate of Execution, with the design of extending them more or less to the deliberating administrative bodies. So may we also admit that there may be more than one method proper to regulate what is called the succession to the throne; for there is a latitude of opinion to be either a Republican or a Monarchist, according to several varieties.

If it is enquired, and I have no doubt that the enquiry will be made, what is my opinion with respect to the hereditary right of the Monarch Elector. I answer, without hesitation, that, in good theory, an hereditary transmission of office, whatever it is, can never accord with the laws of a true representation. Hereditaryship, in this sense, is as much an attaint upon principle, as an outrage upon society. But let us refer to the history of all Elective Monarchies or Principalities. Is there one in which the elective mode is not still worse than the hereditary succession? Is any man so insensible as to intend any blame upon the National Assembly, or to reproach them with want of courage?

What more than they have done could have been performed in the two years past by men, at bottom, like others; that is to say, who can judge only by that which they know, and who, for the most part, know that only to be possible which has already been done? And, if they had thought themselves able to enter into the examination of this question, would it have been for them to balance against an absurd, but peaceable, hereditaryship, the equally absurd custom of election, which is also sometimes accompanied with a civil war? At present, indeed, we are habituated to an elective mode, and have sufficiently reflected to believe, that there may exist a great variety of combinations in that respect.

There is certainly one very applicable to the first public function. It appears to me to unite all the advantages attributed to *hereditary*, without any of its inconveniences; and all the advantages of election, without its dangers. Nevertheless, I am far from thinking that circumstances are favourable for producing a change in this respect of the decreed Constitution, and I am very glad to deliver my opinion strongly upon this subject. The obstacles, I admit, are no longer the same; but have they therefore all disappeared, and have not some new ones arisen? Would an interior division be an indifferent transaction, at the æra in which we are placed? The National Assembly is secure of the union of all parts of France for the Constitution, as already known.

An universal wish appears for the completion and the confirmation of it throughout with uniformity, and with a force capable of giving empire to the law. Would it be reasonable to take this moment for throwing an apple of discord in the midst of the departments, and of hazarding incongruities in the decrees, to which it be hereafter so difficult to place limits? If the nation will one day explain itself by a constituent Assembly as to the place of the Monarch, whether it shall become elective, or remain hereditary, we need not, on that account, lose Monarchy, since there will always remain what is its essence, an individual decision, as well on the part of acting Monarchs as of the Monarch elector. In short, I hope, that as the public opinion is simplifying more and more in political matters, the *triangle* Monarchy will be generally perceived to be more suitable than the republican *platform* to that division of powers, which is the true bulwark of public liberty.

"I understand by a Republic," says Mr. Paine, "a government founded upon the principles of the Declaration of Rights." I do not see why this government should not be a Monarchy.

"Principles," says he, "with which many parts of the French constitution are in contradiction." This is possible; and it is probable, that if it was proposed to form a Republic, offences might be committed against the Declaration of Rights. But who does not see that these contradictions may be remedied without an abolition of the Monarchy? Mr. Paine will permit me to tell him a second time, that, since I do not require him to support any particular Republican form, it is right that he should allow me the same liberty with respect to Monarchy.

I desire, that our discussion, if it takes place, may not depart from the *spheres of theory*. The truths which we shall establish may descend too slowly, or too fast, to be applicable to facts. But I have already said enough to make it understood, that, at present, I feel much more powerfully the instant necessity of establishing the decreed Constitution, than of reforming it.

The Declaration of Rights of France and America are only one and the same thing in principles, and nearly so in words. So much the worse. I could wish that ours might be the best, and it would not be difficult to make it so.

And this is the Republicanism which I have undertaken to defend against what is called Monarchy and Aristocracy. A man who lives in France, or any other part of Europe, will allow, that if we are to take the words Republic and Monarchy only in their common acceptation, we shall be sufficiently disgusted by the mere mention of them. Have I not an opportunity, if I was to follow the example given me by Mr. Paine, to cast some discredit upon that which is called Republic and Aristocracy? Would a Senate of Execution be less aristocratical, than Ministers acting under the free and irresponsible choice of a Monarch, whose evident and palpable interest would be always inseparable from that of the majority?

I have, perhaps, done wrong in making so early a discovery of my doubts as to the excellence of the Republican system. How far are those from understanding me, who reproach me with not adopting a Republic, and believe, that not to proceed so far is to stop upon the road! Neither the ideas nor the sentiments which are called Republican, are unknown to me; but, in my design of advancing always towards the *maximum* of social liberty, I ought to pass the Republic, to leave it far behind, and to arrive at *true Monarchy!* If I am in error, I declare, that is neither for want of time or attention; for my researches and results preceded the Revolution.

I acknowledge, that, for a note, this is become very long; but I was desirous of providing, that if our discussion took place, it would not degenerate into a dispute of words. It will result, I believe, from the perusal of the above, that men who are willing to speak in precise terms will not permit themselves to suppose that Republicanism is the opposite of Monarchism. The correlative of *one* is *many*. Our adversaries are *Poliarchists—Policrates*; those are their true titles. When they call themselves Republicans, it should not be by opposition to Monarchy: they are Republicans, because they are for the *public* interest, and certainly we are so too.

The public interest, it is true, has been for a long time sacrificed to private views; but has not this evil been common to all known States, without regard to their several denominations? If, instead of adopting clear notions, happily suggested by etymology itself, it is determined to persist in a confusion of words which can be useful to no possible end, without doubt I shall not obstinately oppose it. I will permit the word "Republic" to be taken as synonymous to "Representative Constitution"; but I declare, that, after having taken it in this sense, I shall feel a necessity of enquiring, after all, whether they would wish that our Republic should be Monarchic or Poliarchic. Let us then, if we can, establish the question in these terms—"In a good Republic, is it better that the government should be Monarchic or Poliarchic?"

I finish this Letter by a remark with which I ought to have begun it. My Letter inserted in the *Moniteur* of the 6th of July does not announce, "that I have leisure to enter into the controversy with the Republican *Policrates*." My words are these: "I shall, perhaps, soon have time to develope this question." Why *soon*? Because I am persuaded that the National Assembly will, in a short time, put the last-hand to their work, and that it is upon the very point of being finished.

Until then, it is impossible for me to leave my daily occupations to fill the Journals with any sort of discussion. I may be told, that this question is the *order of the day*, but I do not perceive that it is. Besides, a friend of liberty does not chuse to discuss questions of right under the empire of questions of fact. This enquiry into principles, and the publication of them, has been already so sufficiently laborious, to a man left to his own individual powers, that he should not expose himself to the regret of having wished to speak reason, at a time when the most decided determinations deprive many of the possibility of attending to it, and leave only the resolution of serving, in spite of him, the one or the other party.

EM. SYEYES

CHAPTER 4

Of the Gains of Liberty in Society and in the Representative System

It is with sorrow that I witness attempts to denounce the representative system[a] in the name of liberty itself. This is very unfortunate. If the attempt were to succeed, mankind would enter a disastrous epoch. It will therefore be useful for the instruction of the public and in the interests of humanity to clarify the following question: "Understood or experienced in its purest form, in its full force, does liberty guide us away from the representative system or closer towards it?" A number of our fellow citizens are fanatically preaching what they take to be the truth, or are trying to despotically decree that their opinions be accepted. But there can be no danger or drawback in searching for the truth and in displaying and demonstrating it to those who are willing to understand it.

There exist innumerable treatises on liberty: philosophical, moral, metaphysical, and political. This need not worry us; we know that the questions that are discussed most are not therefore the best understood. And after all, what does it matter do us? It would be strange if we needed a profusion of erudition and the apparatus of science just to know what it is that we want when we want to be free. Liberty preceded science in the history of mankind, and still precedes it every day in the life of the individual; everyone knows its appeal and experiences a passion for it, before a thousand anti-social institutions deprave him and condemn him to servitude. Thus there is no doubt that all men understand well enough what they mean when they speak of liberty. But that is not sufficient: they also need to understand each other, and understand each other well, in order to move ahead together.

Let us therefore begin our inquiry by properly analyzing what liberty consists in. We can certainly consider its presence before the origins or the pronouncements of science, but not before the epoch of reason itself. Liberty without reason is that which drives savage people; it is not human liberty at

a It seems likely that the title includes reference to the remarks about the representative system that Sieyès reserved for the (never published) second part of his essay. We can only speculate about the contents of the projected second part. But it is certain that Sieyès understood "representative system" to refer to the division of labor generally, in a sense that includes but is not limited to political representation.

 | DOI: 10.1163/9789004273993_006

all. If this remark will appear otiose to some of my readers, all the better; I wish everyone saw it my way. Since that is not the case, I had to say it this one time.

If man were a creature without any needs, destined to an existence of permanent repose and contemplation, liberty would reduce to no more than *independence* from all that which might disturb his calm or threaten his existence.

But that is not our condition; we are born with needs. Those needs! They are the first mover of the human machine, the true source of the rights of man, the creative principle of the arts, and more. For creatures moved by ever new needs, and endowed with active faculties, something other than negative liberty is required. Activity is as necessary to man as rest. Therefore even the mere liberty of independence already acquires a further aspect; for you will not consider it to be fully realized unless we remove not only the factors that disturb his peace, but also those that impede his activity.

Let me dwell for a moment on this first aspect of liberty, which I am calling the liberty of independence. According to common usage a man is free when he is not hindered by other men from exercising his will. It is hardly possible to list all those many other conditions, internal no less than external, which may render him dependent and even oppressed: I am thinking of the innumerable obstacles that ignorance, clumsiness, rain, wind, fire, and so on, may pose for his activity or his tranquility. For the purposes of analysis it is always salutary to separate and clearly distinguish between distinct ideas. But in the present context I am happy to make do with the degree of precision contained in common usage, since it will be more convenient to discuss independence from real external causes and independence from involuntary internal causes elsewhere, and with a different terminology.

Let us move on to the second aspect of liberty. Besides independence from whatever may disturb their peace or hinder their activity, men need a liberty of ability [or powers (*liberté de pouvoir*)]. How else can they satisfy their ever new needs, how else engage in useful activity, if not by possessing an actual power, a kind of dominion over external things?

Human beings need to be free not simply in order to be free, but in order to exercise or employ their power, and to steadily increase it. But what good is even command over attainable objects when what is attainable is not useful? What use is a person's power over everything he encounters, if he encounters nothing or little of what he needs? The great objective of liberty is the expansion of this power. The more extensive it is, the freer we become. Natural man, like man in society, strives incessantly to remove obstacles to his activity, and to increase his independence.

In speaking of our power over external things, let us not forget the no less important and no less useful dominion that a person should exercise over himself, over his own faculties; for it is above all his foresight, his imagination, the usefulness of his activities, and the skillfulness of his labor which narrow or expand his dominion over his needs, and thus determine the extent of his liberty.

If I were to aim at the utmost grammatical precision, I would look for other terms instead of 'liberty of independence' and 'liberty of ability'. Those to whom the word 'liberty' means nothing but independence will not find the expression 'liberty of ability' fitting. They may even be puzzled and ask what it could mean to be free to be able or free to be unable. Others, for whom the word 'liberty' evokes nothing but the image of a person who has various options to choose from, and chooses among them at his pleasure, will say that they do not understand what could be meant by a liberty of independence. Both sides make the same mistake: they refuse to allow that we must express accurate thoughts in an imperfect manner in cases when it is not advisable to create a new terminology, and when one is confined to speaking in an idiom that is not yet philosophical. Instead of attending to the analysis, many people focus only on the words. They scrutinize them for what was said, and naturally enough they cannot find it: for the words did not fall from the sky possessing some inherent and divine content. They do not accord in advance with the demands of human inquiry. One can turn them over and over, and yet one will not be able to extract anything from them that one has not first put into them. Words are nothing but what men have chosen to make them into. They do not contain any notions but those that have been attached to them, and we may reasonably assume that no language has yet been invested with ideas that men did not already have. As analysis progresses, language is perfected more and more. In the meantime, we have to take from it what we can. It should have become clear enough that in considering the topic of liberty, I want to speak of the independence and of the ability or power of man, both of which are essential components of liberty and without which the word 'liberty' would be nothing but an empty sound.

I want to draw only one conclusion from all I have said so far, and whoever would dispute it must have misunderstood me. I am claiming that liberty, as I understand it here, is liable to increase and decrease, and that a person will be more or less free as his power and his independence grow or diminish. On the basis of this insight our original question can be easily answered. We can now rephrase it as follows: "In order to continually augment and perfect the ability and independence of man, should we move away from the representative system or closer towards it?" Or alternatively: "Does liberty, in its most useful development, lead us towards the representative system, or not?" Again, in posing this question I am concerned only with the sake of liberty: in order to be guided by it alone, I subordinate all other ideas and considerations to it.

If you wish to go back to savage man and consider him in the most isolated condition, as far as possible removed from any sort of political association, because you imagine such a creature to be more protective of his liberty, I will not object. But this same man will enter into the state of society, and he will do so precisely for the sake of his liberty, properly understood. Why? Because this new condition affords him an increase of ability, and even an increase of independence. For a clarification and demonstration of this first step, I ask you to consider one page from [my] 'Reasoned Exposition of the Rights of Man and Citizen':[b]

> Since every man is so constituted as to will his own good, he may enter into contracts with his fellows, and he will do this if he judges that it is to his own advantage. It has been noted above that men can do much to further each other's well-being.
>
> Thus a society established on the basis of reciprocal utility truly follows from the natural means given to men for attaining their goals. Hence this union is a gain and not a sacrifice, and society should be regarded as a successor and a complementary development to the natural order. Even if men were not unconsciously led towards society in a very real and powerful way by all their natural faculties, their reason alone would have guided them to this end. Thus the reason for uniting in society is to advance well-being. The end of society is not the degradation of men, but rather their perfection and ennoblement.
>
> Thus society does not weaken or reduce the means for realizing his personal ends that are at each individual's disposal when he enters into an association with others. On the contrary, it increases them and multiplies them through a more extensive development of his intellectual and physical powers. It increases them still further through the invaluable addition of public works and assistance, so that a tax subsequently paid to the state by the citizen is only a kind of reimbursement that represents but an infinitesimal fraction of the profit and benefits he has gained from society. It is a joint enterprise which yields large dividends.

---

b See text 2 of this compilation.

> Society does not establish an unjust inequality of right alongside the natural inequality of means; instead, it protects the equality of rights against the natural but harmful influence of unequal means. Law is not designed to weaken the weak and strengthen the strong; on the contrary, its purpose is to protect the weak from the assaults of the strong. Since all citizens find protection beneath its beneficent shield, it guarantees each of them the plentitude of his rights.
>
> Man does not sacrifice part of his liberty upon entering society. Even outside the social bond, no one possessed the right to harm another. This principle holds under all conditions one might imagine mankind to be in. Since liberty has never included the right to harm, it would be a mistake to believe that one loses or sacrifices this right when one enters into an association with one's fellows.
>
> Far from reducing individual liberty, society extends and assures its deployment. It removes a great number of obstacles and dangers to which liberty was too exposed when defended only by individual strength, and safeguards it by the all-powerful protection of the entire association.
>
> Hence, since both the physical and intellectual capacities of man are augmented in society, and since, at the same time, he has freed himself from the worries that once accompanied their exercise, it is true to say that liberty is more complete in society than it could ever have been in what is called the state of nature.

Against this view, a specious objection is made that I believe has not so far been properly disposed of. We grant you, they say, all the things that primitive independence stands to gain by entering society and placing oneself under the protection of the laws. But does not the submission to this great multiplicity of decrees and regulations that govern the political association produce a new sort of dependency? Is it really so easy to draw up a balance sheet of gains and losses to liberty? Which side wins out in the calculation?

Allow me to settle the question in two words. In a badly ordered society, the loss outweighs the gain; in the true social order, the gain outweighs the loss. But this truth can only be established through a further analysis of the different kinds of dependency. The term needs to be clarified.

Since nature has invested us with needs, it has imposed on us the necessity of meeting them. Both our question and our answer should set aside dependency in this sense, as it characterizes all epochs of mankind, both before and after the foundation of society.

Man and his environment are organized or constituted in such a way that he is usually compelled, in order to attain his goals, to employ a series of means, as though they were the steps of a ladder; the object that he wishes to secure for himself lies at the end of a chain of intermediary acts or operations. If, for example, he feels hungry or thirsty, the distance that separates him from the fountain requires him to embark on a more or less arduous path; if the fruit he sees is not within the reach of his hand, he has to use a stick in order to reach it, or to climb up the tree. Similar examples abound both in the social and in the natural order. Let us call the dependency on *ends* that dependency in which a person stands with respect to the objects of consumption, use, or convenience. And let us call the dependency on *means* that dependency in which he stands with respect to the activities, efforts, and intermediary labors that are required for reaching his goals.

Given man's needs, would it be desirable for him to be entirely independent of both ends and means? Or would that not rather amount to complete destitution? Without the double yoke of ends and means, would there be any need for liberty? Consider that it is your affluence, in this respect, which constitutes your power, and that it is the unhindered exercise of your command over means and ends that constitutes your true independence.

It is true that at the present stage of social life, not all of our needs are the work of nature. As everyone knows, habit is a second or even third nature, and it is the source of multiple artificial needs that are sometimes beneficial but more often unfortunate. Moreover, there are also false needs stemming from mere discomfort, and so on. What can we say about this? That the most important goal of morality, and therefore of education, must be to recall the simple and natural needs, the habits and passions that impose only a gentle yoke and are conducive to happiness. I cannot defend, or pretend not to notice, the countless evils that prejudices and unsocial vanities have imposed on slavish generations. But instead of dwelling on ignorance and error, let me appeal to enlightenment and to philosophy; allow me to entertain the possibility of an acceptable state of society—otherwise we can only fall silent.

Moderation in one's needs, abundance in one's ends, wise economy in one's means—these would be three chapters of a new exposition of a reasonable morality. In the meantime, let me point out that the more pressing we find it to clarify the theoretical and practical aspects of needs, ends, and means, the more we should recognize the urgency of a progressive development of public enlightenment, human abilities and labor, and the like; and where could such progress take place, where might it advance without interruption towards the goal of true human happiness, if not in a well-ordered political association?

Imagine two people who are caught by surprise in a violent thunderstorm; both suffer equally from their lack of shelter. An open attic and a ladder are in view. One of the two runs to the ladder, picks it up, props it against the wall, climbs up the steps, and is covered; the other, in order to avoid dependency on the ladder, remains outside shivering and exposed to the thunderstorm. Here you have the independence of the savage, as opposed to the liberty of social man; here you have the difference between depending on means and being independent from them. These considerations should help us appreciate the true significance of submitting oneself to the law.

It seems to me that when I desire something, I enter into an agreement with myself regarding the means for procuring it. We should think of our relations with our fellow men in an analogous way.

Others depend on their will just as we do on ours. It is in our common interest to mutually treat each other as means to our respective happiness, rather than as obstacles. For if it is nature's arrangement that another person's will belongs to the chain of means that are most conducive to realizing our ends, we are likewise instructed by nature to address ourselves to another person's will, rather than to his weakness. The exercise of force would disrupt all social and human relations. One need only observe oneself to understand that man is a means of a more sensitive and more delicate kind than the rest of nature. When your will is directed at the will of a fellow human being, it is as though you were tapping at a resonating body: it responds with a request of its own. So be careful: if you manage to strike the right chord, you will produce consonance; if you pluck the wrong string, horrible dissonance will ensue.

In short: the use of force leads to nothing but domination, oppression, resistance, and all the evils that burden humanity. Consider, on the other hand, the social order that will result if people express a willingness to engage in mutually voluntary exchanges, and to unite by the natural law of contractual fidelity: you will be overwhelmed by the promise of prosperity it holds out.

Thus it is only by freely entering into reciprocal agreements that men can act together so as to enable each other's happiness and liberty. And among these fruitful agreements the most important and valuable one is that which binds each individual's will to the common will of the association, and that is to say, to the law. No further proof is needed of this, since to remove the law would be to remove the social order altogether and to trade all its benefits for the dangers of its absence.

The difficulty has now been sufficiently explained, and the conclusion is in plain sight. Obedience to the law belongs to the theory of contracts. From the perspective of liberty, both legal obedience and contractual agreements originate in our dependency on means. That is all there is to it. Far from imposing a limitation on liberty, obedience to the law is rather its most powerful instrument and its most reliable safeguard.

To return to our basic question: does liberty of itself lead towards the state of society? If you consider how it increases power and independence, and if you do not want to betray its goal, your answer must be: yes.

Note: the sequel will appear in the forthcoming issues.[c]

c The announced sequel on this topic in the *Journal d'Instruction Social* did not materialize.

CHAPTER 5

Sieyès's Views Concerning Several Articles of Sections IV and V of the Draft Constitution [First Thermidorian Intervention]

Read to the Convention on the Second of Thermidor in the Third Year of the Republic; Printed by Order of the National Convention

Like my colleagues, I too am of the opinion that there is no task more urgent than completing the constitution. It is unfortunate that there is always so little time in situations like these; I accept this, though without quite knowing why it is the case. Let me explain beforehand that I would not dare to waste your time if my contribution were limited to a detailed critique of your work. That part of the constitution, which is the subject of your present deliberations, is clearly the most difficult one, and perhaps also the most important. After thoroughly inspecting it, I worry that it may not have the necessary robustness to withstand new revolutionary upheavals and to safeguard the public order. That is my motivation for taking the podium today.

Properly understood, the term constitution refers primarily to the organization of the central public institutions (*l'établissement public central*): that part of the political machine invested with legislative authority, as well as the part that emerges from this first one [i.e., the legislature] and which you have placed in a prominent position in order to guarantee the enforcement of laws throughout the Republic. You want a government that will effectively uphold the rights and duties of each individual. But this will remain only a wish as long as you leave the government, whose importance has been so emphasized by the speakers here, a mere formality, by withholding from it the features it needs to fulfill its designated tasks. Prone as our nation may be to the magic spell of words, it cannot cover the void behind it forever. I therefore believe that the government proposed by your committee, with its conflation of legislative and executive power, cannot satisfy those who care about social order. The arrangements needed to uphold the rights and duties of each individual are not in place. This government is ill-designed: it cannot fulfill its proper purpose with respect to either of the two essential functions I have mentioned. Moreover, the first part, i.e. the legislative one, lacks an indispensable, essential safeguard—the element which guarantees the constitution itself, and which has been neglected by all constitutional projects at all times. Finally, we should

 | DOI: 10.1163/9789004273993_007

attend to the balance that needs to obtain between the different branches of the political order (*l'établissement politique*). In these respects, your draft leaves much to be desired.

Let me get straight to the heart of the matter and submit my proposal to you. As far as governments and political constitutions are concerned, unmitigated unity means despotism, and unmitigated division means anarchy. But the combination of division and unity can provide the sort of political guarantee without which freedom is in constant danger.

(Let me mention in passing that it is not only for the sake of security, but also for the sake of a good order, that whatever [government functions] can be separated should be separated, and whatever [functions] can be united should be united. But it is unnecessary to multiply the motivations, as long as one manages to do the right thing.)

In a representative system, political action is divided into two main parts: ascending actions and descending actions. The former comprise all those acts by which a people directly or indirectly names its various representatives, who are charged with making laws, and with their subsequent execution. The latter encompasses all those acts by which those representatives participate in the making or the execution of laws. In a free nation, the point of departure of this political process can be no other than the primary assemblies. The target of the process is in turn the people as the receiver of the law's benefits. Even without further elaboration, it should be clear that establishing a constitution consists in organizing this circular mechanism. Indeed, the constitution has been achieved as soon as central institutions (*l'établissement central*) have been established, since other subordinated institutions do not have to be established by the constituent power itself.

To be sure, alongside the constitution one might set up important regulations, declare various principles, and produce fundamental pieces of legislation. Nevertheless, strictly speaking a constitution is limited to what we have just outlined; perhaps only fifty articles—certainly not two or three hundred—really make up a constitution. In any case, I ask you to attend to only one particular aspect of central institutions.

The question is how to divide up the powers of government. As I have already suggested, the answer lies in the need to divide in order to prevent despotism, and to centralize in order to prevent anarchy.

In both respects nothing must be done arbitrarily: things are not arbitrary in moral and social matters any more than in nature. Pitiable are those men and those peoples who think that they know what they want, but who in fact only want. To want is the easiest thing. As long as there have been human beings, they have wanted. As long as there have been political associations on earth, they have wanted. Everyone wants to be governed well, to not have their rights swallowed up by despotism and to have them protected from the clutches of anarchy. How can one realize this wish?—by knowing how to combine political unity with political division.

I know of only two systems for dividing political powers: the system of equilibrium and that of cooperation (*concours*)—i.e., a system of counter-weights and a system of organized unity. Notice that this explanation does not amount to the insult of trying to lead you away from the representative system; outside the latter we find nothing but arrogance, superstition and stupidity.

At the outset I need to explain one or two concepts. In dealing with questions isolated from their context, and in relying on language that has been damaged by ignorance and insincerity, such digressions are sometimes necessary.

We all know that in any society there is only one political power, that of the community. But loosely speaking the various permissions that this singular power gives its representatives may also be referred to as 'powers,' in the plural: just as we each individually call ourselves and each other a 'representative,' whether by error or out of politeness. In fact there is only one representative—namely the convention as a collective body—and beyond this there are representatives only in the derivative sense, institutions and individuals who have been charged with certain tasks. All those who discharge these tasks should be called representatives when they act in the way commissioned by the people, and usurpers when they do not.

In society everything is representation. Representation is found in the private realm as much as in the public one; it is the mother of trade and production as well as of social and political progress. Indeed I claim that it is the very essence of social life.

More than two years ago I undertook to show that it is the representative system which allows us to attain the greatest possible degree of freedom and prosperity.[a] At that time, so-called friends of the people[b] halted the printing of

---

a Sieyès refers to his constitutional draft, which he meant to present as an alternative to Condorcet's plan. However, the Jacobins prevented the publication of Sieyès's text in 1793.

b This is a reference to the Jacobins, specifically to the newspaper 'The People's Friend' (*L'Ami du Peuple*), edited by Jean-Paul Marat. To Sieyès the Jacobins were populist and insurrectionary demagogues. Marat's paper played a crucial role in encouraging the overthrow of the monarchy on August 10, and in the subsequent September massacres. It continued to attack the government even after Robespierre came to power and demanded, among other measures, the adoption of the 1793 constitution, which would have granted further democratic rights to the people.

my work after the first page. In their crude ignorance, they considered the representative system incompatible with democracy, as though a building were incompatible with its natural foundation; or rather, they wanted to keep only the foundation, apparently thinking that men in society should be condemned to spending their entire lives under the open sky. I wanted to show that the people has everything to gain by establishing a representative structure for the various kinds of powers which make up the public order (*l'établissement public*), and by reserving to themselves only the power to choose each year a number of reasonable and trusted men to replace the departing representatives. To this proposal I attached a sketch of a list of eligible candidates, of the kind that I had already proposed in 1789.[c] But just as now, there existed then a widespread and false idea with grave consequences: namely, that the people should delegate only powers that it cannot exercise itself. Among some, this principle is held as the very safeguard of liberty. But one may as well try to prove to the citizens who need to send a letter to Bordeaux or elsewhere that they will better preserve their liberty by insisting on their right to carry it there themselves, simply because they can, instead of entrusting this task to the public institution meant to discharge it. Can you discern any credible principles in such flawed reasoning?

It is clear that being represented in as many areas as possible increases one's liberty, while uniting various representative roles in a single person diminishes one's liberty. Look at the realm of private affairs: surely he is most free who has others do the most work for him. Conversely, everyone agrees that a man renders himself more dependent on others the more of his delegated tasks are accumulated in one and the same agent—to the point where he completely alienates his own person, if all his powers come to be concentrated in a single individual.

Instead of encouraging people to reserve to themselves the exercise of all those powers that it is really in their best interest to have represented by others, it would be more useful to advise them as follows: Beware of attaching all your rights to one single representative; distinguish carefully between the various representative tasks, and ensure that the constitution does not allow any group of representatives to overstep their particular jurisdiction. But, you will say, what will then happen to the unlimited powers? The answer is that unlimited

c The need for such a list was Sieyès's constant preoccupation. See, for instance, his text 'Some Ideas on the Constitution, with Respect to the City of Paris' ('Quelques idées de Constitution applicables à la ville de Paris'), in: *Œuvres de Sieyes*, ed. Marcel Dorigny (Paris, 1989), vol. 2, no. 8.

powers are a political monster and a great error of the French people, which it will not commit again in the future. This is an important, yet too-little-known truth, so it bears repeating: the French people as a whole does not have these powers, these unlimited rights, which flatterers attribute to it. When a political association is formed not all the rights of the members, and thus not the sum total of all the individuals' powers, come to be held in common.

Rather what comes to be held in common under the name of public or political power is merely the necessary minimum: only that which is needed to enforce the rights and duties of each individual. It is true that this aggregated power bears a certain resemblance to the exaggerated notions that have come to be associated with the concept of sovereignty. It is indeed popular sovereignty that I am talking about: If there is such a thing at all, this is what it is. But the only reason the word evokes such grandiose ideas is that the French, still captivated by the superstitions of kingship, have invested this concept with the whole tradition of pomposity and absolute powers that once served to glorify usurped sovereignty. Public opinion, in its enormous generosity, has even considered adding still greater powers. Some kind of patriotic pride seemed to demand that however powerful and terrible the sovereignty of the great kings had been, the sovereignty of a great people should still surpass it.

But I hold that with the progress of enlightened thinking, and with the increasing remoteness of the times when one believed to know, while in fact one was merely wishing, the notion of sovereignty will find its proper boundaries again. For, once again, the sovereignty of the people is certainly not unlimited, and numerous highly lauded and respected political systems—including the one which is still believed to make a particularly strong claim on us[d]—will come to be recognized as erroneous fancies, as defective plans for a 're-totality' (*ré-totale*) rather than a 're-public', as harmful to liberty and contrary to public and private interests.

Let me return to the question of the division of powers—or, if you prefer, the various responsibilities which, as I explained, should be entrusted to representative bodies on behalf of the people and their liberty. Some believe that it is easiest to create two or three representative organs and assign one and the same function to each of them. On this view, the political acts whereby the collective law-giving will is extracted from the mass of individual wills would all be carried out by one and the same body, thus erasing the boundaries between constitutional will, law-proposing will, executive will, and legislative

d This is not the only place where Sieyès obliquely condemns Rousseau's doctrine of the general will.

will in the proper sense. Frightened by the immense powers thus granted to one group of representatives, what are the proponents of this scheme going to do next? Instead of keeping these different tasks separate, and retaining only those links between them that ensure their coordination towards the a common end, they keep them united; but they decide to then grant a second body of representatives the very same fullness of powers, i.e., to grant each of the two bodies a power of veto against the other. They pride themselves on avoiding the concentration of powers in one place, which indeed would amount to complete despotism. So there you have the system of equilibrium or counter-weights. But just look at any actual instance of this model, and consider how political affairs are conducted there (for, constitutional mistakes notwithstanding, political decisions must somehow be made). You will see that the political system is able to function only because in practice there is really no such counterweight or equilibrium at all. Instead, through abuse and corruption of the system, what is effectively established is precisely that concentration of power which was meant to be prevented, and which was believed to have been precluded through the institution of veto. Let the most devoted partisans of the English system tell us, for example, whether the king is not in fact the absolute master of both houses of parliament, and whether that famous party of the opposition, which sometimes calls itself the friend of the people, is really anything more than a disgruntled petitioner developing schemes and slanders against the royal favorite in order to take the latter's place in the king's services.[1] I will say nothing of how superstitious and undignified it is to have one chamber[e] of nobles and one of royalist theocrats. These deeply entrenched vices, which are hateful to all free spirits, are not essential parts of the system of counter-weights as such—they are not found in the American version of this system—and I am not in the habit of dwelling on faults that are merely accidental to the views that I criticize. Suffice it to say that even when the system of equilibrium consists of homogeneous counterparts, it is not therefore any more worthwhile, and perhaps even less so, at least with respect to the aims of the legislator. When two agencies invested with the same powers remain independent of one another, there is no certainty in politics; the two houses remain in deadlock, which only resolves when the system disintegrates and

1 As always, we must expect that some honorable men will merely adapt to present circumstances.

e With the ambiguous word 'chamber' (chambre) Sieyès could refer to England or France, or both. The 'chamber of nobles' would refer to the English House of Lords, while the 'chamber of royalist theocrats' would point to the first two estates of the French *ancien régime*.

replaces a chimerical equilibrium with an undivided concentration of powers that exposes the nation to all the dangers of despotism. There is a good image for this: two horses put before the same carriage, and made to pull in opposing directions. Despite their greatest efforts, the carriage will remain stationary unless a royal driver takes his seat and brings them into unison. But we do not want such a royal driver.

The people against whom I am arguing confuse unity of action (*unité d'action*) with solitary action (*action unique*). We need the former; they give us the latter. Consider the different kinds of workers needed to build a house. Even though various different trades and skills are involved, they all work towards a common goal. There is no single unique kind of action, but there is clearly a unity of action. My adversaries, on the contrary, have a different idea of the unity of action. Since, as I just said, they confuse it with solitary action, they will only admit one single kind of worker and force him to perform diverse tasks. Then, when they realize that such an accumulation of power leads to abuse, what do they do? They advise the owner, once the house is finished, to call in a second group of workers, each of whom is again competent for all the different tasks, and to have them rebuild the house from the ground up. Of course an analogy is not an argument, and I do not want to take the comparison too far. But you will agree, at least, that there is a certain resemblance here.

The alternative system of division is already suggested by the simple outline I gave earlier. It does not charge several different representative bodies with constructing—or reconstructing—the same piece of work. Rather, it assigns different tasks to different representatives, so that their distinct activities together reliably yield the desired outcome. This system does not place two or three heads onto the same body, expecting that the defects of one will somehow correct the harm caused by the defects of the other. It carefully separates within a single head the different faculties whose distinct operations have to come together in order to produce wise decisions, and it coordinates these faculties through rules which naturally unify all the different legislative activities into the action of a single mind.[f] I have shown elsewhere that dividing the judgment of the nation into two representative bodies leads to the risk of mistaking false outcomes for the correct ones: the people then have no way to guarantee that the majority decision will become law, but are instead held hostage to the veto of the minority. It is hard to think of anything more harmful for the

f It seems that Sieyès's theological training is striking here. Sieyès uses virtually the same analogy as Apostole Paul in 1 Corinthians 12, where he compares the church to a body with many members. We owe this hint to Jonathan Green.

purposes of social existence. Thus one should stick to the system of concerted action, or organized unity. This should become the French system. Since it is also the natural system, towards which political art directs us with each step along the path of human perfectibility, we may reasonably hope that it will one day be the political system of all free and enlightened peoples.

It is a pleasure to be able to praise your proposal. The institutional arrangement envisioned by it is better than that of any other plan so far, and it proceeds further in the right direction than any other plan. It separates the authority to propose legislation from the authority to decide on legislation, and it divides executive power into two parts, although this division is not very firm. But these elements still need to be integrated and harmonized with one another—and in this process, we may find that certain essential elements are still missing. But it will be quicker to simply explain what I am asking for.

[A.] I am asking, in the first place, for a jury of the constitution (*jury de constitution*)[g]—or, to make my idea sound a bit more French and to phonetically distinguish it from the word *juré* (jury member), a constitutional jury (*jurie constitutionnaire*).[h] This would be a body of representatives with the special task of judging alleged violations of the constitution.

A sensible and useful idea was introduced in 1788: namely the distinction between constituent power and constituted powers. This idea belongs among the discoveries that have moved science forward, and it is owed to the French.[i] But the intrigues that so quickly took the place of reason at the time of the Revolution rendered this idea impotent to shape a new political order. Instead, like many new ideas that quickly come to seem obvious, it was used to justify acts of folly (as is the fate of even the best instruments when placed in the hands of ignorant people). Now is the time to make better use of it. If you want to establish a safeguard of the constitution, a beneficial check to contain all representative action within the bounds of its particular mandate, you should set up a constitutional jury. Indeed its necessity is so obvious that I will directly move on to my second request.

[B.] Do you want to make sure that all the needs of the people are taken into consideration, that its concerns are always heard by the legislator, and that all

g Sieyès treats this topic extensively in his second Thermidorian speech (text 6).

h Here Sieyès shifts back and forth between French and English spellings of "jury." In his second Thermidorian speech he returned to the English spelling.

i Sieyès was himself one of the engineers of this idea; see his 'What is the Third Estate?' (text 1).

the means for satisfying them are discovered, discussed, and presented to the legislator with the full weight of an enlightened public opinion? If so, recall the benefits of the so-called popular societies,[j] these mostly disorderly movements of over-eager petitioners who approached you more from a sense of need than with any knowledge of the right means; add such knowledge to that sentiment, represented in one or several tribunes, and your council of five hundred—a reasonable institution, despite its name and its exaggerated size, and capable of further refinement—will become the tribunate of the French people, quite different from the original Roman one.[k]

But by instituting this French tribunate, my fellow citizens, you will still have met the people's need for representation only half way. When I look at your scheme, I do not see any mention of the government; but the times are past when the government used to be regarded as an anti-popular institution. Do not all the parts of the public institutions exist for the sake of the people? Are not the needs of the government simply the needs of the governed? Do the people not carry the burden when the government lacks the necessary means to fully administer the law? If the contrary view were ever to prevail again, one might as well do away with law, representation, and public institutions altogether.

But if the needs of the government—laws, general regulations, and means of enforcement—are also objects of the legislator's activity, why not include them in the system of representation as well? Should we really believe that they will be sufficiently represented by the tribunate? That would betray poor knowledge of men and their passions. One will frequently see the tribunate attack the government—but come to its aid? No: Such a phenomenon would

j 'Popular societies' (*sociétés populaires*) were radical democratic organizations institutionally and ideologically aligned with the Jacobin Club which offered underprivileged citizens and women a venue for political deliberation. A dense web of such societies cropped up between 1791 and 1793. During the rule of the Jacobins, some popular societies claimed authority over the Convention itself. They also controlled civic festivals and the use of revolutionary symbols, such as cockades. After the fall of Robespierre the Jacobin Club was prohibited. On August 23, 1795, popular societies were officially disbanded as well; Sieyès delivered his speech three days prior. Remarkably, despite his hostility to Jacobinism, he acknowledged and publicly emphasized the potential contribution of popular societies to republican education.

k During the French Revolution, Robespierre and Danton were referred to as popular tribunes. The tribunate has its origins in the Roman republic. Its function was to assert and defend the interests of the simple citizens (the *plebs*) against the nobility (the *patriciate*). In contrast with this estate-based form of political representation, Sieyès's idea of a "tribunate of the French people" aims at a democratic representation of all citizens.

be almost a sign of weakness, it would indicate the agony of a sick patient or the existence of a corrupt part close to being victorious.

I know that my suggestion to place the government above the tribunate will appear worrisome to you at first glance. But let me assure you that I am by no means confusing executive power and government. To the contrary, I consider the division of these two powers within a republic an insight at the frontier of knowledge: its importance be revealed and properly appreciated only in time.

Executive power is wholly action, government is wholly thought; the latter allows for deliberation, the former excludes it at all its levels, without exception. But since we are trying to clarify ideas and to make our language more precise, allow me to remark that the term 'executive power' is not quite adequate for characterizing large parts of the administration of the law.

Who executes the law? Those who observe its rules: first and foremost the citizens, each in the respect that concerns him (this is the largest part of the execution of law); then the public officials, in their different functions or tasks. Every law falls into one of these two categories. Indeed, this is the meaning of the distinction between protective laws and directive laws. The former are executed by the citizens, the latter by the public officials. When there is disobedience or resistance at one of these levels, the public administrators who enforce the law are activated against the protesters and resistors. In any case executive power, understood as the power to enforce the law, must be distinguished from government, which encompasses three large areas:

1. At the highest level of the state, the government functions as a jury with the power to make [legislative] proposals.
2. Once a law has been promulgated, government functions as a jury of execution at the subordinate level of the political order. Committee members, such as you, know that aside from general legislation there are innumerable decisions and regulations to be made, even setting aside executive acts and decisions, which in the heat of the current situation are sometimes referred back to the committees; one might call this a legislature of executive affairs. But recall that the tribunate is charged with preventing the government from overstepping its authority and interfering with legislation proper; nowhere is this provision stronger than in my plan.
3. Finally, the government oversees the executive (*l'exécution*), and in this capacity it appoints the administration (*le pouvoir executive*) and the highest officers and directors of the judiciary. It will be immediately obvious that the leadership of the administration can be distributed among several persons, each overseeing a particular area, without any loss of governmental unity of action. But my aim here is not to explain the structure of the executive. I

want to talk only about the government, and to trace the demarcation line that separates the two powers.

[C.] My third demand encompasses several other provisions:

1. I ask for a unified legislative, that is to say, a single body of representatives charged with establishing by vote what is to be the law, and convening in a single chamber. After providing representation for the needs of the governed, on the one hand, and for the needs of the governed for government, on the other, the national judgment must still be pronounced and thus represented, by a body charged only with legislation. I think of this as a supreme court charged with making binding decisions about proposals that are contested, defended, contradicted, or accepted by one party or another, and with doing so in the light of whether these proposals are useful to the people, whose judgment the court represents.
2. I ask that this legislative body, which is the true center and supreme regulator of the whole institutional system, be the largest of the representative bodies. The best solution in my view would be an assembly composed in about equal parts of members from the three great areas of activity (*travaux*), the three great forms of industry (*industries*) which keep a society alive and make it prosper. I am speaking of agriculture, of urban industry, and of that activity whose place is everywhere, the education of men. One day it will become clear that these are important issues. For now, suffice it to say that the legislative assembly should be the largest of the representative bodies, corresponding to its paramount importance.
3. Finally, I ask that the legislature be disallowed from introducing laws of its own accord, similar in this respect to a well-constituted judicial court. I admit that this is a slightly unusual provision, but bear with me for a moment; if it turns out that I am in error, we can move on without difficulty.

Imagine the freest people on earth, the freest people possible: what would it demand of its legislator? That all those laws that are necessary and useful be enacted.

How does one recognize the necessity or the utility of a law? By the fact that it corresponds to a feeling of need.

Well then, have I not designated bodies for the expression of need—the needs of the governed and the governing?

Have I not created two very responsive forums, in which these two sorts of needs will not fail to be heard, and in which they will even be amplified due to the passionate nature of these arenas?

Try to think of any complaint, any demand or proposal—excepting those individual petitions which fall outside the scope of my considerations altogether—that is not afforded full representation here. Can you imagine two better workshops of public policy? What else could there be? Nothing. It is therefore unnecessary to allow your legislature spontaneous acts of will, or what I have called the introduction of laws of its own accord. You may object: perhaps we will find some very enlightened men with excellent opinions in the legislature. No doubt! But we can—indeed we certainly will—find such men among the simple citizens too. Would you therefore grant everyone the right of legislative proposal? No, you would not want that; but it would still be less unreasonable than to accumulate two distinct political functions, two separate areas of authority, in the same representative body. Those good ideas and those useful opinions will naturally take the path that law and custom proscribe: they will arrive in the legislature in a better and more useful form after they have passed through the constitutionally designated channels.

You should be careful: In the interest of liberty, it is more important than you may think that you withhold from the legislator the right to anticipate people's needs. There are many other important truths waiting to be demonstrated besides this one, but allow me a brief explanation.

Political liberty is the same thing as civil liberty, albeit directed at a distinct object. The liberty of the private person who feels that his rights have been violated consists in his ability to lodge a complaint and in the assurance that justice will be done. This liberty is lost when a judge insists on protecting the person's rights concerning some matter in which no complaint had been made in the first place. And you should not assume that the legislative tribunal (*tribunal legislative*) is in this respect any different from ordinary judicial courts. Both rest their decisions on a superior authority, that of the positive legal code in the latter case, that of the more ancient and more comprehensive body of natural laws in the former. In neither case are their decisions arbitrary. Both can err, but they are not to be blamed as long as their error is one of judgment, rather than stemming from an attempt to overstep the proper bounds of their function.

Quite regardless of their relation towards positive law all juries have the same basic character. No jury takes action, makes decisions, or performs any function whatsoever concerning issues that lie outside its jurisdiction, whether brought to it by individuals or by parties. All juries wait for the request of some person seeking justice, prepared to render it at any time. Thus the foremost task of the legislature is, as I have already said, not to divine some need, but to wait patiently; not to legislate spontaneously, but to respond to their requests. The purpose of all public institutions is individual liberty. Attempting to make either the people or the individual more free than they wish or desire would constitute not liberty but domination and servitude.

You have now heard the requests that I announced to you. If I were to explain to you all the benefits of my project I would never finish—so I have given you only cursory impression.

I have provided a preserver and guardian of the constitution, in the shape of a constitutional jury; an assembly that represents the people's needs and proposes the requisite laws; and an assembly in charge of the people's need for execution of the law. Here we find further reasons why the government should function as a sort of workshop, a jury of proposition—but more on this elsewhere. Allow me to add only that, for one, the government as I envision it has no direct influence on the citizens; the idea that citizens are governed by the public authorities is a misguided one. What is being governed, rather, are the executive institutions for which the constitution (*l'établissement public*) provides. The citizens govern themselves, simply by taking care that they do not violate the law; but the public officials, the administrators, are being governed in their functions. We can expect that this word [i.e., government] will no longer occasion such disquiet or even feelings of hatred as it has in the past. On the contrary, you will find the citizen who wishes to complain about the administration or its leadership, or about any branch of the executive, lodge his complaints with the government itself, which he regards as the natural superior of the former, as a an aid rather than an enemy. And you will find him satisfied that he has received justice when it is owed to him.

Executive power, on its part, acquires a precision, promptness, and security so far unknown to it. No longer is it, as in the system of counter-weights, an opposing element vis-à-vis the people's representatives on the legislative balance. For one, each public official is, within the confines of his task, himself a representative of the people. And secondly, we regard the executive power not as a counter-weight but as the continuation and the complement of society's will, since its task is to realize this will and to ensure the faithful and certain execution of the law.

You all know the extent to which undue deliberation has hindered the work of the administration. I expressed my view on this in the Convention in January 1793:[1] within the system of cooperation there is no deliberation here, and there

1 Sieyès is referring to his report about the organization of the War Ministry, which he presented to the Convention on January 25, 1793: 'Rapport du Comité de Défense pour organiser le Ministère de la Guerre', in: *Oeuvres de Sieyès*, ed. Marcel Dorigny, vol. 3 (Paris, 1989), no. 35. Cf. *Archives parlementaires*, vol. 57 (January 12–28, 1793), pp. 644–653.

is no need for any. Where there is deliberation, there is no full responsibility. The minority who are outvoted take no responsibility for legislation, while the victorious majority complain about modifications to their original proposal. Since the proposal has been adopted in an altered form, how can they be held responsible for all its consequences? I leave aside the separate issue of the slowness of deliberation, which is always harmful and sometimes fatal. My own proposal assigns full authority to the respective leaders of the various administrative units.

In a system of equilibrium, the play of passions that results from the different social positions leads to a constant civil war between popular representatives and executive power. In this conflict, one side will be toppled and capitulate, either as the result of bribes or force. Can this be political liberty? In our system of organized unity, we anticipate the force of these passions: we expect them, but do not fear them.

The tribunate may attack the government, but it has the time and resources to defend itself. Thus this struggle will never endanger liberty, since these two powers are subordinate to a third one—the legislative assembly—which mitigates their excesses and judges their proposals. The constitution assigns the legislature a position above the tribunate[m] and the government. The publicists know that there is no particular problem here. Shielded from the sometimes salutary, yet never truly worrisome political tempests, the executive operates safely under the aegis of the executive jury (*jury d'exécution*). It is able to administer the law swiftly and effectively, without being hindered by a constant and bothersome need to justify its actions. This arrangement conduces to the greatest benefit for the people and to a maximum of individual liberty.

But even as I highlight the demagogic dangers that eager and ambitious members of the tribunate present to the government; as I labor to dig a canal and erect dikes to contain this torrent within its constitutional bounds; as I seek to transform party conflicts into mere disagreements and to safeguard society from the strife and unrest from which wrong-headed people stand so much to gain, and good ones so much to lose; all this without depriving society of that dynamic, living character which lends it energy and which furthers its enlightenment: Can it be possible that some still try to attribute to my ideas implications that are completely contrary to my stated goals?

Citizens, allow me a brief observation. Just as orators often resort to imagery in order to facilitate understanding among their listeners, so some of the latter

---

m The French text has *tribunal*. This must be a misspelling, since Sieyès is clearly referring to the tribunal as the people's attorney.

have the habit of stopping at the level of images. The orator tries to make his subject more conspicuous by placing it under a magnifying glass. But it turns out that his listeners use the glass as a mere toy which consumes all their attention and ends up leading them astray.

I have compared the legislature to a court, and the two juries with the right of proposal (i.e., the government and the tribunate) to attorneys. I worry that instead of focusing on my arguments, some of your minds may be burdened by myriad incidental associations that perhaps stem from your experiences with judges and attorneys. I remain always mindful of a particular lecture on animal magnetism[n] that the gentlemen d'Espréménil and Bergasse[o] gave at the house of M. Messmer a few years before the Revolution. There were many women present, and I have too high an opinion of their natural intellect to believe that they were really unable to understand what was said there. The professor resorted to using a common image and compared something or other to the glass pane of a window. The audience had been nearly dead, but at the word 'window' they all slowly and earnestly turned to look at the windows of the room. Their spirit, empty until that moment, was suddenly revived as each listener thought of his own windows, and of associations between this image and many other ideas. No harm in that, to be sure. But from this moment, farewell silence and attention: there was not one woman who did not have twenty objections, twenty observations to make, each more remote from the topic than the previous one, all of them relating solely to the panes

n Franz Anton Mesmer (1734–1815) defended the thesis that human beings were affected by something analogous to electromagnetic forces. His theory was known as 'animal magnetism'. As early as 1784, a scientific commission set up by the French government (including among its members Lavoisier and Benjamin Franklin) declared Mesmerism inaccurate. Far from abandoning his theory, however, Mesmer emphasized its social and political applications. He claimed that the forces of animal magnetism could generate feelings of solidarity and enable selfless and socially beneficial action. Prominent revolutionaries like Lafayette were convinced by Mesmer. He survived the Terror and, in 1814, published a draft for a constitution of Switzerland, which gave special political importance to pedagogy and medicine. On Mesmerism, see Robert Darnton, *Mesmerism and the End of the Enlightenment in France*, (Boston, 1986).

o Nicolas Bergasse (1750–1832) was a French lawyer and a follower of Mesmer. He published a systematic study of Mesmerism entitled *Considérations sur le magnetisme animal* (The Hague, 1784). During the French Revolution, he helped reform the judicial system. Jean Jacques Espréménil (1746–1794), also a lawyer and member of the National Convention from 1789 to 1791, was a vocal defender of the monarchy. After the toppling of Louis XVI, he retreated to the countryside. He was tracked down during the rule of the welfare committee, and was executed by the guillotine in 1794.

and windows of their respective houses. There you see the danger of imagery ... Citizens, I know to whom I am speaking. I do not intend to insult you with my example, but merely to draw your attention to a source of misunderstanding that is all too common, here as elsewhere.

When I compare the legislature to a supreme court that judges between the proposals of the tribunate and those of the government, one should not be so absurd or unjust as to accuse me of wanting to create a parliamentary court, of wanting to advocate yet more attorneys—as though there were not already enough of them—, or of wanting to introduce judicial bickering and passions into the legislative process. "But you pit two attorneys against one another and then provoke them! Will they not divide the nation into two camps, just as we have seen whole cities divided over certain trials?" But certainly it is not fair to blame an illness on the man trying to cure it. If my proposal is of no use, do not use it. But will the problems I have identified cease to exist?

The presence of two parties similar or analogous to those that are elsewhere called the governing party and the opposition party is an integral component of any type of representative system. In fact, they are found everywhere, regardless of the form of government. Perhaps they are likely to develop too much passion when combined into a single assembly. They will shine more and be less dangerous in the deliberative assemblies of a truly free republic. When two parties make full use of their right to speak and to write, they will come to resemble opponents in a state of nature, as long as they have no recognized superior. But as soon as there is an authority competent to adjudicate between them, both are reduced to the roles of mere attorneys. What? The idea of a tribunal charged with ending the discussions at the instant when they cease to yield insight, and when they threaten to devolve into hostilities, is supposed to bring about those very disputes? The common experience of all human associations, that there is need for a judge to adjudicate quarrels between individuals, does not convince you that it is sensible and prudent to apply in the sphere of politics an instrument so universal and necessary in the civil sphere? When a plaintiff demands redress from another citizen or from the law for some injustice, does it matter whether his complaint takes place *under* the law—as in civil disputes—or is directed *against* the law—as in political disputes? Does it matter whether he is attempting to reform the public will, or merely to alter some individual will? Despite their superficial differences, these acts bear the same essential character. Cannot lawyers and advocates, whether they lodge their complaints in writing or whether they plead directly before the legislative or adjudicative court, submit without worry or humiliation to a natural course of affairs that common sense everywhere ratifies as the only suitable way of redressing wrongs, investigating claims, and administering justice? Citizens, are these the sorts of ideas that are likely to create or perpetuate partisanship, or to make it more dangerous?

What is more, the simile has limits. I need to add this even though the divergences all work in my favor. In court proceedings, independently of the two sides' attorneys, there exist the two parties themselves with distinct and sometimes opposed interests, which on occasion lead to violent hatred. There is a simultaneous presence of two enemies. But on the public stage, there are no combatants or enemies: only the attorneys themselves. And experience teaches that we need not fear that the latter will be unable to come to an agreement when necessary; there is after all only one party, the people. For whom, after all, do all the orators, the writers, the government as well as the tribunate plead? For the people. During these contests, it is in the people's best interest to listen by turns to these rival parties, who debate in more or less good faith. A successful landowner is wise enough to listen to both his steward and his counsel before reaching a decision.

A government is not a public forum, but rather an institution from which the public is excluded. But it makes itself heard in writing, and it is good and useful and just that it should be heard. Like the tribunate, it speaks in the name of the people. It has an equal right of proposal; and in response to the worry that it cannot effectively execute the laws, it should suffice to recall that nobody possesses greater competence in this respect than those who conduct the government. It is false to assume that the government is intent on making things more difficult. After all, there are rivals waiting eagerly to prove themselves more competent, and to replace sitting officials. The constitutional apparatus quietly and almost imperceptibly brings about this sort of renewal when necessary. This is not the place to further elaborate on this point. I am also aware that it is time for me to conclude.

The considerations that I have presented to you do not pretend to complete the task of designing the legislative process. I have passed over the question of the promulgation of laws, which has been unduly neglected in all previous constitutional proposals, and also over the mode of electing the government, about which perhaps only future experience will yield a consensus.

Let me now present you four articles that I ask you to submit to the Committee of Eleven, unless you plan to move directly to the agenda.

First Article

There will be a body of representatives, called the tribunate, whose membership is to be three times the number of departments. Its specific task is to attend to the needs of the people and to propose to the legislature any law, regulation, or measure it deems useful. Its meetings will be public.

Second Article

There will be a body of representatives, called the government, numbering seven members, which will attend to the needs of the people and to the need for implementing the law, and to propose to the legislature any law, regulation, or measure it deems useful.

Its meetings will not be public.

Third Article

There will be a body of representatives, called the legislature, whose membership will be nine times the number of departments. Its specific task is to assess and pronounce upon the proposals made by the tribunate and the government. Its judgments, prior to promulgation, will be called resolutions (*décrets*).

Fourth Article

There will be a body of representatives, called the constitutional court (*jurie constitutionnaire*), numbering three twentieth of the legislature. Its specific task is to assess and judge complaints to the effect that some legislative resolution violates the constitution.

Note. Should these articles be adopted, it would be quite simple to complete them by enacting regulations regarding nominations, functions, renewals, etc., and to add several articles concerning the execution of the law.

CHAPTER 6

The Opinion of Sieyès Concerning the Tasks and Organization of the Constitutional Jury, Submitted on the Second Thermidor [Second Thermidorian Intervention]

Read before the Convention on the Eighteenth of the Same Month in the Third Year of the Republic. Printed by Order of the Convention

I would like to explain to you again the last of the four proposals that I presented on the Second of this month,[a] concerning the establishment of a Constitutional Jury.[b] I have discussed various aspects of my proposal with the Committee of Eleven, to whom you referred me and who have been occupied with my work for several days now. The Committee welcomes the establishment of such an institution. I therefore thought it useful to present my proposal to the Committee in fuller detail. Not all my ideas were accepted: the Committee limited itself to the sections I have already announced and for which the need is most evident. Nevertheless, the Committee wishes that I present to you my original proposal in its entirety. I will try to do this as concisely as possible.

I admit that I am reluctant to detach the part of my plan that the Committee wants to accept from its proper context. It is my view that no aspect of the

---

a Sieyès's proposal was submitted on the Second Thermidor (July 20) of 1795. See text 5 ('First Thermidorian Intervention'). The communication here reproduced took place on the Eighteenth Thermidor (August 5).

b There are several possible renderings of the term *jury constitutionnaire*: 'constitutional council,' 'constitutional committee,' or 'constitutional tribunal.' Contemporary usage suggests the term 'constitutional court.' This translation retains the word 'jury,' since it carried special significance for Sieyès. He associates juries with trials, which he in turn connected with both the idea of the separation of powers and the concept of popular sovereignty. The adjective *constitutionnaire* is intermediate between *pouvoir constituant* and *pouvoir constitué*. Sieyès deliberately avoids the term *jury constitutionnel* since his jury, although a constitutionally established institution (*constitué*), serves as a constitutional legislator (*constituant*). 'Constitutionary Jury' may therefore be the most faithful English translation, but 'Constitutional Jury' is better established in the secondary literature.

 | DOI: 10.1163/9789004273993_008

social mechanism (*la mécanique sociale*)[c] should be left to chance, and that the proper place of each part is determined by its position in the overall institutional structure, which cannot be changed at will.

But even if the Constitutional Jury, as an isolated element, will no longer enjoy quite the same harmonious fit with respect to the other institutions and may consequently lose some of its effectiveness, it can still play a useful part in your plans. This is what my most recent work has been aimed at. The current political situation has encouraged me to leave unaltered the full powers I originally assigned to the Jury, especially the second one, the right to improve the constitution piece by piece. In these times especially, do we not have an acute need for such a means of improvement, which functions almost imperceptibly but nevertheless effectively, in accordance with our increasing enlightenment and growing experience? (I am not referring to revolutionary upheavals, whose prevention is not the task of our Jury.) It is, in other words, a procedure of improvement that accords with fundamental political principles but suits the needs and character of the French people as well.

A preliminary question concerns the need for such a Constitutional Jury. Would a provident legislator abandon a constitution to uphold itself from the moment when it is born? If it is anything at all, a constitution is a body of binding laws—and if it is that, one can reasonably ask who will guard it and who will be the judge of this legal code. We will have to give an answer to this question. To remain silent on such a fundamental matter would be both inconceivable and ridiculous in the social sphere, so why would you tolerate it in the political sphere? Whatever their character, laws admit of being broken, and therefore must be enforceable.

I therefore allow myself to ask you, Whom have you chosen to receive complaints concerning violations of the constitution? Whom have you charged with enforcing the law? Are the civil courts to exercise this eminent role? Remember the prudent directive that prohibits judges from removing administrators for bad performance. How much more should we withhold from judges the power to remove the highest political officeholders (*les premiers corps politiques*)?

To treat the constitution as another part of the civil code would be fundamentally misguided. You are not given to such errors of judgment, and

c Sieyès uses mechanical metaphors to describe the artificial, constructed 'body' of the state, which belongs to the sphere of the *organisation sociale* and is thus an object of political science. By contrast, he draws on organicist metaphors to characterize society itself as an *organisme social*, which is the object of sociology.

accordingly it would be a waste of time to cite more arguments demonstrating the need for some organ of constitutional control.

Let me therefore move on to the truly difficult point: which tasks will we assign to the Constitutional Jury? What will be the extent of its powers, and where exactly are its limits to be drawn?—I expect three things from the Constitutional Jury: (1) that it faithfully watch over the integrity of the constitutional provisions (*dépot constitutionnel*); (2) that it calmly consider proposals for improving the constitution; and (3) that in cases of grave inequity, where the law has failed in its protective function,[d] it offer citizens a means of recourse in the service of civic liberty. In other words, I regard the Constitutional Jury (1) as a court of appeals within the constitutional order; (2) as a committee for considering constitutional amendments; and (3) as a supplement of natural jurisdiction when there are gaps in positive jurisdiction. Let me now further explain these different aspects.

To begin, we should distinguish between two types of constitutional violations: one committed by subordinate officials (*actes responsables*), the other by independent officials. Violations by subordinates can be addressed by ordinary courts, and therefore do not fall under the purview of the Constitutional Jury.

There are different sorts of independent officials. When they overstep the bounds of the authority with which they have been entrusted, or fail to conform to the regulations to which they are subject, they violate the constitution. Such an event can be very serious, and may indeed endanger the entire political order. Who will point out these transgressions,[1] these abuses of assigned powers? Who will prevent or at least remedy acts motivated by ambition, intrigue, or delusion? Surrounded by discretionary institutions (*institutions irréspons-ables*), do you not anticipate the need to be able to restrain those political agents who would otherwise step outside their assigned positions?

To develop this a little further, allow me to enumerate in more detail the classes of persons who may attempt to violate the constitution. It can only be useful to be aware of all the directions from which an attack may come.

I will begin with the simple citizens. When a citizen violates the constitution, his act is an offence. He is personally responsible and may be tried by regular courts. In such cases, the Constitutional Jury need not become involved.

1 I prefer this term (*excédence*) to the term *excession*. There are already many words that have the meaningless ending "ion," and their too-frequent use is tiring to the ear.

d Sieyès's literal term here is "*loi tutélaire*," or tutelary law. However, his focus seems to be the protective function of the law, rather than its paternalistic character.

Subordinate officials, too, may act in violation of the constitution while exercising their functions. They can do so in two different ways—either by abusing power within the scope of their jurisdiction, or by overstepping their jurisdictional bounds altogether. I am not asking about the more or less serious consequences of such abuses of office, nor am I concerned with motives, which may be quotidian or even well-meaning. None of this matters, since what is at issue is solely the guilt incurred through the violation of the constitution.

Citizens—take note of the enormous difference between the public official and the simple citizen in this respect, even though both are held personally responsible. The citizen is free in all actions not explicitly constrained by the law. He is culpable only for what he does *contrary* to the law. The public official, by contrast, is culpable not only when he acts against the law, but when he acts in any way that is not explicitly authorized by the law. This is because the citizen's existence and rights belong to him by nature, and the law serves only to protect them; whereas the public official has existence and a capacity to act only as a legal creature. Any extralegal act on the part of the latter is a usurpation of power and a true offence.

Whatever the nature of the official's offence, there should be ordinary judges to try him just like the simple citizen. (Let me add in passing that the highest court should not adjudicate political matters.) Thus, we still do not find here anything that might occupy a Constitutional Jury. In this respect, the constitution already has a sufficient safeguard in the form of regular courts.

Let us now take a closer look at those officials who have been, or should be, declared independent. Here is not the place to justify the need for this prerogative, or rather this quality, which is inseparable from the specific functions of various public offices. In order to be clear, let me enumerate them one by one. Among the independent offices are: the office of elector (*missions électorales*); most importantly, the office of constitutional legislation (*mission constituante*); the Constitutional Jury, which is my topic here; the assembly charged with representing the national will and with passing laws, the great regulator of society; assemblies that gather and deliberate about legislative proposals and bills; and finally, the constitutionally specified organs of promulgation.

This list is not exhaustive. Within the judiciary, judges and jurors are also independent. This is unsurprising, since there are important parallels between the office of a judge and that of a legislator. When the latter passes a general law, he has given thought to all the particular cases which it covers. He would not know or understand what he was doing, he would not be able to articulate a general rule, or only a false one, if he had not first applied to the particular cases the same acts of judgment that the judge will later only repeat, taking into consideration relevant particular circumstances. Both activities are of the same sort. Jurisdiction can be thought of as legislation for the individual case. It is therefore natural that a certain correspondence has been found between the two: judges are seen as independent representatives, and the principle of the division of powers has been invoked in separating the respective functions of judges and jurors.

My point, to which I hasten to return, is that this last class of independent officials, judges and jurors, is not an appropriate subject area for the Constitutional Jury either. The reason is the same as before. The unconstitutional acts of judges and jurors already have natural limits: jurors who attempt to overstep their authority are limited by judges, and both groups are limited by courts of appeal. No further action is needed to protect the constitution. I will not dwell on the lower ranks of the administration, where we would encounter further independent officials, for example in the sphere of public education. I must stop my investigation at this point, lest it become fruitless.

It remains to suggest the proper scope of the Constitutional Jury's jurisdiction:

(1) Unconstitutional acts of the members of the Council of Five Hundred and the Council of the Elders, acting as independent officials (*personellement irresponsables*). I add the latter qualification because anything outside this category—for example, acts of treason—is subject to ordinary judges and sentences. We do not seek to heal what is not ill.

The problems—rather, I should say, the real dangers—that emanate from the extraconstitutional or unconstitutional acts of these two assemblies should not be dismissed as chimerical. After all, these councils are composed of mere humans, and the positions they occupy inevitably give rise to passions and intrigues. Thus, it should not be difficult to accept my proposal on this point.

I propose (2) that violations of electoral regulations also fall within the scope of the Constitutional Jury. Its jurisdiction should extend to the level of primary assemblies, since they act as the trustees of the nation. This is a well-established principle, even if it appears novel: all that belongs to the discretionary exercise of primary rights should, precisely in the interest of the fullest liberty of those exercising those rights, be subject to a constitutionally established conciliatory authority for the event when disagreements arise.

It is of the greatest importance that the constitution be faithfully observed both in the primary assemblies and in simple elections. This holds wherever there is a discretionary exercise of political rights. It would be wishful thinking to assume that laws can survive without a safeguard, resting only on good will. The law whose observance is founded on nothing but good will is like a house built on the shoulders of its inhabitants. I need not explain what will sooner or later happen to this house.

I have now outlined the nature and limits of the first function that I assign to the Constitutional Jury. We must now consider who should be able to bring appeals before this court. I believe that the general right to appeal should be given both to the Council of Five Hundred and to the Council of Elders. Especially, they should have this right against each other, in case there are reciprocal interferences. They should also have this right in case there are internal disagreements between the majority and the minority, since, in truth, you have not adequately protected these assemblies against this danger. The Constitutional Jury can therefore serve as a force to prevent or remove disturbances threatening the political order, and to end stalemates that are deadly to public administration.

Should you grant the right of appeal to the primary and electoral assemblies? Here as elsewhere, disputes can arise about the proper interpretation and application of the law. You should quickly settle the question of who is constitutionally authorized to make binding decisions in this regard. Otherwise you will regret to see this question settled by force, at the cost of the common good and due to your own negligence.

I have already said it, but it bears repeating: those who see no need to establish an authoritative arbiter in political and constitutional matters—an institution that has long been entrenched in other areas of society—fail to recognize that they are hindering the natural development of the social order. Afraid of altogether assimilating it to the legal order, they in fact keep it in several respects in the brute condition of a state of nature.

Recall the dreary mass of more than three hundred different legal customs which until recently governed the French territory and which entered even into the jurisdiction of the higher courts. Do you want each part of our great and indivisible nation to develop its own constitutional jurisprudence, by refusing to acknowledge that the certainty and uniformity of the constitutional laws is even more essential to political stability than the uniformity of ordinary laws?

At the same time, electoral assemblies should at all costs be prevented from remaining in session beyond the designated period, and from transcending the authority given to them. We should also prevent the primary assemblies from being permanently in session. Their right of appeal can be exercised instead by the representatives of the two Councils. Moreover, we will soon consider the rights of individual citizens.

When the executive officials, or indeed any subordinate officials, or even those independent officials who, as I have explained, do not fall under the purview of the Constitutional Jury, resent the fact that they have no right of appeal, we reply to them, Do you have grievances that might be properly reviewed by a Constitutional Jury? According to my proposal, you should turn to your natural representative, the government, and according to the Committee's plan, you should turn to one of the two Councils.

Given that the executive consists of subordinate officials, it may seem difficult to decide whether it should have a right of appealing to the Constitutional Jury. My proposal eliminates this difficulty, by assigning a completely novel sort of role to the government.

As for simple citizens, it may appear at first glance that the right of appeal should be withheld from them too, and for the same reasons. They can petition one or the other of the Councils; they also have freedom of the press, and so on. But individual liberty should be limited only when a right is harmful, not when it merely seems useless. I agree that we should give to public officials only those rights that are necessary; but the liberty of individual citizens, I repeat, should extend as far as possible, so long as it does not have harmful consequences. Thus, if citizens believe that their freedom is increased by the right of appeal, no further reason is needed for granting it. We should pay this solemn tribute to individual liberty: after all, it is for the sake of this liberty that the political order exists in the first place. I often hear people speak of the final cause of the world, and all that it encompasses. One should speak rather of the final cause of the social world, which is the freedom of the individual.

In order to forestall abuses, there is one condition to which I tie this right, which we accord to each French citizen. I am not aiming to save the judges' work; I merely want to prevent the excessive zeal of some appellants from being detrimental to the freedom of the others. The condition, or rather limitation, consists in a fine to be paid for appeals that the Constitutional Jury finds unfounded.

The only further point I would like to add is that the Constitutional Jury must not be allowed to act on its own initiative, since this would make its influence on the other political institutions (*les parties de l'établissement public*) too great.

Let me now move on to the second question. We have considered the constitutional guardian as a court of appeals, designed to maintain [legal and political] order. We will now consider it as a jury of proposition, which collects ideas for the continued improvement of the constitution. Instead of your plan for constitutional revision (which you have not yet passed), I submit the following procedure. The constitution of a people would be imperfect unless it contained within itself a principle of conservation and of life, like every organism (*être organisé*). But should one therefore compare a constitution to an individual who is born, grows, declines, and dies? I do not think so. Should one instead compare it to a species, and thus to a chain of successively existing individuals? I do not believe that either.

Like any organism, the constitution must be able to assimilate the materials needed for its proper development. We must therefore allow it to continually draw on the knowledge and experience of the past so that it can meet the needs of the present. Its true nature lies in its capacity for increasing perfection, not in periodic recreation.

Once a constitution has been placed on a reliable foundation, it should no longer be exposed to moments of complete renewal. It is not up to us to say to our constitution, "You shall convoke at fixed intervals, and you shall solemnly declare those moments to be signals of your impending destruction." Some like to claim that a constitution, like a phoenix, can rise from its own ashes. In fact, the rebirth of a phoenix is a chimera; the periodic return of a constitutional convention is a calamity.

Without abrogating the right of future generations to choose their own political order, we are permitted—indeed obliged—to note that the true subject of a political constitution is the nation that endures, rather than a passing generation, and the needs of human nature, which is common to all, rather than individuals with all their differences. It follows that (as I have said) our constitution should be guided by a principle of unlimited perfectibility, which makes it adaptable to the needs of different eras, rather than a principle of destruction by total revision, which leaves it at the mercy of contingent events.

As time is short, let me get straight to the point. In my view, the Constitutional Jury should not have the right to modify the constitution of its own initiative, since that would amount to a constituent power. It should not even have the right to make proposals. But in the remote future the constituent activity will be divided among the primary assemblies, the Constitutional Jury, and the legislature.

You would be rightly worried by a proposal that made constituent power permanent. One might just as well have no constitution at all: along with stability, it would lose all those sentiments of love and veneration that a free people devote to it, since those sentiments are incompatible with the versatility that would follow from such an arrangement. More than any other law, the constitution must have a certain immutability. One almost wishes that it had the grand and terrible permanence of the laws governing the universe itself, if only human industry were as skilled and powerful as the eternal artisan (*mécanicien éternel*) who imposed order onto nature. But a work of human hands needs to remain open to the progress of reason and experience.

On the one hand, a permanent constituent power or even just a permanent right of proposal would weaken and indeed undo all the benefits of a constitution. On the other hand, to prevent all change would be to deprive ourselves of the insights that develop over time. This could lead to an unfortunate situation in which we cannot repair oversights in a constitution; and in cases where necessary provisions are missing, we may even be unable to defend our liberty and our descendants' liberty from the intrigues of our enemies.

But in a large nation that is so passionate and lively, where each disturbance can lead to greater harm, is it not dangerous to convoke constituent assemblies, even ceremoniously, at appointed intervals? No matter what we call them these assemblies, which in my proposal are not subject to a division of powers, desire the change of the constitution just as much as the Constitutional Jury desires its conservation. To ask the obvious question, Would this not deliver France to regular unrest and incalculable harm?

Compare these extremes with the mode of revision to be followed by the Constitutional Jury. Every ten years, beginning at the end of this century, in 1800, the Constitutional Jury will publish a collection of proposals for improving the constitution. This collection will be selective: it will present only the best ideas from the preceding decade's proposals. At least three months before the primary assemblies convene, this collection will be submitted to the two legislative chambers and disseminated publicly. The legislative assemblies need not further occupy themselves with it, since they do not have constituent power.

The task of engaging with these proposals falls on the primary assemblies, which convene each year to elect the popular representatives. They must vote *yes* or *no* on the question of whether to temporarily cede part of their constituent power to the legislature. If the majority votes *no*, the revision will be placed on hold for the coming ten years. If they vote *yes*, the legislature, now invested with constituent power, will evaluate the submitted proposals, but will not be able to edit or replace them. It may reject some or all of them, but it will have to cite reasons for doing so.

I cannot think of a simpler procedure for constitutional reform: none that would be better suited to reflect the will of the people without either excluding enlightened wisdom or succumbing to [democratic] illusions; none whose execution would present fewer difficulties; none more likely to inspire philanthropic hope and to assuage grievances; none, finally, that would be more in keeping with our strict principle of the division of powers.

Thus we arrive at the third question, which I will briefly remind you about. We said that the Constitutional Jury should function as a source of natural justice, protecting civil liberties when the legislature neglects its protective role. The Jury supplements natural jurisdiction for lacunae in the positive law. It is sometimes necessary to invest judgments of natural equity with the same obligatory force that attaches to the judgments of ordinary courts. A special court should be established that can pass these judgments, and its members should be drawn from the Constitutional Jury.

Regarding the last point, let me note that this third task is not entrusted to the Constitutional Jury as such. Each year, the Jury will select by lot at least one tenth of its members to form a chamber concerned exclusively with cases of natural equity. I mention this organizational detail now only to set aside practical difficulties that do not properly belong to our subject matter here.

Who among you, citizens, has never witnessed a judge presented with a terrible choice between acquitting a guilty person or—even more painfully—punishing an innocent one, in order to avoid violating the law? Does not this situation—namely, a court forced into an arbitrary or unjust decision—demonstrate the insufficiency of [positive] legislation and the existence of legal gaps, which must be compensated for, since they cannot be simply eliminated?

What man possessed of a right mind and a tender heart did not feel regret when the right of granting pardon was abolished, because it was erroneously conflated with notions of royal prerogative? It is, in fact, the prerogative of an innocent man in danger of death because he is suspected of a crime, the last hope of a man whose misfortune is unparalleled in this world, the consolation of those who have a heart, and who are shaken and saddened to the core by the sight of a wrongly accused person. Now, given that this sort of misery is almost always the fault of the legislator (or, if you prefer, the consequence of his oversight), and considering that the legislator, according to his true intentions, would not apply the law in this case, even though the judge must apply it according to the legislator's ostensible intentions—seeing human liberty endangered in this way, how could one decline to meet my request and remedy all this by appointing a judge of natural equity? If pardoning is a duty, then a right to pardon is necessary. Given that it *is* a duty, it should have another name—it is not an act of mercy, but of justice.

More fundamentally, consider the first and most important of all social principles, individual freedom. My aim is not to move or seduce you: let us reason in a rigorous way. Tell me, Can a man call himself free if he has no recourse when his rights have been violated? You will tell me that the answer is "no."

To be free, a man must be able to take recourse to a judge; he must always be able to find a law that applies to the case he wishes to present—for we are supposing that he has indeed suffered injustice. Who could doubt that this is so?

Even if you were to regard your legislation as perfect (and what an assumption that would be!)—would you claim that you have foreseen or are even capable of foreseeing all the cases and all the complications for which the law should supply a remedy? Reality is in this respect more fertile than the mind of the legislator, and will produce much that has not occurred to him. A political society that thinks itself free and enlightened must therefore establish some source of purely natural jurisdiction, both for smaller offences and for real crimes, in order to allow for legitimate defenses in cases in which the positive law has failed.

You will ask me why I do not simply demand a new positive law. True, this might be a sensible request. But try as he might, a legislator will always have to classify offences in general categories, and he simply cannot account for all their detailed differences. On the other hand, one frequently hears the complaint that there are too many laws. There is an element of truth in this common view, but also a certain degree of falsity and triviality. The needs of society always exceed the capabilities of the legislator—and, for that matter, his obligations. Both considerations lead us to compensate for the gap that arises from what legislation is not required to do and, indeed, cannot do.

Why do I not ask for a positive law? Well then, let us ask for one. But you are well aware that a positive law does not have retroactive force. Once it is passed, it is too late for it to be used to address the problem that prompted its making. If, however, natural law makes its voice heard, if it offers consolation to the unfortunate one and a good example to society, you will not accuse it of operating retroactively. Natural law is timeless: it was promulgated at the beginning of the world, and was written into human nature itself as an indelible sense of justice and injustice.

Let us complete and perfect ordinary civil jurisdiction. Because of it individuals experience the gift of liberty, which consists in being secure in the enjoyment of one's rights. Legislators have not always tried to fulfill this supreme duty, be it from ignorance, negligence, or out of deference to the errors and prejudices of their times. Nowhere have all rights been equally protected by the law. You yourselves have recognized some grave errors of all prior legislation, and our descendants will discover yet more. They will at least have to acknowledge our sincere efforts; they will be indebted to us for finally establishing a court of human rights (*tribunal des droits de l'homme*): for this is the proper name for the moral and political instrument that I propose to you, since all of it refers to the rights of man.

If such a court had existed in the first political societies, the most evident rights of man would not have remained unappreciated for so long, nor have been trampled on and turned against liberty itself. Since the great natural law of what is just and unjust always holds the answer that sometimes fails to come from positive law, let us not permit that, after having prepared the ground for individual liberty so well, there should remain even a single inch exposed to the insults of arbitrary power.

What, after all, do we demand when we ask for carefully selected judges, devoted exclusively to the principles of natural equity? Certainly nothing that offends against our principles. Is not the legislator himself a judge in matters of natural justice? Do not his general decisions appeal to the same code that I propose as a source of guidance in some particular decisions?

To be sure, we must take seriously the danger of arbitrary jurisdiction, and resist it. But is this danger any less real for the legislator himself? You yourselves have already overcome it. Both the legislature and the court that I here propose are restrained by a separation of powers, and hence will not slip into arbitrariness.

Allow me to dwell for a moment on this notion of arbitrariness. It has two senses, which need to be distinguished from one another. As an exercise of unfettered, lawless and unprincipled power—the first sense—arbitrariness is abhorrent, and I accept it no more than you do. May it remain forever banished from our social relations. But if you call 'arbitrary' a decision of equity which the legislator has not foreseen but which, with fuller knowledge, he would in the future write into law, the term should not be applied in a derogatory way. Here we have a useful and respectable practice, and nothing is less arbitrary than this.

The proper precaution consists in withholding the right of initiative from the chamber of the Constitutional Jury charged with enforcing natural equity. It can only be activated by formal requests from outside. The right to make such requests will not be available to everyone, but only to courts, which therefore will not be able to complain that their own functions are being interfered with by an alien will. They, in turn, cannot issue their requests informally and without a clear rationale, but only in cases of a recognized need, which the legislature must characterize in a general fashion.

These, citizens, are the three functions that comprise my idea of a Constitutional Jury. In its first two functions the Jury is subservient to the constitution; in its third function, to the rights of man. It remains to explain how it will be composed, and how it will recruit its members.

The frequency of appointments and the apportionment of the exiting members in each period corresponds to what I have already said about the two Councils. With regard to the mode and prerequisites of election there are some differences. I suggest that one-third of the members of the Constitutional Jury vacates their seats each year, to be replaced from among the exiting members of the Council of Elders and the Council of Five Hundred by election. This provision has the following rationale: a juror should not only express his opinion with frankness and according to his conviction, but with another, no less essential quality: namely, with expert knowledge of the matters on which he must decide. I have never thought of the notions of juror and expert as separable, and indeed this is how I conceived of the role of juror in the plan I offered in 1790.

The Constitutional Jury is to be composed of one hundred and eight members, of which one third—that is, thirty-six—are replaced each year. These thirty-six new members will be selected by the Jury itself from among the two hundred fifty representatives that exit from the two Councils each year. For the first set of jurors, the Convention will draw from the members of the constitutional and the legislative assemblies and from the Convention.[e]

Citizens: if you want this institution—the guarantor of all the other institutions' conformity with the constitution—to be respected by all, and especially by the two legislative chambers, you should ensure that these chambers take an interest in it. Accordingly, appointment to the Constitutional Jury at the end of a legislative career should be considered an object of aspiration, a visible honor granted in appreciation of the great responsibility assumed in the service to the nation. Can you not envision how many delegates will secretly desire this quite republican distinction? It will be the right way of promoting appetites and sentiments that are already present, but which are in danger of being corrupted if left under the sway of mere ambition, without further incentives or guidance.

Unless you grant the Constitutional Jury the right to select its own members, I do not see how you can permanently entrench in both Councils that deep respect for the constitution that must inform the views and actions of their members. What evils could arise from a contrary tendency!

In this way, the delegates of both Councils will regard members of the Constitutional Jury as men who were granted the trust of the people and who now occupy an office that, while not higher than their own, is still sought after by them or by the most respected among them. But it is impossible to foresee in detail all the various motives at play in such matters. Let it suffice to observe that on such a seemingly weak political institution will depend, to a large extent, the social harmony through which the different parts of the legislative process are held together.

---

e Sieyès is referring to the three parliaments of the French Revolution to this point. The constitutional assembly (*assemblée constituante*) was followed on October 1, 1791 by a legislative assembly (*assemblée legislative*). After the storming of the Tuileries on August 10, 1792, that assembly decreed the temporary suspension of the king and the convocation of a national convention (*assemblée conventionelle, convention nationale*), which was charged to draft a republican constitution. The first act of the convention was the abolition of the monarchy on September 20, 1792.

Here is my proposal in seventeen articles:

Title: Of the Constitutional Jury

First Article

There is a guardian and preserver of the constitution, called the Constitutional Jury.

II.

The Constitutional Jury is composed of one hundred eight members, of which one third are replaced each year at the same time when the legislative assemblies are renewed.

III.

This third (i.e., the thirty-six new members) is elected by the Constitutional Jury itself, from among the two hundred fifty members who exit from the two legislative assemblies at a specific time each year.

IV.[2]

The members of the first Constitutional Jury will be determined by the Convention in a secret election. One third of the new members will be elected from the constitutional assembly, one-third from the legislative assembly, and one-third from the Convention.

V.

The meetings of the Jury are not public.

VI.

The Constitutional Jury passes judgment on violations or attempted violations of the constitution by the Council of Elders, the Council of Five Hundred, the electoral assemblies, the primary assemblies, or the court of appeals.

Complaints to this effect may be brought forward by the Council of Elders, by the Council of Five Hundred, or by a citizen in his own name.

The Constitutional Jury will also assess complaints brought by the minority against the majority in one of the constituted bodies named here.

2 This Article should be passed into law separately.

VII.

The decisions of the Constitutional Jury are called *judgments* (*arrêt*).

VIII.

Acts that the Constitutional Jury declares unconstitutional are null and void.

IX.

In cases in which potentially unconstitutional acts are dependent acts, or are related to such acts, the Constitutional Jury can refer complaints to the relevant courts and order them to further investigate the matter, either before or after the Constitutional Jury has passed a judgment regarding constitutionality.

X.

The Constitutional Jury will recurrently consider those proposals to improve the constitution and the declaration of the rights of man that it deems promising. When a majority opinion has been formed, it will be recorded in a designated collection of proposals.

XI.

Once every ten years, beginning in 1800—the eighth year of the Republic and the twelfth of the Revolution—the Constitutional Jury will review the proposals it has collected. The Jury then draws up a constitutional reform bill which it officially submits to the Council of Elders and the Council of Five Hundred, so as to give it the widest possible publicity. This must take place no less than three months before the annual primary assemblies.

XII.

After considering the collected proposals, the primary assemblies will vote on whether to authorize the Council of Elders to decide on them, *yes* or *no*. If a majority in the primary assemblies votes *no*, the collection is void, and the proposals contained therein cannot be brought forward again until ten years have passed. If a majority in the primary assemblies votes *yes*, the constituent power is thereby transferred to the Council of Elders, which will decide on the proposals, without having the right to change or replace any of them.

XIII.

Sessions in which the Council of Elders exercises its constituent power will be devoted exclusively to this purpose. There shall not be more than a total of twelve such sessions, and at most two per decade.[f] Minutes will be taken at these sessions, which will be collected in a special register and solemnly deposited in the archives of the Constitutional Jury.

XIV.

Each year, no less than one tenth of the members of the Constitutional Jury, chosen by lot, will form a court of natural justice. In addition to exercising the two aforementioned powers, this section of the Jury alone will adjudicate official requests from various courts, which ask for a judgment of natural justice in cases that those courts are unable to decide—either for lack of applicable positive law, or on the grounds that the positive law would force them to decide against their conscience.

XV.

Judgments based on natural justice will be executed either by the petitioning court or by some other court, at the discretion of the Constitutional Jury.

XVI.

Judgments of natural justice will be communicated to the Council of Five Hundred within one month.

XVII.

The Constitutional Jury cannot pass judgments of its own initiative.

f This restriction is probably meant to prevent the concentration of *pouvoir constituant* in the hands of one individual constituted power.

CHAPTER 7

Constitutional Observations

Dictated during the last days of Brumaire of the year VIII to citizen Boulay [de la Meurthe],[a] a member of the legislative commission of 500, who has given them [these observations] to me after having them transcribed.[b] The constitution was written on the basis of these ideas; afterwards, it was adopted with apparent satisfaction, subsequently changed, repeatedly modified, and finally abolished.

First Observations

Pure democracy, even if it were possible, would be absurd. The representative system is far superior, since it alone allows for the enjoyment of true liberty and the improvement of the human race. Since democracy is the root of the representative system and the political institutions (*l'établissement public*), the government erected on that basis cannot resemble it; it is necessarily representative [of it]. A representative regime is not only required by the size of the territory; irrespective of this point, the people stand to gain a great deal from organizing their political institutions in a representative fashion.

Yet even the greatest partisans of pure democracy do not propose to extend it to the executive, administrative, or judiciary institutions. They ask for it only in the legislative branch. Our challenge is therefore to extend representation only to the legislative branch, for this is what distinguishes a representative regime from pure democracy. Under such a system, the citizen loses the right that he held against all his co-associates, and retains only the right *of an individual associate.*[c] Thus the individual citizen is no longer politically equal to the citizen-representative: this is the difference between the great mass and the individual. There are two kinds of representation: that which is invested in the individual representative, and that which is embodied by the assembly of

a Antoine Jacques Claude Joseph, comte Boulay de la Meurthe (1761–1840).

b In the original text, the following is crossed out: "Nothing is more incomplete and faulty than a hastily dictated sheet."

c This and subsequent italicized phrases were underlined in the original text.

 | DOI: 10.1163/9789004273993_009

which he is a member. The individual representative has the right to consider, petition, speak, and vote in the name of the represented. The representative body has the right to judge and decide.

Principles

Nobody should be invested with an office unless he enjoys the trust of those over whom he is meant to exercise authority. But in a representative government, further, no official should be appointed by those over whom he will exercise authority. Instead, he should be appointed by higher-ranking persons who represent the nation as a body. The people, as a subject of political activity, exists only at the level of national representation: it forms a body only at that level. The government is essentially national, not local. It arises from the national assembly, in which the people is represented, and not from the simple citizen. For the latter does not have the right to represent the people, nor to endow anyone with power in his own name.

Question

The question is this: How can one reconcile the principle that nobody may be invested with an office without the trust of those over whom it is to be exercised with the other principles I have named? The natural way to reconcile them is to revert to the lists of eligibles which the founders of liberty presented in 1789 and whose importance has not yet been appreciated. Public officials should thus be nominated by those who occupy a superior position on the lists presented by the governed. Under this system, the demand for obedience and discipline comes from a high authority, which is properly national.

The Mechanism of the Different Lists

If we assume that there are thirty million people in France, the group of citizens will be around six million. But if one establishes the correct rules, the *members of the political association* will amount to less than one million, even though no citizen is prevented from becoming one if he so wishes. The citizens of each commune will voluntarily select the ten percent whom they trust most, and this yields a first list, the so-called communal list. I am assuming that a commune will be at least thirty-six square leagues in size. Together, the communal lists will then contain the names of about 100,000 persons eligible for being invested with the public trust. Only those who are on the communal list can serve as officials in a commune.

The citizens who are on the communal list then select the most-trusted ten percent from amongst themselves: this yields a second list—the departmental list—which contains the names of departmental officials (around ten thousand). Ten percent of the citizens on each departmental list are then entered into the national list of around one thousand men. This final list will owe its status as a national list to a decision made further up the institutional hierarchy.

The Annual Revision or Recomposition of Those Various Lists

Each year, those who have died will be erased from the lists; those who have been sentenced will be also removed from them; and likewise will those who are no longer residents, as well as those who no longer enjoy the trust of the governed. A citizen who is no longer on the communal list will no longer have the right to occupy a public office. If he is also on a higher-level list, then whenever that list is next revised there will be a vote as to whether to retain his name on the list or not.

The Selection of National Officials

In order to select the national officials from the national list, we will establish two electoral agencies acting in the name of the people: one for the various parts of the legislative order, the other for the executive officials.

The first of the two electoral functions will be entrusted to a Conservatory College (*collège-conservateur*), which will be the highest magistracy of the constitution, and whose authority will extend to all the so-called "ascendant" functions, as well as to the further tasks that I will describe. This college will choose from the national list: (1) those who will form the Tribunal of Petition (with as many members as there are departments), and (2) those citizens who will form the legislature, of whom there should be 300. The members of the chamber of petition[d] can be drawn from the national list irrespective of origin, whereas there should be at least one legislator from each department.

d In the original text, the synonymous term "popular tribune" is crossed out.

Electoral Executive Power

As part of the executive order, this power will have several important tasks, although none of them will give it the right to carry out, by itself, any executive acts.

The electoral executive power will appoint two consuls to head the government: one for domestic affairs, and one for foreign affairs. The administration of foreign affairs will be divided among four ministers and their four respective departments, responsible for: (1) relations with other governments, (2) the army, (3) the navy, and (4) the colonies.

The consul for domestic affairs will oversee the police, the judicial system, the domestic life properly speaking, the departmental services and half of the fiscal authority.

The State Council,[e] the ministers, and the grand tribunals of political justice will be at the disposal of the consuls. The State Council for domestic affairs will have four main tasks:

(1) to present legislative proposals to the legislative body; in this respect, the State Council stands face to face with the tribunal of popular petition, and has the power to veto proposals made to that tribunal.
(2) to function as a jury of execution for already-passed laws, when ministers ask for an interpretation or a confirmation of a contested directive;
(3) to issue regulations that are binding on officials and public employees (as opposed to laws, which are binding on citizens). These regulations are distinct from ministerial directives, and must not be in the hands of the ministers alone. In this respect, the State Council acts as a *legislature of regulations*.
(4) to adjudicate grievances concerning the ministers, from subordinate officials or citizens; but only when those grievances relate solely to administrative matters, since the Council must not usurp the judicial functions of the political tribunal.

The consul in charge of foreign affairs will also have a State Council, albeit a simpler, smaller, and more secret one. It will have the power to propose laws, issue regulations, make decisions as an executive jury,[f] and adjudicate

e On the "Conseil d'État" see Pierre-Yves Quiviger, *Le principe d'immanence. Métaphysique et droit administratif chez Sieyès. Avec des textes inédits de Sieyès* (Paris, 2008), pp. 214ff. and pp. 329ff.

f The original text has "jury of instruction" crossed out.

grievances concerning the ministers. The two consuls will be presidents of their respective State Councils.

The second means of government available to the Consuls are the ministers who exercise executive power properly speaking.

Each minister will be the sole chief of his department, for, as a general rule, where there is execution there cannot be deliberation. Each minister will have, for his department, a disciplinary council to which he may take his subordinates if they make mistakes. Each minister will delegate some of his authority to subordinate agents, divided into two classes: the first encompasses delegates at the departmental level, charged with the transmission of directives, supervision, administration, and ministerial decision processes; the second encompasses agents at the local or communal level, responsible for the official execution of policies within the communes. The real work of administration and the real administrators will be found at the level of the communes. The purpose of the departmental offices is merely to *transmit*, be it in a descending or in an ascending direction.

The third means of government available to the Consuls are the *Chambers of Justice*, which should not be confused with the tribunals of justice, for it does not *govern* the citizens at all, only the public officials. With respect to the Conservatory College, there will be a High Court (which will meet only intermittently to deal with offenses committed by ministers), State Counselors, and judges in their official functions. The Chamber of Justice, on the other hand, will be permanent, and its jurisdiction will extend to all offenses committed by members of the government in their official functions. This court, which deals with the entire executive branch, will be at the same level as the ministries.

Development of Executive Power as Separate from the Government

As you can see, executive power belongs neither to the electorate nor to the consuls, but is exclusively in the hands of the ministers, with the exception of the State Council.[g] This is how the division of powers should be conceived: from top to bottom according to their natural sequence, so that no link in the chain can be removed from its place.

The ministers are properly speaking the procurers of public service. There are fourteen of them:

g Originally, the text had a plural here ("to the State Councils").

The first is responsible for general subdelegation (*sub-légation*);[h]
the second for public instruction;
the third for public property;
the fourth for national insurance.

These four ministers form the domestic *superintendency*.

The fifth is responsible for the civil and rural police;
the sixth for the tutelary police;
the seventh for judicial prosecution;
the eighth for law enforcement.

These four ministers form the national *magistrature*.

The ninth is responsible for the army;
the tenth for the command of the navy;
the eleventh for diplomacy and foreign affairs;
the twelfth for the French colonies.

These four ministers form the superintendency of foreign affairs.

The thirteenth is responsible for the assessment and collection of taxes;
the fourteenth is responsible for the public treasury.

These two ministers form the superintendency of finance.

Since we want the Conservatory College to have the greatest possible means for protecting the free exercise of political rights, we will establish two further agencies alongside it: (1) one to correspond with the military; (2) another in charge of political rights. Further, we will establish (3) a chamber of accounts; and (4) we also need to take some influence on the power of the purse. The authority that distributes [funds] must not be the same as the one that collects taxes, or the one that classifies them.

---

h Sieyès struck out the prefix "dé" from "subdélégation," thereby emphasizing the meaning of legislation over delegation.

The Organization of the Conservatory College

This college does not belong to the executive branch, nor is it part of the government, nor of the legislative branch. Instead, since a constitutional magistrate is necessary, it serves as a regulative agency between the major independent public agencies.

The preservation of social order is guaranteed by the political institutions. The preservation of civil liberty vis-à-vis the political institutions is guaranteed through a proper division of powers. And the preservation of these powers vis-à-vis one another is guaranteed by the Conservatory College. In all states that are sufficiently well constituted to maintain themselves in existence, there is within the institutional structure—more specifically, at the top of this structure—a moral authority that, through its influence on customs, ideas and even fashion, holds all the particular movements in check and forestalls the excesses of unrestrained ambition.

In monarchies, this includes the monarch, the princes of blood, and the grand officers of the crown. In the ancient republics, it was a hereditary aristocracy.[i] But after removing the deceitful scaffolding that had been attached to a certain type of public service by the needs of the age, we now require a different means of rendering this service. Without it, a national need will go unmet, and the public order will suffer.

We will entrust to the Conservatory College this great influence on customs, virtues, services, names, and even property.

First of all it is necessary that its existence should be independent from that of the other public agencies, for it must not arouse even the least suspicion of collaborating with any of them to overturn the established order (since the interest of the whole [national] body and of each of its members must obviously be the conservation of what already exists). This college will be composed of at least one hundred seats, assigned by territory. A rent of 90,000[j] £ [= livres] will belong to each seat.

Some will say that this amounts to an oligarchy. I would respond that this is the only way to curtail the natural oligarchy of wealth that exists in any large and rich republic. It is the only way to reduce the old aristocratic influence, and to completely align it with the republic.[k] One fifth of the seats in the College should always be left vacant, so that it is always possible to nominate new

i The following was deleted in the original text: "We do not want any of that."

j The original figure was 100,000 £. It was exchanged for 90,000 £ by Sieyès.

k The following was deleted in the original text: "The territorial basis of the Conservatory

candidates from one day to the next, and so that there always remain sufficient funds to pay the common expenses of the institution. The majority of these expenses will come from the judicial officers.[1]

The College will appoint candidates to its vacant seats. The seats will be held for life. Appointment to one of the seats will result in the candidate's immediate resignation from any and all other public offices. An appointee will be guilty of high treason if he continues to exercise his former authority, as are those who continue to recognize his authority. He will be *absorbed* [into his new office].

Appointment to the College thus replaces whatever good there may have been in the ancient institution of ostracism. Absorption is preferable to ostracism. Members of the Conservatory College (*les conservateurs*) are inviolable in the exercise of their office. The further properties of the Conservatory College were laid out in my speech to the Convention concerning the establishment of a Constitutional Jury.

The Grand Elector

He is not a king: for if he were, he would have subjects. Government and the execution of laws take place in his name; officials are accountable to him and are supervised by him, but he does not govern. A stamp proves his signature. He is not a public official (*point responsable*). He represents the majesty of the people, both within and without, and since the people itself does not exercise any executive authority, neither does he. He is represented by his ministers. He sets the executive machine in motion and gives it unity. Independent—above the particular passions and interests of the parties—he will choose and dismiss the government, the ministers, etc., guided solely by his reason and by public opinion (properly understood). By his mere existence he prevents or neutralizes any dangerous ambitions on the part of the government or any other citizens.

College's members should be formed by a radius (about 30 to 40 leagues) around a central town, since it is important that member's political and constitutional influence should be felt in the vicinity of that town."

1 The following was deleted in the original text: "and could serve at the respective residence of the members of the Conservatory College, at their disposition and ready to accompany them upon request."

In relation to other states he represents the nation and protects it against their influence. He[m] supervises the government of the consuls, adjudicates conflicts between them, and maintains harmony.

We can add some clarifications regarding notability. First, the political association consists only of the *active* citizens, those who are engaged in the common social project. The door to participation is open to all who are able to demonstrate their *interest* and *capacity*. I have explained elsewhere how these two qualities are determined. The third, equally voluntary, consists in having paid the *annual political tribute* for a second time. I doubt that are more than a million such people in France. These are the true citizens. On request, they can be inscribed [on a list] by providing the evidence I have mentioned. True citizens will voluntarily travel to the capital of their respective communes, and will there place on record the names of those whom they judge suitable for public office. Since the number of voters is known, one will also know who gains an absolute majority of votes. Those who do will be inscribed on a list of *absolute trust*. This list may grow from year to year. It will remain permanently open to additions. Analogously, the notables on the communal list will register at the departmental capitals the names of those they deem worthy of occupying various departmental offices, as well as higher level offices. The list will contain all those who have gained an absolute majority of votes, and will remain open to further additions. The departmental notables will likewise nominate candidates for the national list (the national notables). At a specified time, they will convene as an electoral college to present candidates for the legislature and for the tribunate, drawn only from the national list. The Conservatory College will appoint them, and will invest with a properly national character both those elected and those eligible for national offices.

m From here to the end of the text, the argument is written by Sieyès (and not transcribed).

Bibliography

Writings

Collection des Escrits d'Emmanuel Sieyès, ed. Carl Friedrich Cramer (Paris/Berlin, 1796). [The editor's foreword is in German, Sieyès's texts are in French. Note that only the first volume has been published].

Les Discours de Sieyès dans les débats constitutionnels de l'an III (2 et 18 thermidor), critical edition, ed. Paul Bastid (Paris, 1939).

What is the Third Estate? Transl. M. Blondel, ed. Samuel E. Finer, introd. Peter Campbell (London 1963).

Qu'est-ce que le Tiers Etat? Critical edition, ed. Roberto Zapperi (Geneva, 1970).

Ecrits politiques, ed. Roberto Zapperi (Paris/Montreux, 1985).

Qu'est-ce que le Tiers Etat? Ed. Jean-Denis Bredin (Paris, 1989).

Œuvres de Sieyès, ed. Marcel Dorigny, 3 vols. (Paris, 1989) [facsimile reprint].

Political Writings. Including the Debate between Sieyès and Tom Paine in 1791, ed. Michael Sonenscher (Indianapolis/Cambridge, 2003).

Essai sur les privilèges et autres textes. Critical edition, ed. Pierre-Yves Quiviger (Paris, 2007).

Was ist der Dritte Stand? Ausgewählte Schriften, ed. Oliver W. Lembcke and Florian Weber, (Berlin, 2010).

Letters and Unpublished Manuscripts

Documents inédits: La jeunesse de l'abbé Sieyès, ed. Oliver Teissier (Marseille, 1897).

'Notes et fragments inédits', in *Ecrits politiques*, ed. Roberto Zapperi (Paris/Montreux, 1985), pp. 45–90 [selected manuscripts on economic issues].

'Manuscrit inédit de Sieyès sur les déclarations des droits de l'homme', in *Les déclarations des droits de l'homme de 1789*, ed. Christine Fauré (Paris, 1988), pp. 403–408.

'Sur l'article Evidence de l'Encyclopédie (1773)', ed. Jacques Guilhaumou, in *Recherches sur Diderot et sur l'Encyclopédie* 14 (1993), pp. 129–143.

'Textes d'Emmanuel Joseph Sieyès' [addendum], in Pasquale Pasquino, *Sieyès et l'invention de la constitution en France* (Paris, 1998), pp. 157–196 [selected political manuscripts].

Des manuscrits de Sieyès. Vol. 1: 1773–1799, ed. Christine Fauré, Jacques Guilhaumou and Jacques Valier (Paris, 1999).

Des manuscrits de Sieyès. Vol. 2: 1770–1815, ed. Christine Fauré, Jacques Guilhaumou and Jacques Valier (Paris, 2007).

'Textes inédits de Sieyès' [addendum], in Pierre-Yves Quiviger, *Le principe d'immanence. Métaphysique et droit administratif chez Sieyès. Avec des textes inédits de Sieyès* (Paris, 2008), 375–460 [collected political manuscripts of the year 1799].

Secondary Literature

Biographies

Bastid, Paul, *Sieyès et sa pensée* (Paris, 1939), part 1 (new edition Paris, 1970).

Bredin, Jean-Denis, *Sieyès: La clé de la Révolution française* (Paris, 1988) [paperback].

Mignet, François August Aléxis, 'Notice historique sur la vie et les travaux de M. le comte Sieyès, lue dans la séance de l'Academie des Sciences morales et politiques du 28 décembre 1836', in *Notices et mémoires historiques*, vol. 1 (Paris, 1843), pp. 1–27.

Encyclopedia Articles

Baker, Keith M., 'Sieyès', in *Dictionnaire critique de la Révolution française*, ed. François Furet and Mona Ozouf (Paris, 1988), pp. 334–345.

Clavreul, Colette, 'Sieyès, Emmanuel Joseph, 1748–1836: Qu'est-ce que le Tiers Etat?', in *Dictionnaire des œuvres politiques*, ed. François Châtelet, Olivier Duhamel and Evelyne Piser (Paris, 1986), pp. 747–757.

Forsyth, Murray, 'Emmanuel Sieyès: What is the Third Estate?', in *The Political Classics: Hamilton to Mill*, ed. Murray Forsyth, Maurice Keens-Soper and John Hoffman, (Oxford, 1993), pp. 44–75.

Lively, Jack, 'Sieyès, Emmanuel Joseph', in *The Blackwell Enyclopaedia of Political Thought*, ed. David Miller et al. (Oxford/Cambridge, Mass., 1995), pp. 475 f.

Sainte-Beuve, Charles-Augustin, 'Sieyès', in id., *Causeries du Lundi*, vol. 5, 3rd ed. (Paris, 1857), pp. 189–216.

Thompson, James Matthew, 'Sieyès', in *Leaders of the French Revolution* (Oxford, 1962), pp. 2–16.

Volumes, Journal Articles etc.

Adler-Bresse, Marcelle, *Sieyès et le monde allemande*, 2 vols. (Paris/Lille, 1977).

Aston, Nigel, 'The Abbé Sieyès before 1789: The Progress of a Clerical Careerist', in *Culture, Theory and Critique* 33 (1989), pp. 41–52.

Avocat, Eric, 'Sieyès orateur à l'Assemblée constituante. Aventures et mésaventures rhétoriques de la langue philosophique', in *Figures de Sieyès*, ed. Pierre-Yves Quiviger, Vincent Denis and Jean Salem (Paris, 2008), pp. 159–175.

Baczko, Bronislaw, 'Le contrat social des Français: Sieyès et Rousseau', in *The French Revolution and the Creation of Modern Political Culture*, vol. 1: The Political Culture of the Old Régime, ed. Keith M. Baker (Oxford et al., 1987), pp. 493–513.—engl.: 'The

Social Contract of the French: Sieyès and Rousseau', in *The Journal of Modern History*, 60 (1988), pp. 98–125.

Baecque, Antoine de, *Le corps de l'histoire. Métaphores et politique* (1770–1800) (Paris, 1993).

Baker, Keith M., *Inventing the French Revolution. Essays on French Political Culture in the Eighteenth Century* (Cambridge, 1990).

Baker, Keith M., 'The Idea of a Declaration of Rights', in *The French Idea of Freedom: The Old Regime and the Declaration of Rights of 1789*, ed. Dale Van Kley (Stanford, 1994), pp. 154–196 and 388–392.

Beaud, Olivier, *La puissance de l'Etat* (Paris, 1994).

Benrekassa, Georges, 'Crise de l'Ancien Régime, crise des idéologies: une année dans la vie de Sieyès', in *Annales. Histoire, Sciences Sociales* 44 (1989), pp. 25–46.

Boulay de la Meurthe, *Antoine Jacques Claude Joseph: Théorie constitutionnelle de Sieyès. Constitution de l'an VIII. Extraits des mémoires inédits de M. Boulay de la Meurthe* (Paris, 1836).

Branca-Rosoff, Sonia/Jacques Guilhaumou, 'De société à socialisme: l'invention néologique et son contexte discursif. Essai de colinguisme appliqué', in *Langage et société* 83–84 (1998), pp. 39–77, 163–164.

Bredin, Jean-Denis, 'L'influence de Sieyès sur la Déclaration des droits de l'homme de 1789', in *Revue des Sciences morales et politiques* 144 (1989), pp. 253–264.

Bredin, Jean-Denis, 'Emmanuel Sieyès et Jacques Necker', in *Annales Benjamin Constant* 23–24 (2000), pp. 63–88.

Brunet, Pierre, *Vouloir pour la nation. Le concept de représentation dans la théorie de l'Etat* (Rouen, 2004).

Clavreul, Colette, *L'influence de la théorie d'Emmanuel Sieyès sur les origines de la représentation en droit public*, Paris 1982 [unpublished PhD thesis].

Clavreul, Colette, 'Sieyès et la genèse de la représentation moderne', in *Droits. Revue française de théorie juridique* 6 (1986), pp. 45–56.

Delinière, Jean, 'Karl Friedrich Reinhard, introducteur de Kant auprès de Sieyès', in *Revue d'Allemagne* 12 (1980), pp. 481–496.

Denis, Vincent, 'Force publique et violence d'Etat chez Sieyès', in *Figures de Sieyès*, ed. Pierre-Yves Quiviger, Vincent Denis and Jean Salem (Paris, 2008), pp. 149–157.

Dorigny, Marcel, 'La formation de la pensée économique de Sieyès d'après ses manuscrits (1770–1789)', in *Annales Historiques de la Révolution française* 271 (1988), pp. 17–34.

Deusen, Glyndon Van, *Sieyès. His Life and his Nationalism* (New York, 1932).

Fauré, Christine, 'Sieyès, lecteur problématique des Lumières', in *Dix-huitième siècle* 37 (2005), pp. 225–242.

Fauré, Christine, 'Sieyès, Rousseau et la théorie du contrat', in *Figures de Sieyès*, ed. Pierre-Yves Quiviger, Vincent Denis and Jean Salem (Paris, 2008), pp. 213–225.

Forsyth, Murray, *Reason and Revolution. The Political Thought of the Abbé Sieyès* (New York, 1987).

Gainot, Bernard, 'Sieyès directeur et la question italienne en 1799', in *Figures de Sieyès*, ed. Pierre-Yves Quiviger, Vincent Denis and Jean Salem (Paris, 2008), pp. 125–147.

Gauchet, Marcel, *La Révolution des droits de l'homme* (Paris, 1989).

Gauchet, Marcel, *La Révolution des pouvoirs. La souveraineté, le peuple et la représentation 1789–1799* (Paris, 1995).

Goldoni, Marco, 'At the Origins of Constitutional Review: Sieyès' Constitutional Jury and the Taming of Constituent Power', in *Oxford Journal of Legal Studies* 32 (2012), pp. 211–234.

Guilhaumou, Jacques, 'Sieyès et la "science politique" (1773–1789). Le seuil de la langue', in *Europäische Sprachwissenschaft um 1800*, ed. Brigitte Schlieben-Lange, vol. 3 (Münster, 1992), pp. 95–108.

Guilhaumou, Jacques, 'Nation, individu et société chez Sieyès', in *Genèses. Sciences sociales et histoire* 26 (1997), pp. 4–24.

Guilhaumou, Jacques, 'Sieyès et la métaphysique allemande', in *Annales historiques de la Révolution française* 317 (1999), pp. 513–535.

Guilhaumou, Jacques, 'Un nom propre en politique: Sieyès', in *Mots* 63 (2000), pp. 74–86.

Guilhaumou, Jacques, *Sieyès et l'ordre de la langue. L'invention de la politique moderne* (Paris, 2002).

Guilhaumou, Jacques, 'Sieyès et le non-dit de la sociologie: du mot à la chose', in *Revue d'Histoire des Sciences Humaines* 15 (2006), pp. 117–134.

Guilhaumou, Jacques, 'Sieyès et la figure nominaliste du métaphysicien: du Grand Cahier métaphysique aux Vues analytiques', in *Figures de Sieyès*, ed. Pierre-Yves Quiviger, Vincent Denis and Jean Salem (Paris, 2008), pp. 241–253.

Hont, Istvan, 'The Permanent Crisis of a Divided Mankind: "Contemporary Crisis of the Nation State" in Historical Perspective', in *Contemporary Crisis of the Nation State?* Ed. John Dunn (Oxford, 1995), pp. 166–231.

Iribarne, Philippe d', 'Trois figures de la liberté', in *Annales. Histoire, Sciences Sociales* 58 (2003), pp. 953–980.

Jaume, Lucien, *Hobbes et l'état représentatif moderne* (Paris, 1986).

Jaume, Lucien, 'Garantir les Droits de l'homme: 1791–1793', in *The Tocqueville Review/La Revue Tocqueville* 14 (1993), pp. 49–65.

Jaume, Lucien, 'Sieyès et le sens du jury constitutionnaire: une réinterprétation', in *Droits. Revue française de théorie juridique* 36 (2002), pp. 115–134.

Koung, Yoeh, *Théorie constitutionnelle de Sieyès*, Paris 1934.

Lahmer, Marc, 'Sieyès lors des débats constituants en l'an III: autopsie d'un échec', in *Figures de Sieyès*, ed. Pierre-Yves Quiviger, Vincent Denis and Jean Salem (Paris, 2008), pp. 43–82.

Laquièze, Alain, 'La réception de Sieyès par la doctrine publiciste française du XIXe et du XXe siècles', in *Figures de Sieyès*, ed. Pierre-Yves Quiviger, Vincent Denis and Jean Salem (Paris, 2008), pp. 83–121.

Larrère, Catherine, *L'invention de l'économie au XVIIIe siècle. Du droit naturel à la physiocratie* (Paris, 1992).

Larrère, Catherine, 'Sieyès, lecteur des physiocrates: droit naturel ou économie?', in *Figures de Sieyès*, ed. Pierre-Yves Quiviger, Vincent Denis and Jean Salem (Paris, 2008), pp. 195–211.

Lembcke, Oliver W./Florian Weber, 'Die Monarchie als wahre Republik. Emmanuel Sieyès' Briefwechsel mit Thomas Paine', in *Berliner Debatte Initial* 19 (2008), pp. 70–82.

Lembcke, Oliver W./Florian Weber, 'Sieyès' Konzept der Staats- und Regierungsform', in *Volkssouveränität und Freiheitsrechte. Emmanuel Joseph Sieyès' Staatsverständnis*, ed. Ulrich Thiele (Baden-Baden, 2009), pp. 139–166.

Lembcke, Oliver W./Florian Weber, 'Revolution und Konstitution: Zur politischen Theorie von Sieyès', in Emmanuel Joseph Sieyès, *Was ist der Dritte Stand? Ausgewählte Schriften*, ed. Oliver W. Lembcke and Florian Weber (Berlin, 2010), pp. 13–89.

Negri, Antonio, *Il potere costituente: saggio sulle alternative del moderno* (Carnago/Varese, 1992) (French edition Paris, 1997).

Loewenstein, Karl, *Volk und Parlament nach der Staatstheorie der Französischen Nationalversammlung von 1789. Studien zur Dogmengeschichte der unmittelbaren Volksgesetzgebung* (München, 1922).

Oelsner, Konrad Engelbert, *Luzifer oder Gereinigte Beiträge zur Geschichte der Französischen Revolution*, ed. Werner Greiling (Leipzig, 1987).

Pasquino, Pasquale, 'Emmanuel Sieyès, Benjamin Constant et le "Gouvernement des Modernes"', in *Revue Française de Science Politique* 37 (1987), pp. 214–229.

Pasquino, Pasquale, 'Le républicanisme constitutionnel de E. Sieyès', in *Droits. Revue française de théorie juridique* 17 (1993), pp. 67–77.

Pasquino, Pasquale, *Sieyès et l'invention de la constitution en France* (Paris, 1998).

Pasquino, Pasquale, 'Constitution et pouvoir constituant: le double corps du peuple', in *Figures de Sieyès*, ed. Pierre-Yves Quiviger, Vincent Denis and Jean Salem (Paris, 2008), pp. 13–23.

Quiviger, Pierre-Yves/Vincent Denis/Jean Salem (ed.), *Figures de Sieyès*. Actes du colloque des 5 et 6 mars 2004 organisé à la Sorbonne par le Centre d'Histoire des Systèmes de Pensée moderne et l'Institut d'Histoire de la Révolution Française (Université Paris I) (Paris, 2008).

Quiviger, Pierre-Yves, 'Sieyès et Spinoza', in *Figures de Sieyès*, ed. Pierre-Yves Quiviger, Vincent Denis and Jean Salem (Paris, 2008), pp. 227–239.

Quiviger, Pierre-Yves, *Le principe d'immanence. Métaphysique et droit administratif chez Sieyès. Avec des textes inédits de Sieyès* (Paris, 2008).

Quiviger, Pierre-Yves, 'Sieyès as a Reader of John Locke: Metaphysics, Politics and Law', in *Locke's Political Liberty: Readings and Misreadings*, ed. Christophe Miqueu and Mason Chamie (Oxford, 2009), pp. 127–142.

Redslob, Robert, *Die Staatstheorien der französischen Nationalversammlung von 1789. Ihre Grundlagen in der Staatslehre der Aufklärungszeit und in den englischen und amerikanischen Verfassungsgedanken* (Leipzig, 1912).

Rials, Stéphane, 'Sieyès, la délibération sans la prudence', in *Droits. Revue française de théorie juridique* 13 (1991), pp. 123–138.

Rosanvallon, Pierre, *Le sacre du citoyen: histoire du suffrage universel en France* (Paris, 1992).

Rosanvallon, Pierre, *La démocratie inachevée. Histoire de la souveraineté du peuple en France* (Paris, 2000).

Scheuerman, William E., 'Carl Schmitt's Critique of Liberal Constitutionalism', in *The Review of Politics* 58 (1996), pp. 299–322.

Sewell Jr., William H., *A Rhetoric of Bourgeois Revolution. The Abbé Sieyès and 'What is the Third Estate?'* (Durham/London, 1994).

Sonenscher, Michael, 'The Nation's Debt and the Birth of the Modern Republic: The French Fiscal Deficit and the Politics of the Revolution of 1789. Part II', in *History of Political Thought* 18 (1997), pp. 267–325.

Sonenscher, Michael, *Before the Deluge. Public Debt, Inequality, and the Intellectual Origins of the French Revolution* (Princeton/Oxford, 2007).

Sonenscher, Michael, *Sans-Culottes. An Eighteenth-Century Emblem in the French Revolution* (Princeton and Oxford, 2008).

Spitz, Jean-Fabien, *John Locke et les fondements de la liberté moderne* (Paris, 2001).

Spitz, Jean-Fabien, *La liberté politique: essai de généalogie conceptuelle* (Paris, 1995).

Thiele, Ulrich 'Volkssouveränität—Menschenrechte—Gewaltenteilung im Denken von Sieyès', in *Archiv für Rechts- und Sozialphilosophie* 86 (2000), pp. 48–69.

Thiele, Ulrich (ed.), *Volkssouveränität und Freiheitsrechte. Emmanuel Joseph Sieyès' Staatsverständnis* (Baden-Baden, 2009).

Trevor, Daphne, 'Some Sources of the Constitutional Theory of the Abbé Sieyès: Harrington and Spinoza', in *Politica* 1 (1935), pp. 325–342.

Troper, Michel, 'Sieyès et le jury constitutionnaire', in *Mélanges en l'Honneur de Pierre Avril. La République*, ed. Michel Ameller (Paris, 2001), pp. 265–282.

Troper, Michel, 'Sieyès et la hiérarchie des normes', in *Figures de Sieyès*, ed. Pierre-Yves Quiviger, Vincent Denis and Jean Salem (Paris, 2008), pp. 25–42.

Tyrsenko, Andrej, 'L'ordre politique chez Sieyès en l'an III', in *Annales historiques de la Révolution française* 319 (2000), pp. 27–45.

Tyrsenko, Andrej, 'Les principes politiques de Sieyès d'après ses manuscrits de thermidor et de brumaire', in *Figures de Sieyès*, ed. Pierre-Yves Quiviger, Vincent Denis and Jean Salem (Paris, 2008), pp. 177–191.

Weber, Florian, 'Verfassungsschutz als Demokratiefürsorge? Zur Theorie eines Verfassungswächters bei Fichte, Sieyès und Constant', in *Der Staat* 44 (2005), pp. 112–137.

Zweig, Egon, *Die Lehre vom Pouvoir Constituant. Ein Beitrag zum Staatsrecht der Französischen Revolution* (Tübingen, 1909).

Index

Administration 27–28, 39, 41, 52, 63, 85, 92, 138, 140, 161, 164, 174–175, 189–190
Adunation 18, 23, 25, 27
Ancien Régime 2, 28, 33, 157
Art social 17, 22, 24, 38
Assemblée législative 3, 182
Assemblée nationale 2–5
Assimilation 18
Authority 3, 7, 9, 13, 15, 20, 21, 23, 36, 37, 40–41, 65, 75, 90, 98, 102, 104, 108, 110, 129–132, 152, 159–161, 163, 165, 167, 172, 174–175, 187–193

Bicameralism 30, 38–39, 81

Church 2–3, 6, 44, 46–47, 52, 57, 64, 68, 83, 104, 158
Citizen viii, xi, 4, 12–17, 19–20, 22, 24–30, 32, 35–37, 44–50, 52, 55–58, 60–68, 71, 75–87, 91, 94–97, 99, 100, 102, 105, 107–119, 121–125, 127, 129–133, 144, 147–148, 155, 160–167, 172–173, 175–176, 179, 181–183, 186–189, 193–194
Civil rights 7, 35, 50, 57, 61, 77, 90, 100, 108, 127
Clergy 2–3, 34, 46–48, 57, 62–64, 69, 82, 97–98, 102–105
Collège des conservateurs (Conservatory College) 25, 42, 188, 190–192, 194
Community 2, 9–14, 16–17, 19, 24–26, 28, 30, 68, 88, 90, 154, 187–188, 190, 194
Competence 8, 31, 73, 88, 168
Conseil d'Etat 41, 189
Constituent power (*pouvoir constituant*) viii, 18, 20, 22, 24, 34–35, 89, 119, 126–127, 153, 159, 170, 177–178, 184–185
Constituted power (*pouvoir constitué*) 89, 170, 185
Constitution xi, 3–6, 8, 12, 15–17, 20–26, 28, 30–31, 34–38, 40–42, 50, 53–54, 67, 78–81, 84–86, 97, 100, 102–103, 105–110, 119, 124–127, 129, 132, 134–135, 138–139, 141–142, 152–159, 161, 164–166, 169, 171–174, 176–178, 181–184, 186, 188
Constitutionalism 21, 27, 29, 33, 40, 42
Consultation 52–53, 70, 73, 94, 96, 107
Cooperation 6, 29, 32, 38, 72–73, 154, 164
Council of Five Hundred (*conseil de 500*) 160, 174–175, 181, 183–185
Court 16, 26, 29, 34–35, 40, 51–52, 59, 76, 82–83, 96, 162–163, 166–181, 183–185, 190

Decision 16, 18, 20, 24–25, 27, 29, 30–32, 54, 56, 63, 67, 83, 85, 90–91, 95, 97–98, 105–107, 119, 128, 140–141, 157–158, 161–163, 168, 175, 179, 181, 184, 188–190
Deliberation 39, 72, 79, 99, 102, 104, 106, 108, 140, 152, 160–161, 164–165, 167, 173, 190
Democracy 4–5, 9, 16, 19, 21–29, 31–32, 38, 40–42, 101–102, 155, 160, 178, 186
Department 4, 28, 38, 52, 91, 124, 139–141, 168–169, 188–190, 194
District 28, 61, 67, 77
Division of powers 141, 156, 174, 178, 190, 192
Dominion 145–146

Education viii, 1, 18, 38, 55, 61, 63, 125, 149, 160, 162, 174
Elections 3, 7–8, 21–22, 25–26, 28, 37, 41–42, 50, 52, 56, 67, 69, 82, 112, 139, 174, 183, 194
Elite 2, 6, 8, 26, 29, 36
England 30, 35–36, 58, 79–82, 84–86, 92–93, 96, 102–103, 135–136, 157, 159, 170
Enlightenment 1, 18, 38, 58, 61, 70, 77, 79, 84, 86, 94, 116, 125, 149, 165–166, 171
Estate vii–viii, x–xi, 1–3, 17, 20, 22, 30, 33–36, 43–117, 127, 157, 160
Ethic(s) 11, 18–19, 33
Ethocratie 18
Executive 6–7, 27, 31, 33, 37–42, 52, 85, 89, 91, 96, 113, 126, 136, 138–139, 152, 156, 159, 161, 164–165, 175–176, 186, 188–190, 192–193

Federalist Papers 33–34
Freedom 9–15, 17, 20, 22, 24, 33, 37–38, 48, 57, 58, 61, 71, 85, 98, 108, 111–112, 115, 145, 153–154, 176, 179

General will (*volonté générale*) 10, 13, 16–17, 19, 21, 38, 52, 54, 61, 104, 107, 128, 132, 156
Government (*gouvernement*) 4, 7–9, 12–15, 21, 24, 26–33, 37–39, 41, 45–46, 53, 60, 67, 71–72, 79, 81, 85, 88–90, 93, 102, 124, 126, 133, 135–143, 152–154, 160–169, 176, 186–187, 189–190, 192–194
Grand Electeur 41–42

Happiness 11, 13–14, 108, 111, 120, 149–150
Hierarchy 2, 23, 26, 64, 188
Human rights viii, 12–16, 20–21, 23, 35–36, 40, 180

Judge 40, 42, 53, 61, 83, 87, 91, 97, 106, 121, 140, 147, 163, 165–167, 169, 171, 173–174, 176, 179, 181, 187, 190, 194
Jurisdiction 21, 41, 76, 155, 163, 172–175, 178, 180–181, 190
Jury xi, xii, 20, 22, 26, 39–42, 85, 159, 161, 163–165, 170–179, 181–185, 189, 193

Leadership 6, 8, 31, 41, 53, 93, 161, 164
Legislation 2, 11–12, 16–17, 24, 26–27, 30–31, 35–36, 39–42, 47, 60, 66, 76–78, 80, 84, 88–93, 96, 102, 107–108, 110–115, 126–127, 136, 138, 140, 152–153, 156–171, 173–174, 177–183, 186, 188–189, 191–192, 194
Legitimacy viii, 4, 11–12, 15, 21–22, 24–25, 29, 34–35, 59, 81, 90–91, 108, 110, 121, 125, 138, 180
Liberty vii, viii, xi, 26, 37–38, 55, 58–59, 71, 76, 85, 91, 100, 106, 108, 111–112, 116, 122–125, 127, 135–137, 141–151, 155–156, 163–165, 172, 174, 176, 178–180, 186–187, 192

Majority will (*volonté de tous*) 6–8, 19, 22, 31, 34–35, 37, 62, 66, 71–72, 83, 94–96, 98, 103, 105–106, 109–110, 114, 128, 140, 142, 158, 165, 175, 178, 183–184, 193–194
Military viii, 5, 8, 49, 64, 75–76, 124–125, 130–131, 191
Mixed constitution 9, 29, 32–33
Monarchy 4–6, 30–32, 36–37, 48, 52, 74, 82–83, 99, 102, 135–142, 154, 166, 182, 192
Moral(s) 3, 10, 17–19, 28, 46, 87, 91, 100, 109, 114, 135, 144, 154, 180, 192

Natural law 11–14, 20–21, 27, 89–90, 121, 150, 180

Obligation 11, 14, 16, 26, 36, 106, 119, 121, 127
Office 2, 7–9, 15, 21–22, 24, 27, 32–33, 36, 41, 48, 50, 56–57, 59, 64, 70, 75, 81, 110, 128–129, 132–133, 140, 161, 171, 173, 182, 187–188, 190, 192–194
Organism 23, 171, 176–177

Parliament 4, 6–9, 25, 30, 38–39, 42, 93, 103, 136, 157
Polyarchy 31
Privilege viii, 3, 13, 30, 34–35, 46, 49, 51, 69, 76–77, 82–83, 112, 128–129, 131
Property 12–15, 25–26, 38, 45, 47, 55, 59–61, 64, 67–68, 74, 76, 78, 99, 110–111, 122–123, 127, 129–132, 191–192

Representation viii, xi, 3–5, 10–11, 13, 19, 21, 23–24, 28–30, 34, 37, 47, 49–50, 52–54, 57, 59, 61, 63, 68–70, 72, 84, 98–99, 104, 107, 110, 116–117, 135, 138–140, 144, 147, 153–154, 160, 162–163, 167, 186–187
Republic 4, 7, 22, 31–32, 37, 38–39, 137–139, 141–143, 152, 160–161, 167, 170, 184, 192
Resistance 4, 15, 81, 83, 131, 150, 161
Responsibility 27, 29, 31, 40, 52, 76, 94, 121, 128–130, 133, 139–140, 142, 156, 164–165, 172–173, 182, 189–191
Revolution viii, 1–9, 21, 26, 30, 34–37, 41, 84, 101, 137, 142, 159–160, 166, 184

Social contract 13, 15–17, 21, 72, 112
Sovereignty 9, 16, 19–23, 34, 36, 39–42, 59, 156, 170
State of nature 10, 12, 14, 20, 22, 91, 93, 122, 148, 167, 175
System of cooperation 29, 164
System of equilibrium 29, 154, 157, 165

Tribunate 160–161, 165–169, 194
Trust 8, 22, 24, 28–29, 57, 58, 61, 87–88, 114, 130, 133, 184, 187–188, 194

United States of America 30, 40

Veto 4–5, 30–31, 39, 66, 79, 157–158, 189
Virtue 18, 49, 68, 76, 93, 101, 109, 111, 113, 125

www.ingramcontent.com/pod-product-compliance
Lightning Source LLC
LaVergne TN
LVHW010657300926
849161LV00005B/1153